Larkin's
BLUES

Larkin's
BLUES

JAZZ

POPULAR MUSIC

AND

POETRY

B. J. LEGGETT

LOUISIANA STATE UNIVERSITY PRESS
Baton Rouge

Designer: Amanda McDonald Scallan
Typeface: Minion
Typesetter: Crane Composition
Printer and binder: Edward Brothers

Library of Congress Cataloging-in-Publication Data:
Leggett, B. J. (Bobby Joe), 1938–
    Larkin's blues : jazz, popular music, and poetry / B.J. Leggett.
      p.   cm.
    Includes bibliographical references (p.   ) and index.
    ISBN 0-8071-2342-0 (cloth : alk. paper)
    1. Larkin, Philip—Knowledge—Music.   2. Popular music—England—
History and criticism.   3. Blues (Music) in literature.   4. Music
and literature.   5. Jazz in literature.   I. Title.
PR6023.A66Z748   1999
821'.914—dc21   98-43704
                                        CIP

CONTENTS

ACKNOWLEDGMENTS

Earlier readers of Larkin to whom I am indebted are apparent in my citations and notes, but I want to call attention to several works to which my debt is especially great. Anthony Thwaite's edition of Larkin's letters and Andrew Motion's *A Writer's Life*, both at the heart of the recent controversy about Larkin's status as a national monument, were invaluable sources in charting what Larkin called his jazz life. These two works have, for better or worse, altered our sense of Larkin as a poet and public figure, and this study, in its present shape, would not have been possible without them. I have referred frequently to two collections of essays, Anthony Thwaite's edition of *Larkin at Sixty* and Dale Salwak's *Philip Larkin: The Man and His Work*. Readers will also find numerous references to recent works by Janice Rossen, A. T. Tolley, and Andrew Swarbrick. Barbara Everett's essays have also influenced my view of Larkin's poetry, and Blake Morrison's *The Movement* has helped me to see it in a larger perspective.

Of the scores of volumes on jazz and blues I consulted, those that I found most helpful in writing about the confluence of poetry and music were Ted Gioia's *The Imperfect Art*, Eric Hobsbawm's classic *The Jazz Scene* (first published under the pseudonym Francis Newton), Albert Murray's revisionist *Stomping the Blues*, a host of blues studies by Paul Oliver, and a recent collection of essays edited by Krin Gabbard, *Representing Jazz*. Its companion volume, *Jazz Among the Discourses*, is not cited here, but it was also helpful in exhibiting the manner of contemporary academic writing on jazz.

Among the many commentaries on popular music now available, I found the work of Simon Frith the most useful for my own project, especially the essays of his collection *Music for Pleasure.* I have also profited from Dave Laing's *The Sound of Our Time;* Philip Furia's *The Poets of Tin Pan Alley;* two works by Richard Middleton, *Pop Music and the Blues* and *Studying Popular Music;* and almost everything by Greil Marcus. Christopher Ricks appears here in several roles, as a Larkin critic, a Bob Dylan enthusiast, and a commentator on the state of the cliché. The theorist to whom this study is most indebted is Michael Riffaterre, as will be evident, although he would no doubt disavow my loose version of his more rigorously theoretical intertextuality.

I wish to thank *Twentieth Century Literature* for permission to reprint, with slight alteration, the material that makes up chapter 2. I am grateful to the John C. Hodges Fund of the English Department of the University of Tennessee and to Allen Carroll for providing the time to complete a portion of the book. I also wish to express my gratitude to LSU Press's sharp-eyed anonymous reader for many valuable suggestions. Quotations from Larkin's *Collected Poems* are copyright © 1988, 1989 by the Estate of Philip Larkin and reprinted by permission of Farrar, Straus & Giroux, Inc., Faber & Faber, and the Marvell Press.

ABBREVIATIONS

Philip Larkin's works, Anthony Thwaite's edition of the letters, and Andrew Motion's biography are cited in the text as follows:

AWJ   *All What Jazz: A Record Diary, 1961–1971.* New York, 1985.
CP   *Collected Poems.* Edited by Anthony Thwaite. New York, 1989.
Jill   *Jill: A Novel.* Woodstock, N.Y., 1976.
RW   *Required Writing: Miscellaneous Pieces, 1955–1982.* New York, 1984.
Letters *Selected Letters of Philip Larkin, 1940–1985.* Edited by Anthony Thwaite. New York, 1993.
Life   Andrew Motion. *Philip Larkin: A Writer's Life.* New York, 1993.

Larkin's

BLUES

1

INTRODUCTION

A writer's reputation is twofold: what we think of his work, and what we think of him. What's more, we expect the two halves to relate: if they don't, then one or other of our opinions alters until they do.

—Larkin, "The Real Wilfred"

I can't believe I am so much more unpleasant than everyone else.

—Larkin, Letter to Monica Jones

THE title *Larkin's Blues* now carries implications I could not have anticipated when I first began looking at the confluence of jazz and poetry in the Larkin canon. At that time Philip Larkin was the most highly regarded English poet since Auden, the "unofficial laureate of post-1945 England" and "the best-loved poet of his generation."[1] By

1. The first characterization is Donald Davie's in *Thomas Hardy and British Poetry* (London, 1973), 64. The second is Anthony Thwaite's in a volume of essays celebrating Larkin's sixtieth birthday, although he is repeating Davie in a review of Larkin's *Oxford Book of Twentieth-Century English Verse*. Thwaite adds, "Many would call him the finest living poet writing in English" ("Introduction," *Larkin at Sixty*, ed. Anthony Thwaite [London, 1982], 11).

the time the study was well under way he was, in a *New Yorker* profile of Alan Bennett, "the late, disgraced Philip Larkin," depicted now as a foul-mouthed bigot whose generally wretched state had been relieved, Ian Hamilton notes, principally by pornography, jazz, gin, and Mrs. Thatcher. Calling attention to Larkin's "steady stream of casual obscenity, throwaway derogatory remarks about women, and arrogant disdain for those of different skin colour or nationality," Lisa Jardine reports that Larkin is not taught much now in her Department of English, the sort of remark that led John Carey to observe, "Contempt for Philip Larkin is in vogue." *Larkinesque* now had a new meaning. Where it once suggested qualities "both lovable and glum," a "somewhat poignant type of artist, wry, subtle, elegiac," Hamilton observes, it now means "foul-mouthed," "four-letter words and hateful views." He cites a newspaper article on the rap performer Ice Cube, whose misogynist and racist language is characterized by the article's author as "incessantly Larkinesque." Larkin's present decline has also given rise to a new coinage. To be *Larkinized* is to have one's reputation as an artist questioned on the basis of personal beliefs or attitudes, as in the case of Anthony Lane's remark that "there is every danger that Eliot is now in the process of being Larkinized."[2]

Larkin's fall from grace is well documented, its point of origin easily fixed. It began at the end of 1992 with the publication of Anthony Thwaite's edition of *Selected Letters of Philip Larkin,* a "hateful and disgraceful book," as described by Davie, who had earlier awarded Larkin the title of unofficial laureate. The symbolic date for the fall might well be marked as November 6, 1992, when in a response to a review of the letters in the *Times Literary Supplement* Tom Paulin concluded with the most memorable phrase of the Larkin letters controversy, a reference to "the sewer under the national monument Larkin became." The phrase

2. Stephen Schiff, "The Poet of Embarrassment," *New Yorker,* September 6, 1993, p. 92; Ian Hamilton, "Bugger Me Blue," *London Review of Books,* October 22, 1992, p. 3; Lisa Jardine, "Saxon Violence," *Guardian,* December 8, 1992, sec. 2, p. 4; John Carey, "Mail Chauvinism," *Sunday Times,* October 25, 1992, sec. 6, p. 5; Ian Hamilton, "Self's the Man," *Times Literary Supplement,* April 2, 1993, p. 3; Anthony Lane, "Writing Wrongs," *New Yorker,* March 10, 1997, p. 91.

itself helps to explain the vehemence of some readers' responses to the revelations of the letters and of Andrew Motion's biography, which appeared a few months later and added to the already ugly portrait an account of Larkin's selfish and devious relationships with the women in his life. If Larkin had not become a national monument, Paulin's figure implies, then the discovery of the sewer would not have appeared quite so shocking. We have been deceived, and the deception, he argued, may extend to Thwaite's editing of the letters. Thwaite's editorial cuts appeared to Paulin to be used "to minimize the full force of [Larkin's] prejudices,"[3] a charge that led to further exchanges in the pages of the *Times Literary Supplement* and to a postscript in the next edition of the letters explaining the basis for the cuts.

Ironically, then, the poet whose major theme is the uncovering of the deceptions by which we live is now charged with deceiving us, as is his editor. Deception is also the theme of Alan Bennett's long review of Motion's *A Writer's Life*. (The review's title, "Alas! Deceived," clearly recognizes the ironic relationship between Larkin's first important volume of poems and his present fate.) Bennett, who had contributed a very funny and appreciative essay to the commemorative *Larkin at Sixty* in which he characterizes Larkin's poems as speaking directly to his own experience, is now not so sure. "Because his poems spoke in an ordinary voice and boasted his quiescence and self-deprecation one felt that here was someone to like, to take to and whose voice echoed one's inner thoughts," he writes in the review. The "unexpected outpouring of regret when he died showed this sentiment to have been widespread." But "what one is left with now is a sense of betrayal which is quite difficult to locate," and the constituency Larkin had acquired through the "public intimacy" of his poetry was equally deceived.[4]

There is a small difficulty here about the matter of deception, as Bennett recognizes. He admits that Larkin never attempted to mislead readers about his character, but one could go much further. Many of

---

3. Donald Davie, "Letters from Hull," *PN Review,* XIX (1993), 4; Tom Paulin, Letter to the Editor, *Times Literary Supplement,* November 6, 1992, p. 15.

4. Alan Bennett, "Alas! Deceived," *London Review of Books,* March 25, 1993, p. 6.

the qualities objected to in the letters—the obscenity, the conservatism and insularity, various prejudices, defenses of selfishness, arguments against marriage—were present in his texts (not only the poems but the reviews, articles, and interviews) almost from the beginning. He told Ian Hamilton in a 1964 interview, "I wouldn't want to write a poem which suggested that I was different from what I am." One of his criticisms of earlier poets was that "they said one thing and did another, a false relation between life and art." And far from seeking to mislead the public about his private self (as he constructed and projected it), Larkin proclaimed his likes and dislikes whenever the occasion presented itself. To take the matter of his taste for the obscene, *shit, piss, fuck, tits,* and *cunt* had all appeared in his poems. Should we have been surprised that the letters are also laced with obscenities? And there is a further difficulty. It is not simply that we were aware of Larkin's obscenity; we applauded him for it. It was a part of the antipretentious common-language style he shared with other Movement writers. It was an essential part of an attitude, a persona, that made him the best-loved poet of his generation. "For three decades Larkin's mockery of anything that smacked of high-mindedness in art proved to be his most endearing feature," Joseph Bristow writes, "—until, that is, his letters appeared."[5]

Bristow has examined the issue of Larkin's obscenity in the context of his recent fall from grace, attempting to explain how his most endearing feature, a mocking unpretentiousness amounting to philistinism, could become the occasion of his undoing. His explanation, curiously enough, is that readers turned against Larkin once they recognized (from the letters) that he "actually *meant* what he was saying" in his poetry and reviews. "What were once rhetorical gestures that had a wholly plausible, if not ennobling, place in his art have become palpable evidence of a politics that for the majority of left-liberals has since proved to be intolerable." But it was not only that he meant what he was saying; it

---

5. Ian Hamilton, "Four Conversations," *The London Magazine,* IV (1964), 75; Joseph Bristow, "The Obscenity of Philip Larkin," *Critical Inquiry,* XXI (1994), 158.

was as well the targets of his obscenities, among them, as Bristow notes, his Pakistani neighbors, trades unionists, and women.[6]

Of the Larkin vices of Ian Hamilton's list, including pornography, gin, and Mrs. Thatcher, it turns out to be his adoration of Mrs. Thatcher that is the most damaging in the end. What is it, Bristow asks, about Larkin's obscenity "that has become posthumously so anachronistic in its 'chummy democratic' appeal"? It is not that *piss* and *fuck* have become more shocking. "It is rather that the letters went on sale at a time of immense political turmoil that enabled us to understand, much to our frustration, how Larkin's four-letter words issued from a conservatism that the nation had increasingly come to despise." Presumably, then, had Larkin's obscenity been associated with a liberal agenda, it would not have occasioned the outrage that it did. "Only in the light of the economic and social damage done by Thatcherism," Bristow argues, "have English intellectuals been able to see more clearly than before where Larkin stood in relation to those at whom he angled his 'wonderful line in obscenity.' "[7]

As an outsider I decline to enter the political area of the controversy, to defend or to attack him, but no one writing on Larkin these days can ignore the event of Larkin's "almost overnight transformation from the bard of the nation who spoke both of and to an Englishness we could cherish into the man from whom we could only recoil."[8] I accept Bristow's political explanation for Larkin's present decline in England; presumably, however, the charge of Thatcherism is not so shocking to Larkin's American readers, who did not cherish Larkin's Englishness (or did not realize that it was his Englishness that they cherished). And yet those with the stamina to last through the more than 1,300 pages of the letters and the biography will find plenty of evidence that Larkin could be, especially in his later years, an unpleasant, opinionated, intoler-

---

6. Bristow, "Obscenity of Philip Larkin," 161, 158–59.

7. Ibid., 160. The quotation "He had a wonderful line in obscenity" is from Jean Hartley, the former wife of George Hartley, publisher of *The Less Deceived*.

8. Ibid., 161.

ant man. (They will also find evidence that he could be compassionate, self-deprecating, and outrageously funny.)

Alan Bennett ends his long review of Motion's biography by adopting a position with which I sympathize. "There remain the poems," he writes, "without which there would be no biography. Reading it I could not see how they would emerge unscathed. But I have read them again and they do, just as with Auden and Hardy, who have taken a similar biographical battering."[9] He might have added Eliot, Frost, and Yeats to the list of poets whose biographies exposed them as reactionary, intolerant, or, as Auden says of Yeats, "silly like us." The *reason* the poems emerge unscathed, Bennett concludes, is expressed in Auden's elegy for Yeats, a poet whose political views he despised. Time, Auden wrote in lines later dropped from the poem, "Worships language and forgives / Everyone by whom it lives." Time may eventually forgive Larkin his Thatcherite politics. Whether English academics can forgive him is another matter.

Larkin presumably will never again be the spokesman for twentieth-century Englishness, but there remain the poems. (I cannot agree with the view of Tom Paulin and, I presume, Lisa Jardine, that we are no longer allowed to "promote" writers whose works "are structured by key beliefs to which we can no longer subscribe."[10]) My own interest in the fall has less to do with Thatcherism than with the insight into the Larkin persona, the voice of the prose as well as the poetry, that the controversy has produced. We now see certain elements of Larkin's assumed philistinism more clearly than before. We recognize, for example, that what attracted us to him was also what brought on the reaction against him. We see—most importantly for my subject here, the convergence of his music and his art—that his jazz, his rise to the position of unofficial laureate, and his present decline proceeded from the same complex of attitudes and ideas that (the letters show) began forming

9. Bennett, "Alas! Deceived," 9.

10. Jardine, "Saxon Violence," 4. Jardine ascribes this view to Paulin, but I assume that she cites it approvingly and that she believes Thwaite's editing of the letters is an example of the dishonesty and corruption of values of which her review speaks.

at Oxford. Larkin's jazz is an essential part of the philistine manner that dictated, among other things, his antimodernist stance, the persona he assumes in his poems and reviews, his common language, his clichés and obscenities, his conception of his audience, and his position on the direction English poetry should take in the mid–twentieth century. The place of jazz in Larkin's texts—jazz as an essential Larkin intertext—is the subject of the following chapters, but by necessity they also consider issues such as those above. It is difficult to discuss Larkin's account of the evolution of jazz, for example, without reference to his view of modernism, and it is not surprising that his most sustained attack on modern art and literature occurs in his introduction to the jazz reviews. Before coming to Larkin's jazz, however (and jazz is a shorthand way of referring to a range of popular music considered here), it is instructive to look briefly at the philistinism that incorporates his jazz and that has figured so largely in the controversy surrounding his letters and biography.

"Is Jorge Luis Borges the only other contemporary poet of note who is also a librarian, by the way?" Larkin was asked in a 1982 interview. "Are you aware of any others?" "Who's Jorge Luis Borges?" Larkin responds (*RW*, 60), typically depicting himself as the common reader of limited range (and perhaps mocking as well the pretentiousness of the interviewer's reference to a writer whose primary appeal was to academics). It was not the letters or the life that first revealed Larkin's philistinism. He had perfected that role much earlier, and a reader who knew only this *Paris Review* interview would have a relatively clear picture of the persona Larkin projected. What is his daily routine? "Work all day, then cook, eat, wash up, telephone, hack writing, drink and television in the evenings" (*RW*, 57). What does he think of the academic world? "I should think that chewing over other people's work, writing I mean, must be terribly stultifying. . . . It would be death to me to have to think about literature as such, to say why one poem was 'better' than another, and so on" (*RW*, 60–61). What does he think of poetry readings? "I don't like hearing things in public, even music" (*RW*, 61). Has he ever considered writing a play? "I don't like plays. They happen in public" (*RW*, 66). What has he learned from his study of earlier poets? "Oh, for Christ's sake, one doesn't *study* poets! You *read* them" (*RW*, 67). What does he mainly read now? "Detective stories: Gladys Mitchell, Michael Innes, Dick Francis. . . . Nothing difficult" (*RW*, 70). What does he think of American poetry? "I'm afraid I know very little about American poetry" (*RW*, 70). Why does he distrust modern art? "It seems to me undeniable that up to this century literature used language in the way we all use it, painting represented what anyone with normal vision sees, and music was an affair of nice noises rather than nasty ones. The innovation of 'modernism' in the arts consisted of doing the opposite" (*RW*, 72). How does he defend his selections for *The Oxford Book of Twentieth-Century English Verse?* "I made twentieth-century poetry sound nice" (*RW*, 73).

Janice Rossen argues that "the philistine pose was a clever projection, designed to create a self-protective image," a refinement of a persona he had first developed at Oxford, and to read carefully one of the texts such as the *Paris Review* interview that projects Larkin's philistinism is to be convinced that it *was* to some extent a protective pose. Anyone familiar with the letters or the reviews of *Required Writing* will spot at once the deception of Larkin's account of his lightweight reading. A. T. Tolley devotes a chapter of his recent study of Larkin to *Required Writing* and concludes that "it is quite clear from Larkin's reviewing that his reading of English poetry of any era was extremely extensive," and this includes the literature of modernism.[11] The supposed naïveté of "Who's Jorge Luis Borges?" works only if we assume, mistakenly, that Larkin was responding directly to the interviewer. In fact, the interview was conducted, at Larkin's insistence, by mail, and he wrote his answers at his own pace, having the opportunity to check anything he wasn't sure of. Had he wished to adopt a different pose, he might have learned who Borges was, even in the unlikely event he did not know. (Borges had received an honorary degree from Oxford in 1971, the same year Larkin was a Visiting Fellow at All Souls College working

11. Janice Rossen, *Philip Larkin: His Life's Work* (New York, 1989), 99; A. T. Tolley, *My Proper Ground: A Study of the Work of Philip Larkin and Its Development* (Ottawa, Ontario, 1991), 152–53.

on *The Oxford Book of Twentieth-Century Verse.*) And he might have resisted calling special attention to his "hack writing," his drinking, and his nightly television viewing. When he sent his answers back to Robert Phillips of the *Paris Review* he wrote, "It has taken a long time because to my surprise I found writing it suffocatingly boring" (*Life,* 491). Finally, he claims to know very little about American poetry, but then almost immediately makes a joke about John Ashbery.[12] He also provides some rather esoteric information about Archibald MacLeish's appointment as Librarian of Congress, conducts a sophisticated argument on the false analogy between poetry readings and musical performance, and refers to the sense of class in the works of John O'Hara.

Yet so pervasive was Larkin's projection of himself as the common man "sprawled out on the couch of an evening, watching wrestling on the telly,"[13] that John Carey, one of his defenders, professes what must now seem an ironic sense of shock in reading the letters. He discovers an *antiphilistine* Larkin. "For most of his adult life . . . he passed himself off so successfully as a reactionary curmudgeon that it is a shock—and a gladdening one—to find in his early letters a young idealist, burning with the pure flame of art." In Carey's argument, all of Larkin's worst features are placed in the service of his art. For Larkin, "[a]rt and life are antipathetic." The philistinism was a part of his construction of a facade designed to protect his art from the intrusion of life.[14] This is one of the themes as well of Andrew Motion's biography, as its title, *A Writer's Life,* implies. Larkin's devotion to art "challenges the idea of himself as a writer that he liked to promote." Larkin understood, however, "that the relationship he had created between 'high' art and 'ordinary' existence was a remarkable one." In every phase of his life, his ordinary existence was dictated by his dedication to his art. "The friends he made, the jobs he took, the habits he formed, the places he lived in, the people he loved—all were chosen so that he could concentrate on

12. Both Rossen and Robert Crawford point out this discrepancy in the interview. Crawford is quoted in Rossen, *Philip Larkin: His Life's Work,* 99.

13. This is Andrew Motion's description, as reported to Rossen, of the way Larkin pictured himself to friends (Rossen, *Philip Larkin: His Life's Work,* 96).

14. Carey, "Mail Chauvinism," 5.

his writing, which is what mattered to him most. In the strictest sense, his was a writer's life" (*Life*, xix–xx).

And it is the place of Larkin's presumed philistinism—or at least one aspect of it—in his writing, his art, and not in his life that concerns me here. I am interested in the significance of jazz, blues, and popular music intertexts and conventions in particular works, but I recognize that many of the issues raised in this pursuit are also the issues raised by attention to Larkin's low-brow persona, questions about levels of language, for example, or the use of the cliché or the poems' audience.

Blake Morrison has raised some of these questions in *The Movement*, suggesting that Movement writing in general may be read as a tension between "academicism" and philistinism, and in his recent study Andrew Swarbrick finds in Larkin a tension similar to that Morrison sees in the Movement as a whole, arguing that Larkin's entire career can be read as a largely unresolved conflict between philistinism and aestheticism. The book traces the conflict from Oxford, where this cleavage first becomes apparent, to *High Windows*, where the philistinism, now more insistent, threatens to overwhelm the verse. It is Swarbrick's contention that Larkin's discovery of his "voice" in the poems of *The Less Deceived* is in fact his discovery of a way of "exploiting rather than suppressing" his philistinism. "The poems in *The Less Deceived* which established Larkin's particular identity as a poet—debunking, unillusioned, wittily rueful and irreverently ironic—represent the expression of the philistine in Larkin which begins to triumph over the aesthete who wrote *The North Ship*." Toward the end, the triumph of philistinism, however, becomes more problematical. The satirical poems of *High Windows* "reveal the most damaging aspects of Larkin's philistinism. In them, Larkin's political prejudices are all too vulnerably exposed."[15]

Swarbrick's study appeared after the letters controversy, and it demonstrates perhaps how the reaction against Larkin has begun to color

---

15. Blake Morrison, *The Movement: English Poetry and Fiction of the 1950s* (London, 1986), 135; Andrew Swarbrick, *Out of Reach: The Poetry of Philip Larkin* (New York, 1995), 51, 48, 141.

our reading of the poems. His manner of dealing with the paradox of a defining philistinism that is both the making and the undoing of a poet is to suggest that, as with cholesterol, there is both a good and a bad philistinism. The good philistinism is that described by Barbara Everett in "Art and Larkin." It includes the evocation of "that densely actual commonplace existence that all Larkin's poems 'invent' as their subject," the love of everyday things, the "sweet middle ranges of 'philistine' experience," the "flight from 'Art' " and the "drive to extinguish the false artistic ego," the poems' sense of artlessness, their sense of place and of factuality, and a modesty that suggests that the "artist as such has no standing." Swarbrick's bad philistinism features such impulses as hatred of "abroad" and foreign poetry, dogmatism, political bigotry, stereotyped attitudes, and sentimental cliché.[16]

The splitting of Larkin's philistinism into good and bad does not resolve what has become for some readers a moral issue. Swarbrick's assumption is that Larkin's bad philistinism produces bad poems. (He offers "Homage to a Government," "Going, Going," and "The Card-Players" as examples.) But many of the earlier successful poems—"Deceptions," "Places, Loved Ones"—issue from impulses that are now being condemned, and some of the most blatantly bad-mannered poems of *High Windows*—"Annus Mirabilis," "This Be the Verse," and the title poem—are to my mind among the most successful, certainly among the most frequently written about. The whole of Swarbrick's intelligent reading of the *Collected Poems* illustrates, however, the manner in which the philistine poet has become the focus of Larkin commentary.

Larkin's jazz addiction is only a part of a larger complex of attitudes and ideas, but it is central to it and epitomizes it in ways that have become evident to readers. As Swarbrick has noted, jazz was one of the earliest guises of Larkin's developing philistinism at Oxford. A "passion for jazz, which became the qualification for entry to the Larkin-Amis circle, was part and parcel of their defiant unpretentiousness, their irreverent rejection of the pieties associated with 'highbrow' arts." "This

16. Barbara Everett, "Art and Larkin," in *Philip Larkin: The Man and his Work,* ed. Dale Salwak (London, 1989), 130–35; Swarbrick, *Out of Reach,* 131, 141.

was something we had found for ourselves, that wasn't taught at school," Larkin recalls, "and having found it, we made it bear all the enthusiasm usually directed at more established arts" (*AWJ*, 16). A. T. Tolley writes that jazz "was to become for Larkin an epitome of the accessible, unself-conscious art that the modern world seemed to have turned away from," and he reminds us that the "no-nonsense relationship to the arts that jazz seemed to encourage was one that Larkin and Amis desired for all the arts at the time of the Movement." Clive James has also argued for the centrality of Larkin's jazz to his antimodernist art. Referring to his jazz aesthetic, he writes, "The same aesthetic underlies his literary criticism and everything else he writes. Especially it underlies his poetry."[17]

The question of the extent to which Larkin's poetry has absorbed his jazz, his blues, and his other musical addictions is the burden of this study, although it approaches the larger question through a series of smaller ones and it attempts to remain at the level of particular texts. To what extent did Larkin's "jazz life," as he referred to it, furnish a paradigm for his conception of all the arts? Tolley and other readers obviously believe that it did, but it is instructive to trace the development of this paradigm in Larkin's letters, his writings on jazz, and his critique of modernism. What are we to make of the contradictions and gaps of the introduction to *All What Jazz*, the differences between the attitude toward modern jazz in the introduction and that in the reviews that immediately follow? The first issue I have taken up is the connection between Larkin's jazz aesthetic, the way he conceives of jazz, and his conception of the development of all the arts in the twentieth century.

Do jazz and blues inform Larkin's poems in the way that they inform his views of twentieth-century poetry? This is a more difficult question to approach, especially since I am less interested in music as an influence on Larkin than in the significance of musical intertexts and conventions in the poems. The difference between the two interests may seem minor but it dictates the kind of reading I wish to pursue. To state it simply, I am more concerned with questions that arise in reading the poems

---

17. Swarbrick, *Out of Reach*, 70; Tolley, *My Proper Ground*, 138, 145–46; Clive James, "On His Wit," in *Larkin at Sixty*, ed. Thwaite, 103.

than with questions about how they came to be written, their sources or influences. Can there be much question that in the traditional sense Larkin's music was an "influence" on his poetry? But the more interesting issue, it seems to me, is the *significance* of the poems' musical intertexts, the ways in which jazz or popular song can shape our reading of a particular poem, at times without making an obvious appearance.

Michael Riffaterre draws a distinction between significance and meaning that helps to clarify my intent here. Meaning in his sense is the contextual understanding of a statement or text, dictated by its grammar and syntax, the words' references to other words. Only ordinary linguistic competence is required to understand a poem's meaning. Significance, however, is the product of a second reading stage that goes beyond grammatical meaning to explain "ungrammatical" features of the text. To see a text's significance the reader requires literary competence, since the significance of a poem may be incompatible with its contextual or grammatical meaning, referring the reader instead to an intertext or set of intertexts—cultural or literary texts, conventions, descriptive systems, clichés, or commonplaces it has absorbed. Riffaterre notes that "ungrammaticality within the poem is a sign of grammaticality elsewhere, that is, of belonging in another system. The systemic relationship confers significance."[18]

My method of reading Larkin, then, would have to be called intertextual in a general sense, but it is, I hope, an informal and unpretentious intertextuality in keeping with its subject. I have, in effect, appropriated and freely adapted a theory of reading for practical purposes. I require a method of writing about relationships between popular music and poetry, and Riffaterre's variety of intertextual theory provides a set of assumptions about reading texts I find useful. It assumes, for example, that all texts have absorbed other texts (using *text* in the broadest possible sense), and that the significance of a text is dictated by its relationship to its intertexts. It assumes that intertextual reading completes something otherwise incomplete in the text, that it is a product of the reader's collaboration with the text. It assumes that intertexts may range from

18. Michael Riffaterre, *Semiotics of Poetry* (Bloomington, 1978), 164–65.

cultural practices and conventions to identifiable literary (or musical) texts.

Tolley argues that "there is little use of intertextuality (conscious or unconscious) in Larkin's work: the reference to other literatures as a dimension of understanding . . . was anathema to him." It is true that Larkin railed against the modernist practice of self-conscious allusion and declared that he had "no belief in 'tradition' or a common myth-kitty or casual allusions in poems to other poems or poets" (RW, 79). This attitude is of course a part of his official philistine creed that he occasionally violated, as he does when he alludes to Gray's "Elegy" in "For Sidney Bechet" or Tennyson's The Princess in "Lines on a Young Lady's Photograph Album" or Robert Louis Stevenson's "Requiem" in "This Be the Verse" or Hamlet in the title of The Less Deceived. Intertextuality in the sense in which I use it, however, has little to do with The Waste Land manner of allusion. It is closer to the kind of intertextuality Larkin knew well in his own jazz and blues. It could be argued that jazz and blues furnish the purest model of the way intertextuality functions in all the arts. "Every artist is a jazz musician," Larry Beinhart writes, "running new riffs on old tunes."[19] The extent to which blues songs depend on a "common myth-kitty," a storehouse of phrases, lines, and conventions, has always been evident (Larkin refers to it in All What Jazz [249]). One may even come to feel that every blues song begins "Woke up this morning."

Larkin's "Aubade," in fact, begins with its own version of "Woke up this morning," and it furnishes an instance of one of the many forms musical intertexts may take in Larkin's poems. "Aubade" is of course not a blues—officially, its title identifies it as a morning song, a lyric about the coming of dawn—but its first line immediately dispels the impression given by the title and its most distinctive features, I argue, may best be read in light of the blues conventions it has incorporated. In only one line of the poem do the blues make a direct appearance, yet the poem as a whole is shaped by an attitude that is closer to the

19. Tolley, My Proper Ground, 177; Larry Beinhart, American Hero (New York, 1993), 128.

music of the American South than to the poetry of a long English tradition. It signifies in part through its relation to an absent blues intertext.

Jazz is overtly present, or at least it appears to be, in other Larkin poems, poems that are in effect responses to jazz or the blues. One of the informing fictions of such poems is that music is playing during the poem's performance—Bechet's soprano saxophone in "For Sidney Bechet," for example, or King Oliver's "Riverside Blues" in "Reference Back." Yet even in these poems the musical intertext around which the poem is shaped and to which it responds is, for most readers, an absence. These poems reproduce the situation of all intertextual reading. The text through which the work achieves its significance may not be recoverable by the reader even as its presence is indicated by an incompleteness in the work.

These "jazz poems," poems *about* jazz, or perhaps more correctly about *listening* to jazz, provide some of the most instructive examples of the manner in which his texts are informed by his jazz. So completely are poems such as "Reasons for Attendance" and "Reference Back" shaped by the conventions and assumptions of the jazz world that they have been misread when the jazz intertext is ignored. "Reasons for Attendance" is not, as has been assumed, a defense of the speaker's art of poetry. The appeal to art by which the poem finds its resolution is an appeal to jazz as an art form and not to poetry. ("For Sidney Bechet" is also, in part, an argument for taking jazz seriously as art.) "Reference Back," on the other hand, is not, as it first appears, a tribute to the music of King Oliver, yet the actual recording—the performance—of "Riverside Blues" in Chicago in 1923 by King Oliver's Creole Jazz Band is crucial to a complete reading of the poem.

The significance of poems such as these, I suggest, rests on jazz and blues conventions that must be read as a part of the poems' system of intertexts. "Reference Back" and "For Sidney Bechet," for example, both find significance in the jazz distinction between the work as artifact and the work as performance, jazz as an irreproducible art that exists only at the moment of its creation. "Reasons for Attendance" turns on the jazz aficionado's assumption that jazz is a music for listening and not for dancing, that dancing is an inauthentic response to jazz. The notion of the jazz "lover," jazz as the love object and not the music that accompanies love, is essential to the resolution of "For Sidney Bechet." A rare musical text may at times be identified in the poetry—George and Ira Gershwin's "But Not for Me" or Cole Porter's "At Long Last Love"—but it is the conventional quality of the "Cole Porter song" rather than an identifiable song that is at issue in "Lines on a Young Lady's Photograph Album." And the musical intertext of "Aubade" or "Two Guitar Pieces" is not a single blues song but an entire system of assumptions and practices together with a storehouse of adaptable lines and phrases known as the blues.

To think of the relation between "Aubade" and the blues or "Lines on a Young Lady's Photograph Album" and a Cole Porter song or "Annus Mirabilis" and pop music is to raise a number of other questions about the poetry. Almost all of them can be related to the current focus on Larkin's philistinism, but I have, for the most part, avoided the term in what follows since it tends to tilt the discussion toward Larkin the poet and to offer too pat an answer to the issue at hand. To suggest, for example, that the presence of blues conventions in "Aubade" is simply another case of Larkin's philistinism (whether good or bad) doesn't say anything about the place of the blues intertext in our reading of the poem.

The same is true of the issue of the audience for whom the poems appear to be written. One of the conventions of Larkin's poetry is that it is directed to the "common reader," the audience for popular music and popular literature. And his harshest accusation against modernism is that it lost the only audience that matters, the "cash customers" of poetry who read for pleasure and who have been replaced by an academic audience. One could dismiss all of this as a part of the philistine pose (or applaud Larkin for attempting to capture a larger audience for serious poetry), but my concern is with the way Larkin's "popular" poems position their readers, especially "serious" or academic readers. In this discussion music at times serves more as an analogue or a lens through which to view the poems than as an intertext. Since a poem like "Annus Mirabilis" or "This Be the Verse" pretends to be addressed to a popular audience, a reader who devotes the kind of attention to them one would devote to a poem by Yeats or Auden is put in much the same position as a young Larkin listening to Louis Armstrong or Pee Wee Russell (or an older Larkin listening to the Beatles). He says of his Oxford jazz circle, "I suppose we devoted to some hundred records that early anatomizing passion normally reserved for the more established arts" (*RW*, 22). A critic who sets out on a rigorous analysis of a poem that begins "They fuck you up, your mum and dad" may feel a kinship with this point of view.

The suggestion that Larkin has re-created in his poetry the conditions of his own enjoyment of popular music is a way of saying what has been said before, that popular music, jazz in particular, furnished the model for a kind of poetry to set against the modernist poem. I will attempt to get beyond that general observation (with which I agree) to look at a number of the immediate and specific consequences of reading poems in which the "epitome of the accessible, unself-conscious art"[20] to which they aspire is jazz or some other genre of popular music.

Some of these consequences—and I will use them here as examples that represent a wider range—may be grouped under the general heading of *authenticity* (in several different senses) as it relates to Larkin's poetry. There is, first and famously, the legend of Larkin's discovery of an authentic voice through his rejection of the consciously poetic Yeats and his adoption of the unpoetic Hardy. The point of this story, created by Larkin and repeated in countless Larkin commentaries, is that poems don't come from other poems, as he told an interviewer—they are not intertextual—but from real life. In the story Hardy teaches Larkin to escape artifice and thus to become the poet of the authentic, the real. The opening poem of *The Less Deceived*, "Lines on a Young Lady's Photograph Album," it has been suggested, announces his realist aesthetic. It is a poem about "a real girl in a real place," and its exemplary art form is the photograph.

A part of our sense of Larkin as the philistine poet in Barbara Everett's positive sense is of course Larkin as the poet of the commonplace, of

20. Tolley, *My Proper Ground*, 138.

the world of everyday things, whose poems wear the guise of artlessness. There is a danger, however, of confusing the guise of artlessness with the absence of art, of thinking of Larkin—as he thought of himself—as having broken from convention and artifice to arrive at the threshold of the real. A great deal of the early criticism implies, sometimes without saying it outright, that Larkin became a great poet when his poems began to forsake the poetic and to incorporate the details of actual experience. This is very close to the blues musician's claim that the blues are not artifice but reality. It is relatively easy to show that the blues are among the most rigidly conventional of all musical forms; it is more difficult but nevertheless possible to show that a "realist" poem like "Lines on a Young Lady's Photograph Album" takes its voice and its attitude not from the photographic or the documentary but from the opposite pole. The poem is, one might argue not altogether whimsically, Larkin's version of the "Cole Porter song." My contention is that Larkin's poems frequently achieve the effect of authenticity—they sound unpoetic—not because they have somehow managed to incorporate unmediated reality, not because they *are* artless, but because they have employed conventions and artifices that readers identify with something other than the classical poetic tradition. There is no one set of conventions to be identified in the poems, but some of the poems have clearly absorbed the conventions of American popular music.

Authenticity is also a concern of the poems themselves, especially the jazz-related poems, which focus, for example, on the authenticity of jazz as an art set against other kinds of music or the authenticity of the speaker's reception of jazz set against that of an inauthentic audience. I argue that the concept of authenticity in the poems is tied to another of their underlying themes—the assumption that the real is always elsewhere. Larkin's poems treat this theme directly, as in "The Importance of Elsewhere," but more often indirectly, as in "Annus Mirabilis," which is in part about the speaker's exclusion from the "authentic" sexuality of the Beatles generation. The sense of exclusion and the notion of authenticity are in turn related in an interesting way to Larkin's jazz. His own account of his introduction to jazz emphasizes a link between the authenticity of the music and the fact that it was not a part of his own culture but something appropriated from outside. In this respect the appeal of jazz to Larkin was typical of the more general English appropriation of black American music, a music that was authenticated by the fact that its "real" audience was elsewhere.

Simon Frith has shown how the early reviews of jazz in England reveal the extent to which it was an elite taste, not something embraced by the "common reader." They also reveal, Frith suggests, the extent to which the reception of jazz in England was involved with "the urge to 'authenticity' ": "In this world," he writes, "American music—black American music—stands for a simple idea: that everything *real* is happening elsewhere."[21] The middle-class English audience attributed authenticity to an American jazz from which they were effectively excluded—truly authentic jazz was played by black musicians for black audiences, as one of the early reviewers pointed out—and it is intriguing to compare this sense of authenticity to that attributed to Larkin's verse by academic readers who are similarly excluded (at least conventionally) from poems that pretend to be written for someone else.

Larkin's readers have also called attention to what William Harmon labels the "authenticating function" of Larkin's use of obscenity and slang,[22] and I am interested in the function of cliché toward the same end. Swarbrick argues, in effect, that obscenity loses its authenticity once it is turned into art, but one of the effects of the Larkin poem is that its language appears to retain its authenticity by its resistance to becoming art. Its pretense of being unself-conscious entertainment, when set against the reality that it makes its appeal to sophisticated readers, gives a Larkin poem like "This Be the Verse" the peculiar status of "two-audience" music—jazz or blues performed at once for the dance hall and the concert hall.

One of the obvious effects of the use of cliché in Larkin's poems is also to impart to them the status of popular music, of unself-conscious entertainment. "For what could a popular song be which scorned or

---

21. Simon Frith, "Playing with Real Feeling—Jazz and Suburbia," in *Music for Pleasure: Essays in the Sociology of Pop* (New York, 1988), 61.

22. William Harmon, "Larkin's Memory," *Sewanee Review,* XCVIII (1990), 217.

snubbed cliché?" Christopher Ricks asks of a Bob Dylan song,[23] and I have found it useful to compare the effect of the cliché in popular songs such as those of Dylan and in poems by Larkin. (It happens that the same cliché is the basis for a Dylan song and a Larkin poem.) Approaching Larkin's use of cliché through popular music, however, entails other questions about the performance of cliché. What accounts, first of all, for the appeal of the cliché in popular music and does it have a similar appeal for Larkin? Popular music commentators have offered a number of explanations for their music's embrace of commonplace expressions—that pop lyrics are in some sense *about* ordinary language, about themselves as songs, for example, or that the effect of popular music lyrics is to "defamiliarize" the language of everyday, or to bring the listener's attention to the language itself, or to transform to poetry the stale and familiar.

Larkin's devotion to the cliché could be explained along similar lines. His poems are of course *about* the use of a certain level of language, about using *fuck* in a "serious" poem, and there is no question that Larkin's poems bring the reader's attention to the ordinary language itself—the bride's "*I nearly died*" in "The Whitsun Weddings" as a characterizing phrase or the speaker's "Most things may never happen: this one will" in "Aubade" as an example of what can be done with the most commonplace words. Larkin's poems do transform the familiar into art, but to leave it at that is simply to revert to the concept of the philistine poet and to explain Larkin's embrace of the cliché and of ordinary language in general as a part of his effort to reclaim the "common reader" modernism supposedly drove away. Rather than asking about the appeal of the cliché for Larkin, however, we can pose the question in a way that leaves his own motives aside—how does the cliché function in particular Larkin texts?

J. R. Watson observes that Larkin associates clichéd language with social positions and lifestyles and uses clichés to identify and characterize his speakers and the people they observe, and Andrew Swarbrick simi-

---

23. Christopher Ricks, "Clichés," in *The State of the Language,* ed. Leonard Michaels and Christopher Ricks (Berkeley, 1980), 61.

larly notes the tendency of the poems to capture attitudes and social location in a representative cliché. Clearly one of the functions of the cliché is to "place" speakers and characters sociolinguistically, but I am interested in another related effect of the cliché that is suggested by the popular song analogy. One of the effects of clichéd language in popular song lyrics, it has been argued, is to establish the "reality" of the world the song creates and therefore the basis for its reception. In the music of Buddy Holly or the Everly Brothers, for example, the "universe" of the song may be defined, as Dave Laing suggests, by the high school courting code or another similar set of references that are immediately accessible to the teenage audience. The cliché, that is to say, is perceived as a source of the "authenticity" of the song since it is a part of the song's base in the everyday world, and the "reality" of the everyday world is no more or less than the language ordinarily used to evoke it. I follow Riffaterre here in assuming that a text is seen as "true" because it conforms to "a mythology that the reader carries within him," which is itself "composed of clichés and commonplaces."[24] It is obviously a short step from this point to an examination of the role of the cliché in the perceived "authenticity" of a typical Larkin poem.

If we adopt Riffaterre's theory of reading, we would have to conclude that a culture's clichés and commonplaces are essential to *all* reading at whatever level it occurs. What is distinctive about a Larkin poem like "Next, Please," however, and what makes the musical analogy meaningful, is that it uncovers what is hidden or disguised in the texts of "high" culture. In Riffaterre's method of reading, any poem may be reduced to the cultural commonplaces shared by the poet and the reader, but since these commonplaces have been so radically altered by the poet's language or so deeply buried, this may be a difficult task. In many of Larkin's poems, however, and in the lyrics of popular music, the clichés and commonplaces are brought to the surface, openly displayed.

---

24. J. R. Watson, "Clichés and Common Speech in Philip Larkin's Poetry," *Critical Survey,* I (1989), 150; Swarbrick, *Out of Reach,* 3; Dave Laing, *The Sound of Our Time* (Chicago, 1970), 101; Michael Riffaterre, *Text Production,* trans. Terese Lyons (New York, 1983), 185.

A successful reading of some of these poems—"Next, Please" and "Wires" are two examples—depends on the reader's possession of the cliché that serves as a kind of intertext, and I have used the cliché-dependent popular song (and its commentary) as the basis for my own examination of the cliché's performance in these poems.

In the interview with *Paris Review* discussed earlier, Robert Phillips, through a long leading question, gave Larkin the opportunity to discuss the "art" of his use of "common phrases." Were they for irony, to "bear more meaning than usual"? Were they added late "to add texture," or were they "integral from the beginning"? Refusing to take the bait, Larkin answered, "They occur naturally" (*RW*, 70–71), as if to oppose the artful with the natural, to deny the implication that the cliché could be artfully employed in "serious" poetry. By this point of course, the early eighties, Larkin was rigidly fixed in the philistine pose that had such unexpected consequences. I have avoided an appeal to the philistine pose as diligently as Larkin avoided an appeal to high art. Although Larkin's jazz and his nod toward pop music were a part of his rejection of what high art had become, I have taken him seriously as an artist. I have assumed throughout that the Larkin canon merits the same scrutiny as the poems of the high modernists, that whatever his current status as cultural icon, he is, if no longer the best-loved, still the best poet of his generation. Before the publication of the letters, it would not have been necessary to affirm his place among twentieth-century poets, but Larkin's posthumous blues have finally allowed him the deprivation he claimed for himself during his lifetime.

2

JAZZ AND MODERNISM

The wonderful music that swept the world during the first half of this century
. . . was of limited appeal, but that appeal was new and definite: a certain area
of musical and rhythmic sensibility was being played on for the first time.
—Larkin, "Wells or Gibbon?" in
All What Jazz

Russell, Charles Ellsworth "Pee Wee" (b. 1906), clarinet and saxophone player
extraordinary, was, *mutatis mutandis,* our Swinburne and our Byron.
—Larkin, Introduction to *Jill*

OFFERING an explanation for the source of his poetry ("unhappiness") and the source of his popularity ("writing about unhappiness"),
late in his career Larkin told an interviewer that deprivation was for him
what daffodils were for Wordsworth (*RW*, 47). Although unhappiness is
a state we readily associate with Larkin's poetry, *deprivation* as a description of the circumstance of his life doesn't quite ring true, perhaps
because it is dictated by the alliterative echo of *daffodils* (and wit seems
an inappropriate mode for expressing deprivation). Or perhaps it is
because the postbiography-and-letters Larkin appears now to have
indulged himself to a degree even exceeding the norm in that traditional

triad of worldly pleasures wine, women, and song, which he termed in an unfinished poem "Drink, sex and jazz—all sweet things" (*CP*, 154). Whatever the case, a more persuasive argument might be made that it was not the fact of deprivation but the musical and rhythmic sensibility of deprivation, the blues, which were for Larkin what daffodils were for Wordsworth. For Larkin, the "hallmark" of the blues was exactly their capacity to express the "solitary anguish" (*AWJ*, 86) of the African-American's life of deprivation. His praise for the blues and for jazz in general—that is, the music for which the blues serve as foundation— is based, ironically, on an admiration for the sort of emotional honesty missing in the comparison with Wordsworth.[1] He characterizes the blues as "a kind of jazz that calls forth a particular sincerity from the player ('Yeah, he's all right, but can he play the *blues?*')," and he argues that the "Negro did not have the blues because he was naturally melancholy. He had them because he was cheated and bullied and starved" (*AWJ*, 87, 224). The deprivation-daffodil parallel more aptly applies to the makers of the music to which Larkin was addicted and through which he experienced his privation secondhand.

It is perhaps decisive for Larkin's own version of jazz and the blues that his jazz sensibility was formed in adolescence. "I became a jazz addict at the age of 12 or 13," he remembers (*Letters*, 416), so he might also have said, preserving the alliteration, that jazz was for him what juvenescence was for Wordsworth. At a time when Wordsworth was, by his testimony, bounding like a roe o'er the mountains, Larkin was entering his subscription to *Down Beat* and learning to play the drums.

---

1. In *Stomping the Blues* (New York, 1976), Albert Murray quotes (disapprovingly) the definition of the blues offered by the *Standard Dictionary of Folklore, Mythology, and Legend*—the "tender, ironic, bitter, humorous, or typical expression of a deprived people" (74). On the issues of the blues as the music of deprivation and the blues as fundamental to both jazz and rock and roll, see, for example, *AWJ*, 36, 86, 87, 234–35, 266 and *Life*, 46–47, 57. In general, Larkin thinks of the blues both as a kind of jazz and as the basis of all jazz. Very early in his jazz career he came to the conclusion that "there is only one kind of jazz, and that's Blues, or music based on the Blues" (*Life*, 46). In *All What Jazz* he writes that "blues lie at the heart of rock," which is "only certain elements in the blues isolated, coarsened and amplified" (266).

And while Wordsworth remembers the "very Heaven" of being young at the time of the French Revolution, Larkin's later reflection on his youth was that it was his particular bliss to have been young at the only time he could have experienced the pleasure of jazz. Had he died on 9 August 1922 instead of being born then or had he been born a decade or so later, he would have missed it all (*AWJ*, 28), since, he notes, jazz was the "emotional excitement" peculiar to one generation, his own, that "came to adolescence" between the two world wars. "In another age," he suggests, "it might have been drink or drugs, religion or poetry" (*Letters*, 416; *AWJ*, 15). Or daffodils or revolution. Larkin's claim to have substituted jazz for the inspirations and excitements of other ages is something more than his characteristic philistine pose, even if it is also that. Jazz was, along with poetry, the great passion of his life ("In many ways I prefer it to poetry")[2] and his reader may well wonder about the extent to which the two passions intersect.

Larkin has given readers cause to think that the popular music of his time was a part of the climate in which his conception of poetry took shape. In a 1972 review of a book on Cole Porter he reminds us of the sophistication of the typical Cole Porter song, "that feat of rhyme and reference," and he adds that "those who were exposed daily to such products grew up thinking that songs (and perhaps even poems) were skilfully made things, requiring thought as well as feeling" (*RW*, 227). In a 1979 interview he makes clear that he is referring to his own exposure to such products and to his own assumptions about how songs and poems are made:

I must have learned dozens of dance lyrics simply by listening to dance music. I suppose they were a kind of folk poetry. Some of them were pretty awful, but

---

2. This is quoted from a 1968 *Guardian* interview in Rossen, *Philip Larkin: His Life's Work*, 100. The whole passage is of interest because of Larkin's explicit comparison of jazz and poetry: "In many ways I prefer it to poetry. I listen to it while dressing in the morning, turning to it in a way I should turn to poetry if I were living my life according to Vernon Watkins's standards. What did Baudelaire say, man can live a week without bread but not a day without poetry. You might say I can live a week without poetry but not a day without jazz."

I often wonder whether my assumption that a poem is something that rhymes and scans didn't come from listening to them—and some of them were quite sophisticated. "The Venus de Milo was noted for her charms / But strictly between us, you're cuter than Venus / And what's more you've got arms"—I can't imagine Mick Jagger singing that; you know, it was witty and technically clever. (*RW,* 50)

We too may wonder what part of Larkin's poetic assumptions and practices came from his musical addictions. The question of the significance of jazz in the Larkin canon—does jazz haunt Larkin's poems in the way that nature haunts Wordsworth's?—encompasses too many other issues to be tackled in the space of a chapter, but one of these issues, the confluence of jazz, poetry, and modernism in what Larkin called his "jazz life" (*AWJ,* 17), invites a more circumscribed reading, and I will examine it as a preface to the larger question. I want to look particularly at Larkin's attitude toward jazz as a measure of all the arts—the sense we have in reading his letters and criticism that Larkin's music is often the perspective from which all else is seen—and I want to examine in some detail the odd pairing of jazz and literary modernism in his collection of jazz reviews.

"The art-form I associate with Philip at Oxford was not any sort of literature but jazz," Kingsley Amis writes, and others who remember Larkin at Oxford make the same association. Nick Russel recalls that in their first meeting Larkin immediately abandoned his mission (drumming up support for the university English Club) when he spotted on Russel's table a copy of Hugues Panassié's *Hot Jazz.* Russel also recalls that Larkin had the most remarkable ear of the dozen or so undergraduates who belonged to the unofficial jazz club: "he could distinguish accurately between Johnny Dodds and Albert Nichols, say, or King Oliver and Armstrong." Larkin appeared to Russel to make little distinction in value between discussions of the work of Sidney Bechet and Pee Wee Russell and discussions of Lawrence, Joyce, and Yeats.[3]

3. Kingsley Amis, "Oxford and After," in *Larkin at Sixty,* ed. Anthony Thwaite (London, 1982), 24; Nick Russel, "Larkin' About at St John's," in *Philip Larkin, 1922–1985: A Tribute,* ed. George Hartley (London, 1988), 83.

Among those who belonged to the unofficial club at Oxford jazz soon became the language into which literature and the other arts were translated. The Romantics became "Bill Wordsworth and his Hot Six—Wordsworth (tmb) with 'Lord' Byron (tpt), Percy Shelley (sop), Johnny Keats (alto and clt), Sam 'Tea' Coleridge (pno), Jimmy Hogg (bs), Bob Southy (ds)."[4] Larkin and his circle applied to jazz the kind of scrutiny that at another time would have been given to poetry:

I suppose we devoted to some hundred records that early anatomizing passion normally reserved for the more established arts. "It's the *abject entreaty* of that second phrase. . . ." "What she's actually singing is *ick-sart-mean*. . . ." "Russell goes right on up to the first bar of Waller. You can hear it on Nick's pick-up." "Isn't it marvellous the way Bechet . . ." "Isn't it marvellous the way the trumpet . . ." "Isn't it marvellous the way Russell. . . ." (Introduction to *Jill*, 15)

That a music so exotic—a "form of Afro-American popular music that flourished between 1925 and 1945," as Larkin defined it (*AWJ*, 246)—should have spoken directly to an Oxford undergraduate perhaps requires explanation, especially in light of Larkin's later statement that he was "not fond of exotics (botanical term meaning introduced from abroad)" (*AWJ*, 197). Both Larkin and Amis (who shared Larkin's passion for jazz at Oxford) have offered explanations that arrive at similar conclusions. The appeal of jazz, in Larkin's view, was precisely that it was *not* foreign; it was something his generation took as their own because they had discovered it for themselves. One's parents knew nothing about it, "[n]o one you knew liked it" (*AWJ*, 15), and it provided a private language that those outside the unofficial club had difficulty understanding. "For us, jazz became a part of the private joke of existence, rather than a public expertise," Larkin says of his group at Oxford; "expressions such as 'combined pimp and lover' and 'eating the cheaper cuts of pork' (both from a glossary on 'Yellow Dog Blues') flecked our conversations cryptically" (*AWJ*, 17). More than that, it was an unpretentious art built on a simple and direct emotional appeal that did not depend on an extensive musical education. Jazz was a "form

4. Amis, "Oxford and After," 26.

ideally suited to those with enough—but no more—music in them to respond intensely to a few strong simple effects," Amis says. Larkin's explanation contains an implicit recognition of what should have been the distance between American musician and English audience:

[T]hose white and coloured Americans, Bubber Miley, Frank Teschmacher, J. C. Higginbotham, spoke immediately to our understanding. Their rips, slurs and distortions were something we understood perfectly. This was something we had found for ourselves, that wasn't taught at school (what a prerequisite that is of nearly everything worthwhile!), and having found it, we made it bear all the enthusiasm usually directed at more established arts. (*AWJ*, 16)

A. T. Tolley characterizes Larkin's love of jazz as a kind of "cultural iconoclasm," and he observes, correctly, that "the sense that one valued something, not because it was felt to be culturally important, but because it spoke to one with immediacy, was to remain for him a touchstone of the arts." Amis agrees that the appeal of jazz lay somehow in its lack of cultural authority, the fact that its commentary had not yet been written. His generation was the first to encounter it, and there were no precedents. Jazz was a "world of romance," he writes, "with no guide, no senior person to point the way."[5]

For Larkin, conversant with this world, everything from painting to a sore throat had its jazz analogy or allusion. He writes to art student Jim Sutton, formerly his fellow jazz enthusiast at King Henry VIII School, Coventry: "There is great hope for your painting. Look at Armstrong's crude beginnings & his lyric height. Or even the third-stage crudeness of Pee Wee Russell" (*Letters*, 18). Another letter to Sutton mentions "a cough & generally Armstrongish throat" which is "fine for bawling blues with ('Ah'm sorry babe . . . sorry to mah heart . . .')" (*Letters*, 7). An early spring day is "as wonderful as hearing Earl Hines after a YMCA piano-basher" (*Letters*, 114), and Auden's integrated style in *Paid on Both Sides* is "like Teschmaker's clarinet or Pee Wee Russell" (*Life*, 75). The blues form especially was adaptable to any sort of utter-

---

5. Kingsley Amis, "Farewell to a Friend," in *Philip Larkin: The Man and His Work*, ed. Salwak, 4; Tolley, *His Proper Ground*, 2.

ance, even the apology to Sutton in Italy (*Letters*, 81) that a previous letter would be late because it was too heavy to be sent airmail:

> 'Sent you a letter, but it had to go by boat
> I said I sent you a letter, but it had to go by boat,
> Er—pardon me a moment while I pour some
> whiskey down the inside of my throat . . .'

Larkin's most extravagant jazz analogy appears in an essay written during his last year at Oxford in which he argues that jazz "is the closest description of the unconscious we have" (*Life*, 57). The argument begins with the Eliot-like assumption of a decay of ritual that has resulted in the deprivation of the unconscious, "which finds its daily fulfilment in such ritual." The predicament of the unconscious is reflected in turn by a general upheaval in all the arts, and most particularly in the emergence of American jazz. Every quality of the new music is analogous to the situation of the unconscious. The stridency of jazz symbolizes the urgency of the problem. The subjection of the unconscious is symbolized by the music of a subject people. The imprisonment of the unconscious is captured by the unvarying monotony of jazz's 4/4 rhythm, and the unconscious's panic is captured by the texture of the jazz tone. "Jazz is the new art of the unconscious," Larkin concludes, "and it is therefore improvised, for it cannot call upon consciousness to express its own divorce from consciousness" (*Life*, 57).

The tendency to use jazz—that is, early jazz—as a reference point or, more frequently, as a touchstone by which authenticity may be determined (including the lack of authenticity of later jazz) persists into post-Oxford life. Decades later Larkin counters, with a quotation from Pee Wee Russell, Yeats's statement that a poem is a piece of luck: "The more you try, the luckier you are." And in 1981 the twenty-seven years since the publication of Amis's *Lucky Jim* is made real for Larkin once he converts it to the chronology of jazz: "That shakes me. Longer than between Oliver's first record and Basie's" (*Letters*, 81, 638). The most elaborate entanglement of jazz and the other arts is the introduction to the 1970 *All What Jazz*, where jazz and modernism are paired in ways that (Larkin believes) expose qualities of both. Jazz reveals the excesses of modernism very clearly, Larkin explains in a later interview, "because it's such a telescoped art, only as old as the century" (*RW*, 72). In a review included in the second edition of *All What Jazz*, he goes so far as to suggest that the short history of jazz recapitulates in a condensed form (and therefore unmasks what is more difficult to see in the longer histories of the other arts) the stages into which any art may be segmented. In jazz we see "a capsule history of all arts—the generation from tribal function, the efflorescence into public and conscious entertainment, and the degeneration into private and subsidized absurdity" (*AWJ*, 259).

All What Jazz is a collection (along with a polemical introduction) of the jazz reviews Larkin began writing for the *Daily Telegraph* in 1961,[6] and it invites a somewhat closer and more skeptical reading than Larkin's casual comments on jazz. A rereading of the collection with its introduction reveals, among other things, that Larkin had also been rereading the pieces and in the process had discerned a "story" lying hidden in the progression of seemingly innocuous record reviews. Larkin's account of his rereading is almost certainly feigned to a degree; he presents himself as an innocent reader coming upon a group of music reviews that reveal collectively a latent text more interesting ("entertaining" is his word) than the manifest content, but of course he knew the story long before he reread the pieces. It is, however, a crucial narrative of Larkin's jazz career and it merits retelling, although we may well be suspicious of his own version. The story is in part an explanation for his inability to appreciate postwar or modern jazz, but, since jazz is Larkin's touchstone for all the arts, it becomes as well his explanation of a distaste for the whole of modernism, exemplified by the alliterative triad of Parker (Charlie), Pound, and Picasso, names that become his shorthand for the pioneers of modernism and "every practitioner who might be said to have succeeded them" (*AWJ*, 27).

Larkin's story revolves around a gap in his jazz career that is both

---

6. The reviews continued until December 1971. The first edition of *All What Jazz* (1970) contains the reviews between 1961 and 1968. The second edition (1985) adds the reviews of the last three years.

the problem to be explained—something missing from his appreciation of jazz—and the explanation—a chronological gap during which he is divorced from jazz: "on leaving Oxford I suffered a gap in my jazz life" (*AWJ*, 17). The explanation is disappointingly simple; in beginning his career as a librarian in 1943, Larkin lived in a series of lodgings where he was forbidden to play his gramophone. Since jazz, unlike poetry, cannot be enjoyed in silence and moreover depends notoriously on the individual performance—"it is not 'Weary Blues' we want but Armstrong's 1927 'Weary Blues' " (*AWJ*, 60)—Larkin, separated from his records and without access to new performances, lost touch with jazz for almost five years. In 1945, for example, he reports to Amis that he has received for his birthday a copy of "Jazz Me Blues" by the Lewis-Parnell Jazzmen: "This is I believe (though only having heard it once I can't be sure) one of the best records ever made in England. I suppose the best was 'Waltzing the Blues.' . . . But as I have no gramophone here all this is rather academic" (*Letters*, 107). When he was reunited with his collection in 1948, he "was content to renew acquaintance with it and to add only what amplified or extended it along existing lines" (*AWJ*, 17–18). He was further isolated from contemporary jazz by his resistance to the long-playing record, introduced in the mid-fifties: "it seemed a package deal, forcing you to buy bad tracks along with good at an unwantedly-high price" (*AWJ*, 18). He was vaguely aware of something now called modern jazz: "What I heard on the wireless seemed singularly unpromising, but I doubt if I thought it would ever secure enough popular acceptance to warrant my bothering about it" (*AWJ*, 18).

Uncannily, Larkin's gap after Oxford in 1943 was being duplicated at almost exactly the same time by a gap in jazz created by the American Federation of Musicians' ban on recorded music imposed in July of 1942. "It is a significant date," Larkin says in a review of a jazz discography. The disruption "closed the era of swing music. When the ban was lifted two years later, jazz had split into what seemed two irreconcilable camps, be-bop and trad revival, and things were never quite the same again" (*AWJ*, 161). Larkin's implication is that the coincidence of the two gaps caused him to miss the advent of modern jazz, so that when he began reviewing jazz records for the *Daily Telegraph* in 1961, he was "patently unfitted to do so" and took on the job only because of the depth of his ignorance of the new jazz: "I didn't believe jazz itself could alter out of all recognition any more than the march or the waltz could. It was simply a question of hearing enough of the new stuff" (*AWJ*, 18–19). But when the records arrive, the extent of the gap in Larkin's jazz is revealed:

[T]he eagerness with which I played them turned rapidly to astonishment, to disbelief, to alarm. I felt I was in some nightmare, in which I had confidently gone into an examination hall only to find that I couldn't make head or tail of the questions. It wasn't like listening to a kind of jazz I didn't care for—Art Tatum, shall I say, or Jelly Roll Morton's Red Hot Peppers. It wasn't like listening to jazz at all. (*AWJ*, 19)

In this multiplicity of gaps there is one further gap that the first two are meant to account for—the real motive for the story Larkin supposedly discovers—and that is the gap between the conception of jazz in Larkin's introduction to *All What Jazz* and that in the reviews it introduces. A number of readers of the collection have noted the contradiction—a bitter denunciation of modern jazz and its practitioners in the introduction and a fair-minded and appreciative view of the same music and musicians in the essays that immediately follow. To take the most obvious example, in the introduction Charlie Parker (as a member of the Parker/Pound/Picasso trinity) comes to represent everything that is wrong with modern jazz. Larkin holds him personally responsible for the advent of the new music, which is characterized as "Parker and his followers" (*AWJ*, 20), and he comes to epitomize the worst of modern jazz's mannerisms, the "impression of mental hallucination," a "kind of manic virtuosity," and the "substitution of bloodless note-patterns for some cheerful or sentimental popular song as a basis for improvisation." Parker's playing was "fast and showy," he "couldn't play four bars without resorting to a peculiarly irritating five-note cliché" from "The Woody Woodpecker Song," and his tone was "thin and sometimes shrill." He repeats, finally, one jazz critic's testimony that "if he played Charlie Parker records to his baby it cried" (*AWJ*, 20–21, 26).

This is not, however, the Charlie Parker of a 10 June 1961 joint review of Parker and Sidney Bechet. Here the two musicians represent two different but equally legitimate branches of jazz:

Parker ... had when he died, aged 34, seen jazz re-fashion itself pretty well in his image and heard his own solos coming back at him from a thousand horns. His technique and invention were prodigious, whereas no one would pretend Bechet had any more of either than he needed. Yet both alike on these records display unquestioned individual authority, unclouded and absolute. This is jazz and this is Bechet (or Parker) playing it. (*AWJ*, 40)

Parker is praised as a musician who "not only could translate his ideas into notes at superhuman speed, but who was simultaneously aware of half a dozen ways of resolving any given musical situation." Interestingly, Larkin's own traditional jazz is now referred to as "the ossified platitudes of 1940 big-band jazz" against which Parker's modern jazz was in part a reaction. The review ends with one of those unexpected and affecting figures that the Larkin reader sometimes stumbles across in the last lines of a poem: "But on the evidence of these solos alone it would be absurd to call Parker's music a reaction. As well call leaping salmon a reaction" (*AWJ*, 42–43). The elation of the leaping salmon and the generosity of coupling Parker with Bechet, Larkin's representative of all the best qualities of jazz, will at first seem odd to a reader who, a few pages earlier in the introduction, has seen Parker coupled with another traditional jazz musician: "I used to think that anyone hearing a Parker record would guess he was a drug addict, but no one hearing Beiderbecke would think he was an alcoholic, and that this summed up the distinction between the kinds of music" (*AWJ*, 20).

It is the gap between the two Parkers that Larkin seeks to fill with the story he claims to have discerned in rereading the reviews. Contemporary criticism thrives on gaps and contradictions of various kinds—the reader-response critic's blanks, the poststructuralist's aporias, Macherey's Marxist lapses and hollows. These critics discover disruptions even where the surface looks perfectly smooth; it is difficult to come up with another instance of a writer opening a chasm as wide as that Larkin opens in *All What Jazz*. And in attempting to bridge one gap, the two Parkers (I will follow Larkin's lead in using Parker as an icon for the whole of modern jazz), he introduces another that is equally troubling. Larkin's explanation for the contradiction between the two Parkers involves a confession that would seem more damning for a reviewer than the charge of inconsistency. He confesses that for the first two years or so of his career as a record reviewer he faked his responses to the music under review.

What prevented him from publishing his honest response? Larkin's explanation is that he found himself in the awkward position of coming upon the traditional-modern controversy twenty years too late. It was in the late forties (during the gap in his jazz life) that the battle had been fought; to adopt the traditional viewpoint once again in 1961 would have been "journalistically impossible," since the issue had long since been decided. By the time Larkin could enter the fray "Parker was dead and a historical figure, in young eyes probably indistinguishable from King Oliver and other founding fathers. There was nothing for it but to carry on with my original plan of undiscriminating praise" (*AWJ*, 21). In short, he became the jazz equivalent of the literary "whores who had grown old in the reviewing game by praising everything" (*AWJ*, 19). Larkin's "slow approximation" through the reviews to the position taken in the introduction is the amusing narrative he finds in the collection—"watching truthfulness break in, despite my initial resolve" (*AWJ*, 25).

Larkin's figure for himself as the jazz whore seems particularly damning here in light of his attitude toward modern jazz. In taking up his column for the *Daily Telegraph,* he would be to reviewing what prostitution is to sexual desire, and it turns out that his formulation— the counterfeit that is the antithesis of the thing it feigns—approximates the relationship of modern jazz to real jazz. "When Parker and the rest started bopping," he says in a review included in the second edition of *All What Jazz* (by which time truthfulness had broken in), "their aim was to sell something as unlike jazz as possible to jazz audiences." What they produced was "the conscious opposite of jazz" (*AWJ*, 260). Borrowing an argument from A. E. Housman, Larkin declares that the music of Parker and the rest was not *bad* jazz; it was simply not jazz at all, and to appropriate the name for something different amounts to a kind of dishonesty. "What Parker, Monk, Miles and the Jazz Misanthropes are playing can be Afro-American music for all I care, but it isn't jazz" (*AWJ*, 261): "Now I am a simple soul. If someone offers me salt instead of sugar, or a waltz instead of a march, or bop instead of jazz, then I can't help pointing out that there's been some mistake" (*AWJ*, 160).[7] Using the same argument, one would have to say that if Larkin's introduction is truthful, then a good part of *All What Jazz* offers us reviews that are not reviews at all.

One of these reviews sets out to define the essence of jazz reviewing. What is the one quality that the jazz critic must possess? It turns out to be exactly that quality betrayed by the first two years of Larkin's reviews. The jazz critic is "only as good as his ear":

His ear will tell him instantly whether a piece of music is vital, musical, exciting, or cerebral, mock-academic, dead, long before he can read Don De Micheal on the subject, or learn that it is written in inverted nineteenths, or in the Stygian mode, or recorded at the NAACP Festival at Little Rock. He must hold on to the principle that the only reason for praising a work is that it pleases, and the way to develop his critical sense is to be more acutely aware of whether he is being pleased or not. (*AWJ*, 156)

By this test as well Larkin's foray into jazz criticism was an act of dishonesty—unless, of course, Parker's solos *did* afford him some small pleasures and his metaphor of leaping salmon was not altogether contrived. This is to say that there is the possibility of another equally amusing interpretation of the two Parkers and of Larkin's story justifying them: the antimodernist theory of the introduction is simply not sophisticated enough to incorporate Larkin's own practice as a critic in the reviews. In order to say one thing about modernism in the introduction (to alter a Marxist formulation on ideology) there are other things that cannot be said. Unfortunately for Larkin he had already said them in the reviews of the first two years.

---

7. Housman argues against extending the word *poetry* to verse that does not merit the term. Rather than calling it bad poetry we should not call it poetry at all: "If we apply the word poetry to an object which does not resemble, either in form or content, anything which has heretofore been so called, not only are we maltreating and corrupting language, but we may be guilty of disrespect and blasphemy." See "The Name and Nature of Poetry," in *A. E. Housman: Selected Prose*, ed. John Carter (Cambridge, 1961), 174.

To put the issue another way, why would a reviewer publish two years of faked reviews and call his readers' attention to it in the introduction? Clearly because the values his story reveals and conceals are more important to him than the impropriety of confessing to fakery (and of course the emphasis of his version of the story is that he *eventually* told the truth). Here is Nietzsche's manner of questioning this sort of revelation: "When we are confronted with any manifestation which some one has permitted us to see, we may ask: what is it meant to conceal? What is it meant to draw our attention from? What prejudice does it seek to raise?"[8] Pierre Macherey in *A Theory of Literary Production* extends Nietzsche's argument to ask of texts what it is they cannot say. In Macherey's theory the kind of gaps that we confront here can be traced to the text's relation to ideology. A text produced under a particular ideology—a conception of literary modernism, for example—cannot say something that would contradict that ideology. Yet in attempting to avoid one contradiction the text is driven to other disruptions that are the inevitable result of the limits and gaps inherent in all ideologies.[9]

I am not suggesting that Larkin's criticism is more ideological than that of any other critic; my point is simply that directing attention to the ideological stance of his writing on jazz helps us to understand the shape it takes. I use the term *ideology* in its Althusserian sense of a representation of an *imaginary* relationship to the set of conditions in which one lives. An ideological explanation in this sense is not simply false consciousness but a necessary and universal social condition, an effort to impose a unified meaning on disparate materials and to disguise or repress those elements that would expose the explanation *as* ideology. The repressed contradictions may appear in the text as gaps (illustrated most notably in Macherey's *A Theory of Literary Production*) and such openings enable the reader to unmask the ideology, the *imaginary* expla-

---

8. Friedrich Nietzsche, *The Dawn of Day,* trans. J. M. Kennedy, Vol. IX of *The Complete Works of Friedrich Nietzsche,* ed. Oscar Levy (New York, 1964), 358.

9. I have used Nietzsche and Macherey in a similar manner in *Early Stevens: The Nietzschean Intertext* (Durham, 1992). See chapter 2, "Stevens Reading Nietzsche," for a more extended discussion of Macherey's symptomatic reading.

nation, in the text. But one does not have to resort to a symptomatic reading of *All What Jazz* to be aware of the kind of disruptions Macherey's theory searches out. Larkin's own rereading uncovers obvious contradictions and he tells a story to account for them. Later readers have come upon these and other gaps and have attempted to resolve them in quite different ways. Clive James charts Larkin's reviews of John Coltrane and Miles Davis through the volume and explains the discrepancy between the fair-minded Larkin of the early reviews and the vitriolic Larkin of the later ones as an instance of a reviewer shifting his taste over time. In 1962, for example, he was still of "two minds" about Coltrane ("Coltrane's records are, paradoxically, nearly always both interesting and boring, and I certainly find myself listening to them in preference to many a less adventurous set" [*AWJ*, 65]), but by May of the following year he was of one mind, and Coltrane thereafter became a name that conjured up all the dreariness and boredom of modern jazz. Similarly, after early favorable reviews, "he became progressively disillusioned with Miles Davis."[10] This quite reasonable explanation, it should be noted, goes against Larkin's own story, in which he was of one mind about Davis, Coltrane, and Parker from the very beginning; it was simply "journalistically impossible" to tell the truth.

Other readers' responses to the gaps in Larkin's jazz criticism open other fissures. Janice Rossen finds that the reviews give the impression of having been written for "two different and opposing kinds of audience." Portions of the reviews sound as if they were directed to open-minded readers receptive to modern jazz; other portions seem to have been written for an audience "he feels certain will agree with him about the 'nightmare' of the contemporary scene and the horror of the new generation of impudent youth." There is some irony in the suggestion here that Larkin, one of the twentieth-century writers most immune to fashionable opinion, should have compromised his critical position by trying to placate the moderns, and Cedric Watts sees a larger irony in the gap between the theory of the introduction and the practice of the

10. James, "On His Wit," 99, 101.

reviews. It can be stated in several ways but it amounts to this: the "untruthful" Larkin of the reviews often seems more trustworthy than the sincere Larkin of the introduction.[11]

Many readers, especially those who know the records under review, must have experienced this reaction. Tolley finds it puzzling that "someone who hated Parker's music so much" could write "so perceptively about his concert recordings," and Watts, who prefers the insincere Larkin of the reviews, suggests that "the discipline of striving to write fairly may actually have liberated more of his intelligence than did the freedom he enjoyed in that Introduction."[12] It is easy to agree with Watts's premise that the reviews are more interesting, more intelligent, more acute than the introduction and still question the adequacy of his explanation, since it depends on our accepting Larkin's story that the introduction represents the truth and the reviews the pretense.

Behind the scenes, Larkin's own attitude toward the introduction is equivocal, as is indicated by his remarks to Donald Mitchell, to whom *All What Jazz* is dedicated, and Peter Crawley, sales director at Faber & Faber. He told Mitchell that the introduction was "not perhaps to be taken very seriously" (*Letters*, 408). To Crawley he said of the thesis of the introduction—that "post-Parker jazz is the equivalent of modernist developments in other arts": "I don't think this has actually been said before, and, while it may not be wholly defensible, I think it is sufficiently amusing to say once" (*Letters*, 417).

When we look closely at the conception of modernism that Larkin brings to his discussion of jazz in the introduction, we recognize that it is the kind of ideological statement that could never sanction thoughtful criticism of modernism or modern jazz. Any sophisticated discussion of Parker or Davis (or Eliot) would contradict it since the introduction relegates all the productions of modernism, including jazz, to the realm of nonart, unworthy of serious consideration. Modernist works "are

---

11. Rossen, *Philip Larkin: His Life's Work,* 112–13; Cedric Watts, "Larkin and Jazz," in *Critical Essays on Philip Larkin: The Poems,* ed. Linda Cookson and Bryan Loughrey (London, 1989), 24.

12. Tolley, *His Proper Ground,* 144; Watts, "Larkin and Jazz," 22–23.

irresponsible exploitations of technique in contradiction of human life as we know it. This is my essential criticism of modernism, whether perpetuated by Parker, Pound or Picasso." The modern work "will divert us as long as we are prepared to be mystified or outraged, but maintains its hold only by being more mystifying and more outrageous: it has no lasting power" (*AWJ*, 27). The genesis of modernism is related to an imbalance between the two tensions that produce art, the tensions between the artist and the material (that is, a concern with technique) and between the artist and the audience (a concern with being read or heard or seen): "in the last seventy-five years or so the second of these has slackened or even perished" (*AWJ*, 23). In consequence the artist has become overconcerned with technical experimentation and has no interest in giving pleasure to an audience (or perhaps even delights in producing outrage in the audience). "The tension between artist and audience in jazz slackened when the Negro stopped wanting to entertain the white man," Larkin writes. "From using music to entertain the white man, the Negro had moved to hating him with it" (*AWJ*, 24).

The final logic of Larkin's theory is the Housman argument that he incorporates in a later review: if we apply the word *poetry* or *jazz* to something that does not resemble in content or form the thing that has heretofore been called by that name, we are corrupting the language. "By this time I was quite certain that jazz had ceased to be produced," Larkin writes in the introduction. "The society that had engendered it had gone, and would not return" (*AWJ*, 25). In a later review that reflects the introduction, Larkin has found a name for the new music—"the jazz that isn't jazz" (*AWJ*, 87). In a 1967 review titled "Credo" he returns to Housman's conception of poetry in "The Name and Nature of Poetry":

I like jazz to be jazz. A. E. Housman said he could recognize poetry because it made his throat tighten and his eyes water: I can recognize jazz because it makes me tap my foot, grunt affirmative exhortations, or even get up and caper round the room. If it doesn't do this, then however musically interesting or spiritually adventurous or racially praiseworthy it is, it isn't jazz. If that's being a purist, I'm a purist. (*AWJ*, 174)

What Parker and his fellow musicians are playing "isn't jazz. Jazz is dying with its practitioners, Red Allen, Pee Wee Russell, Johnny Hodges" (*AWJ,* 261). To develop a concept of poetry or painting or jazz that holds that the work under examination simply does not merit the name by which the art is customarily evoked is a legitimate enterprise; it is not, however, a promising basis for a collection of reviews of such works, especially since the loving attention and carefully drawn distinctions of the reviews will seem to be in contradiction to the theory.

If we assume that the more one conforms to an ideology of art the more one comes up against things that cannot be said or sensibilities and pleasures that must be repressed, then the introduction of *All What Jazz* may be read not as the sincere Larkin who confesses to insincerity in the reviews but as the ideological Larkin whose ideology of modernism tempts him to discredit his more honest attempts to understand modern jazz. From the time of Oxford, Larkin had viewed literature and the other arts through the lens of jazz. In two discussions of jazz and modernism (quoted earlier) that follow the first edition of *All What Jazz* he also gives the impression that it was jazz that allowed him to understand modernism (*RW,* 72; *AWJ,* 259); but in fact, if we can accept his account of his moment of revelation, he reverses the relationship and allows his version of modernism to explain jazz. By this time, however, jazz and modernism have become so entangled that it is impossible to say which is the perspective through which the other is seen, and at different points in the introduction each serves as paradigm. The critical jargon of modern literary criticism, Larkin says, helped him to understand what was happening in modern jazz, but, at the same time, his *definition* of modernism, which involves the artist's overconcern with material and technique and lack of concern with audience, almost certainly derives from his sense of exclusion from contemporary jazz after the gap in his jazz life. That is, the mystery of how a jazz lover, indeed a connoisseur of the art, could be so thoroughly alienated from the latest phase of jazz is solved once he sees that the musician of modern jazz has no interest in *him,* feels no responsibility for entertaining or even being understood by an audience. Thus his conclusion that the defining quality of the term *modern* applied to art is "irresponsibility" (*AWJ*, 23).

To return to Larkin's narrative of his awakening to the true history of jazz, he fixes its moment of inception to the confluence of the language of jazz criticism and the language of modernist criticism of poetry and painting. Faced with the task of writing a column on music no longer familiar to him, he begins reading jazz critics and historians:

[T]here was something about the books I was now reading that seemed oddly familiar. This *development*, this *progress*, this *new language* that was more *difficult*, more *complex*, that required you to *work hard at appreciating it*, that you *couldn't expect to understand first go*, that needed *technical and professional knowledge* to evaluate it *at all levels*, this *revolutionary explosion* that *spoke for our time* while at the same time being *traditional* in the *fullest*, the *deepest*. . . . Of course! This was the language of criticism of modern painting, modern poetry, modern music. *Of course!* How glibly I had talked of modern jazz, without realizing the force of the adjective: this was *modern* jazz, and Parker was a modern jazz player just as Picasso was a modern painter and Pound a modern poet. (*AWJ*, 22)

Perhaps the most revealing moment in Larkin's account of his revelation is the relief that comes flooding in once he can feel that the problem is not a gap in *his* understanding or sensibility but a gap in the history of the arts. "All I am saying is that the term 'modern,' when applied to art, has a more than chronological meaning: it denotes a quality of irresponsibility peculiar to this century, known sometimes as modernism, and once I had classified modern jazz under this heading I knew where I was" (*AWJ*, 23).

All-encompassing ideologies such as Larkin's formulation of modernism have both positive and negative functions, as Althusserian critics point out. Positively, they allow us to hold on to comforting beliefs and attitudes by offering what look to be natural and seamless explanations; negatively, they allow us to take imaginary explanations for real ones. They also force us to suppress any element of the formulation that would expose it as ideological and to attempt to cover over the contradictions the explanation produces. Once Larkin has classified postwar jazz under the general heading of modernism, it is true that he knows where he is; he now has a way of explaining every feature of the music of Parker, Coltrane, and Davis. Unfortunately, this also means that jazz must now conform to his paradigm of modernism, and this produces a somewhat eccentric history of jazz.

An obvious example is Larkin's attack on the university in the introduction to *All What Jazz*. The chief villain of literary modernism for Larkin is, strangely, not the artist but the academic critic. In "The Pleasure Principle" (1957) he charges that poetry has lost its true (that is, pleasure-seeking) audience through a kind of conspiracy among the poet, the literary critic, and the academic critic, three classes so indistinguishable that "the poet has gained the happy position wherein he can praise his own poetry in the press and explain it in the classroom" (*RW*, 81). The audience that reads poetry for pleasure has been replaced by an audience of students who learn from their (mystifying) professors that "reading a poem is hard work" (*RW*, 81). The university professor is the subject of some of Larkin's most biting prose and verse. He is the narrator of "Naturally the Foundation Will Bear Your Expenses," he is Jake Balokowsky of "Posterity," and he is the speaker of the follow passage, designed to demonstrate how the academy has aided the conspiracy to deceive the contemporary audience:

[D]on't trust your eyes, or ears, or understanding. They'll tell you this is ridiculous, or ugly, or meaningless. Don't believe them. You've got to work at this: after all, you don't expect to understand anything as important as art straight off, do you? I mean, this is pretty complex stuff: if you want to know how complex, I'm giving a course of ninety-six lectures at the local college, starting next week. . . . After all, think what asses people have made of themselves in the past by not understanding art—you don't want to be like that, do you? (*AWJ*, 23–24)

As an argument about modern poetry, which flourishes to such an extent in the college classroom, this has some cogency, and Larkin was not alone in holding the position. (Blake Morrison reports that Larkin's friend and fellow conservative Robert Conquest suggested in a 1966 interview that a conspiracy existed between universities and poets to promote ambiguity and difficulty, thus keeping university professors employed.) But in applying the argument to jazz—which he also tries to move into the academy via "concert halls" and "university recital rooms" (*AWJ*, 24)—Larkin produces only a caricature of art history. Jazz as an art form and jazz musicians as artists are notoriously unacademic. "It lacks the embedded institutions of the other arts," Ted Gioia has noted of jazz, and he adds that the "group norms, exercised perhaps through academia or other mechanisms of standardization, would probably have stifled some of jazz's greatest talents."[13] How is it possible for Larkin to argue that the sounds of Charlie Parker or Miles Davis are the result of a conspiracy of university professors? In large part because of the confluence of jazz and poetry, later to be mixed with conceptions of modernism, that began when Larkin became a jazz addict at the age of twelve or thirteen.

And such a confluence may have implications for all the streams that converge. Larkin's jazz criticism is informed by a conception of literary modernism. It may be that a reader of the poetry who brings to the reading a sense of Larkin's jazz life will find in the verse various manifestations of that life, some of them difficult to separate from a style or quality we now think of as Larkinesque, although such a reading will require a more rigorous and extensive examination of both the poems and musical texts and conventions. It may also be that, apart from poems that openly embrace jazz—"Reasons for Attendance," "For Sidney Bechet," "Reference Back," for example—the traces left by jazz and blues in Larkin's verse are so elusive, so deeply submerged as to be nearly inaccessible or to be retrievable only through more speculative readings. Still, it is intriguing to conceive of a jazz/blues intertext inhabiting the Larkin canon that may be glimpsed now and then, as in the opening of the late poem "Aubade" (*CP*, 208)—"I work all day, and get half-drunk at night," a line that, read in another context, could as easily be attributed to Sleepy John Estes or Blind Lemon Jefferson.

13. Morrison, *The Movement*, 128–29; Ted Gioia, *The Imperfect Art: Reflections on Jazz and Modern Culture* (New York, 1988), 83.

3

JAZZ POEMS

Larkin: It seems to me undeniable that up to this century literature used language in the way we all use it, painting represented what anyone with normal vision sees, and music was an affair of nice noises rather than nasty ones. The innovation of "modernism" in the arts consisted of doing the opposite. I don't know why, I'm not a historian. You have to distinguish between things that seemed odd when they were new but are now quite familiar, such as Ibsen and Wagner, and things that seemed crazy when they were new and seem crazy now, like *Finnegans Wake* and Picasso.

    Interviewer: What's that got to do with jazz?

    Larkin: Everything.

—Larkin Interview, 1982

ROBERT PHILLIPS, the *Paris Review* interviewer, puts directly to Larkin the question I have raised and one Larkin raises explicitly in his criticism and perhaps implicitly in his poetry—what does his attitude toward modernism have to do with jazz? Larkin's response here suggests both the centrality of jazz in his thinking about art and the specific part played by jazz in his conception of modernism. The short history of jazz shows everything about modernism, he tells Phillips, because it is the paradigm for all the arts ("a telescoped art, only as old as the century"

[*RW*, 72]), and Charlie Parker's seemingly single-handed wrecking of jazz provides a model for thinking about Picasso or *Finnegans Wake* or *The Waste Land*. It is perhaps not an analogy that bears close scrutiny, but whatever we may feel about the persuasiveness of his point of view, it is nevertheless true that Larkin's interviews, letters and reviews, and, most powerfully, his introduction to *All What Jazz* indicate quite clearly that jazz is a haunting presence in his conception of modern art. The question that follows is perhaps obvious—does jazz haunt Larkin's art in the way that it haunts his *conception* of art? Does it constitute one of the fundamental intertexts of Larkin's poetry—a presence as spectral and elusive as Hardy or Auden or Yeats?

The figure of haunting I borrow from *Rereading*, Matei Calinescu's recent study of the dynamics of reading, since this trope suggests, on several levels, the nature of my engagement with Larkin's poetry here. As Calinescu points out, there are, first of all, texts that haunt us, that cannot be forgotten, and I locate a number of what I think of as Larkin's jazz poems—poems *about* jazz or the blues or poems informed by them—in the category of texts to which I keep returning. I will reread some of these poems with a focus on jazz texts and conventions that have not thus far been uncovered. Calinescu also points out that there are "texts that haunt other texts, in the sense that they appear in them as expected or unexpected visitors," and the phenomenon of intertextuality is of particular importance in the case of Larkin's jazz. That is, the *significance* of certain of Larkin's poems, the manner in which they signify, appears to depend on the presence within them of jazz or blues texts. Finally, Calinescu notes, it is we, the readers (or rereaders), who are haunting the texts, who insist on revisiting them partly because we want to understand why they attract us.[1] The questions I pose about Larkin's jazz poems are primarily in terms of my own reading, my revisiting (armed with jazz and the blues) of texts, rather than in terms of Larkin's composition of them.

One of the essential intertexts of these poems is, however, the rich jazz life that preceded them, and reading them with an eye to what they

---

1. See Matei Calinescu, *Rereading* (New Haven, 1993), xi–xii.

have absorbed will necessarily incorporate Larkin's own account of the confluence of jazz and poetry and the accounts of his contemporaries. What one gathers from Motion's biography, the letters, and the recollections of friends like Kingsley Amis is that in Larkin's earliest imaginative endeavors jazz is unguardedly and overtly present. In his first "successful" work, the Oxford novel *Jill*, where we might well expect to encounter jazz, it is surprisingly absent, and I will speculate briefly on its absence before turning to the poems.

Death in Swingham, a mystery novel written while Larkin was still a student at King Henry VIII School, is about a famous saxophonist who is poisoned; one of his first compilations of poems is titled *Nine O'Clock Jump* (*Life*, 29, 34). At Oxford he and Amis collaborated on a story called "I Would Do Anything for You," where, Amis says, "The interest was divided between jazz and lesbianism":

[I]t was about two beautiful lesbians in somewhere like Oxford. . . . In their digs there was a mysterious cupboard full of jazz records Philip and I had heard of but never heard. It was Mr So-and-so who had left them there and might come back for them one day. We were especially interested in Wild Bill Davison, whom we'd read about, and one of the girls—Marsha, who went in for avowals of love—found "On a Blues Kick." Philip admired it so much he said he'd rather she found anything but that, and wrote in the next paragraph, "As the heavy steel needle, which they never changed, clumped into the first groove. . . ." (Quoted in *Life*, 86)

Also at Oxford Larkin produced (without Amis) two novels, *Trouble at Willow Gables* and *Michaelmas Term at St Bride's,* and a group of poems called *Sugar and Spice*—all written under the pseudonym Brunette Coleman. The name, as Andrew Motion has discovered, was adapted from a jazz group of the time, Blanche Coleman and her Girls' Band (*Life*, 86), but it also anticipates uncannily Larkin's great modern jazz nemesis Ornette Coleman, whose music, Larkin once said, gave the effect of "watching twenty monkeys trying to type the plays of Shakespeare" (*AWJ*, 188).

Jill was begun immediately after this period of his deepest immersion in jazz, and his 1963 introduction (added to Faber's reissue) is as much an account of jazz at Oxford as it is of the circumstances of the novel's inception, which makes the absence of jazz in the novel the more striking. *Jill* is built on a working-class boy's first term at Oxford and his painful period of adjustment to the middle-class manners of his boorish room-mate and the roommate's circle of friends. At the time it was first conceived (as a short story), Larkin's own summary of his protagonist's plight is this:

As a result of adverse conditions, and also of telling his room-mate that he had a sister a year younger than himself (or two or three years)—which is untrue— he begins to construct a complicated sexless daydream about an imaginary sister, who serves as a nucleus for a dream-life. Then he meets a girl who is exactly like this imaginary sister (the sister-aspect having by now changed into rather a more emotional relationship) and the rest of the story, in action and in a long dream, serves to disillusion him completely. (*Letters,* 61–62)

In a later addition to the introduction to *Jill* Larkin says of his hero John Kemp that "over the years I can see that I have been to some extent identified with him" (*Jill,* 18). That has indeed been the case, and, taking account of the personal nature of the novel and its setting— Larkin's identification of jazz with the social life of the university— readers might expect a glimpse of the musical world of Oxford featured so prominently in its introduction. A parallel instance is Amis's first novel *Lucky Jim,* clearly shaped by Amis's musical tastes. Music is central to the first half of *Lucky Jim,* especially the pivotal chapters devoted to the "arty week-end," and Welch's musical events are occasions for some of the book's most hilarious moments. Jim Dixon's character is in part defined by his popular musical biases—his representation, for example, of "serious" music as "Brahms rubbish," "a violin sonata by some teutonic bore," "some skein of untiring facetiousness by filthy Mozart," and his lampooning of the local band's attempt at jazz lyrics at the Summer Ball.[2] In *Jill,* however, jazz is suppressed and it is interesting

2. See Kingsley Amis, *Lucky Jim* (London, 1965), 36, 45, 64, 117, 127. The links between Larkin and *Lucky Jim,* which is dedicated to Larkin, are complicated and disputed. "Filthy Mozart," it has been suggested, was Larkin's own expression, and Larkin has been identified as the model for Jim Dixon, although Amis has denied it (see Rossen, *Philip*

to speculate on the significance of its absence. About two-thirds of the way through the novel, as John Kemp is returning to his quarters, we are told that "the distant sound of jazz could be heard as usual" (*Jill*, 173). Oddly, to this point—and it is the only time the word appears in the novel—we have had no inkling that the sound of jazz was ever present at Oxford.

Larkin said in the note he added to a later edition of *Jill* that his purpose in writing an introduction to the novel was to make clear that his own Oxford life was different from that of his hero (*Jill*, 18), and one difference is suggested by the numerous references in the introduction to Larkin's jazz life and to friends like Amis and Nick Russel who shared it. Such a life is precisely what is missing in John Kemp's first year at Oxford. Jill—the imagined Jill—is for Kemp in the novel what jazz is for Larkin in Motion's *A Writer's Life*. Motion's picture of Larkin in *his* first year at Oxford is this:

In rooms after dinner, in pubs, when he should have been attending lectures or preparing for tutorials, the excitement of jazz did more than anything else to persuade Larkin that he was "beginning to enjoy Oxford." The music was a focus for powerful feelings which were blocked in more orthodox contexts; it was the means by which his stammering shyness could be set aside; it was his most enjoyable way of feeling part of a community. (*Life*, 47)

John Kemp has no such inner resources, and his romantic fantasy of a sister named Jill is created to fill the void. She is imagined in association with music (playing the piano) and America (she has a phobia about things American and refuses to eat a certain kind of breakfast cereal because it comes from America). Kemp's invention of

---

Larkin: His Life's Work, 96, 150n). According to Eric Jacobs in *Kingsley Amis: A Biography* (London, 1995), *Lucky Jim* began as a story about Larkin and his girlfriend Monica Jones. However, "in the course of pondering the character Larkin dwindled and disappeared" (144). The only traces left, Jacobs argues, were the name Dixon, taken from Dixon Drive, where Larkin had lived in Leicester, and the character Margaret Peel, who continued to resemble Monica Jones (145–46). Since Amis's and Larkin's musical tastes were quite close, it is difficult to know how much of Jim Dixon's musical vocabulary can be attributed to Larkin.

her life (incorporating some of Brunette Coleman's *Trouble at Willow Gables*) furnishes the romantic sensibility that jazz provides for the Larkin of the Oxford chapters of *A Writer's Life*. Larkin said in an interview: "John's being working-class was a kind of equivalent of my stammer, a built-in handicap to put him one down" (*RW*, 63). And Jill is a kind of equivalent for the jazz that allowed him to get around the stammer. If Jill is for Kemp what jazz was for Larkin, then the absence of jazz in the novel is understandable and inevitable, since it finds its expression in another form. In "For Sidney Bechet" Larkin refers to the fantasy awakened in the listener by Bechet's jazz as an "appropriate falsehood," and Hugh Underhill sees a link between the poem's fantasy theme and that of the novel. One sense of *appropriate,* he notes, is "that which may properly be indulged since we have to get through somehow," and Kemp's fantasy of Jill, which "enables him to survive his first traumatic term at university," is an early treatment of the "appropriate falsehood" later associated with Bechet's jazz.[3]

In *A Writer's Life,* Motion points out obvious links between Kemp and Larkin, and he argues that since Larkin wanted to recreate in Kemp the shyness and uncertainty he himself had felt when he arrived at Oxford, he could not allow Kemp to form the "circle of friends who shared his interests and enthusiasms," chief of which was the music that became, Motion argues, "a focus for powerful feelings which were blocked in more orthodox contexts" (*Life,* 107, 47). One could go a step further to suggest that there is in *Jill* a rough equivalency between two forms of boyhood infatuation and fantasy that might well be recognizable to the jazz fan.

From the time of its reputed beginnings in the New Orleans brothels—evoked by Larkin in "For Sidney Bechet"—jazz has always carried erotic associations (in one of the earliest Freudian studies devoted to jazz, it comes to represent, for Aaron Esman, "the id drives that the superego of the bourgeois culture sought to repress"). Larkin and Amis made the identification of jazz and erotic fantasy in their jazz/lesbian

---

3. Hugh Underhill, "Poetry of Departures: Larkin and the Power of Choosing," *Critical Survey,* I (1989), 185.

fiction; their title, "I Would Do Anything for You," is at the same time an invitation to sexual license and a jazz standard (four versions of which Larkin reviews in *All What Jazz* [48, 80, 104, 106]). Amis's more moderate attempt to account for the appeal of jazz at Oxford many years later—a representation of a "world of romance"—is perhaps more in keeping with the relatively innocent eroticism of *Jill*, jazz as adolescent first love. In *The Jazz Scene* Eric Hobsbawm cites a comparison of the initial impact of jazz to the "first love of teen-agers in the era when such emotions, however fleeting, were supposed to be unforgettable." Hobsbawm observes that "the jazz fan, however knowledgeable, is fundamentally a lover. While old-style pop music . . . crystalized and preserved the relation of human beings in love ('They're playing our song'), jazz, more often than not, is itself the love object for its devotees."[4] The convention of the jazz "lover"—jazz as the love object rather than the background music for love—is marginally relevant to a reading of *Jill* in the sense that it may have shaped the text in certain ways; it is, however, crucial to readings of two of Larkin's later jazz poems, "Reasons for Attendance" and "For Sidney Bechet," as will become apparent.

To read *A Writer's Life* beside *Jill* is to recognize that the absence of jazz on the surface of the novel is in fact an indication of its having been so thoroughly absorbed. In regard to such decisive absences, Pierre Macherey has noted that "in order to say anything there are other things *which must not be said,*"[5] since their saying would compromise in some way what *is* said. And the "not-said" is the link to the ideology that shapes what is said or the intertext that has been absorbed by it. One has only to read Larkin's introduction to *Jill* and letters written during

---

4. Aaron Esman, "Jazz—A Study in Cultural Conflict," *American Imago*, VIII (1951), 222; Amis, "Farewell to a Friend," 4; Eric Hobsbawm, *The Jazz Scene* (New York, 1993), 306. *The Jazz Scene* was first published in 1959 under the pseudonym Francis Newton. The revised edition above, which also contains essays published in the *New York Review of Books* and the *New Statesman*, was published under Hobsbawm's own name. I have maintained the distinction between the two editions by referring to the author of the first as Newton and that of the later edition as Hobsbawm.

5. Pierre Macherey, *A Theory of Literary Production*, trans. Geoffrey Wall (London, 1978), 85.

its composition to see that the world of jazz and the jazz lover is a part of the "not-said" of the novel, and it has perhaps shaped the text in ways that a more rigorous examination might expose.

To take one example, we may note that musical references in the novel have been cleansed of their jazz associations. When the narrator tells us of Kemp's sudden elation after an apparent act of kindness from his roommate, he turns to a musical analogy that could more easily be adapted to the improvisations of a jazz band:

There are numerous passages in music where the whole orchestra, which has previously been muttering and trifling along some distracting theme, suddenly collects itself and soars upwards to explode in a clear major key, in a clear march of triumph. Any of these movements would have described John's feelings exactly as he bent over the drawer, repeating again and again to himself that Christopher had called him by his first name. (*Jill*, 55)

Kemp's excited feelings after telling Christopher a story from his fantasy of Jill are "like the mutterings of the orchestra before the overture to an opera" (*Jill*, 119). After meeting the actual Jill and inviting her to tea, Kemp awakens the following morning and tries to bring to mind some extraordinary thing that he knows has happened the day before: "It was as if the world lay silent as an orchestra under the conductor's outstretched arms. Then the moment of remembrance set every nerve in his body trembling, as a movement by the conductor might send a hundred bows to work" (*Jill*, 195). The habit of picturing emotions as musical experiences echoes Larkin's Oxford practice of viewing everything through the lens of jazz—hoarseness is an "Armstrongish throat" and a break in the weather is "hearing Earl Hines after a YMCA piano-basher" (*Letters*, 7, 114)—but in *Jill* jazz has been evaded, whether consciously or not, in a maneuver that illustrates what Terry Eagleton calls "determinate absences," intertexts that shape texts from which they are themselves excluded. "Absences," Christopher Ricks notes in another context, "as in Larkin's poem of that title, make themselves felt."[6]

6. Terry Eagleton, *Criticism and Ideology* (London, 1976), 89; Christopher Ricks, "Like Something Almost Being Said," in *Larkin at Sixty*, ed. Anthony Thwaite (London, 1982), 123.

It is clearly not the case that Larkin regarded jazz as inappropriate for "serious" literary texts. Shortly after the publication of *Jill* he attempted a direct treatment of a jazz form, an evocation of the blues in the first of a pair of poems called "Two Guitar Pieces" (*CP*, 8). The poem has attracted little interest or commentary, perhaps because it seems at first reading no more than a collection of exotic images that trail off inconclusively. It does, in fact, have something to say, but because what it says depends more on jazz and blues conventions than on traditional attitudes toward art, its matrix is difficult to retrieve. It has also assimilated, oddly, an Auden text that complicates its tone and, to some degree, works against its blues elements. It is easy to dismiss as an early failure, but I want to examine it in some detail—more than it may appear to merit—since it raises issues that surface in later and more successful poems that have assimilated jazz conventions.

The title "Guitar Pieces" suggests that the two poems are in some way analogous to musical compositions, and in both, in different ways, the sound of a guitar serves as the musical intertext to which the verse responds. In the second (which I pass over as uninteresting except for its Eliot-like atmosphere) the speaker's friend strums a guitar while the speaker rolls a cigarette, stares out the window, and ponders the effect of the music, which is "Spreading [him] over the evening" like J. Alfred Prufrock. In the first, set in the American South, a black man plays a guitar, the notes wandering aimlessly into the southern heat:

> The tin-roofed shack by the railroad
> Casts a shadow. Wheatstraws[7] in the white dust
> And a wagon standing. Stretched out into the sun
> A dozen legs are idle in dungarees,
> Dark hands and heads shaded from the sun and working.
> One frowns above a guitar: the notes, random
> From tuning, wander into the heat

---

7. "Peetie Wheetstraw, the Devil's Son-in-Law" was well known for his early recordings of the blues (see Samuel B. Charters, *The Country Blues* [New York, 1975], 175, 192–93), although the poem gains very little from our incorporating him into a reading.

> Like a new insect chirping in the scrub,
> Untired at noon. A chord gathers and spills,
> And a southern voice tails out around one note
> Contentedly discontent.

This is evidently not an attempt to create a poetic equivalent of the blues—in the manner of Auden's "Refugee Blues" for example—but a response to the blues, another "appropriate falsehood," a scene suggested to a particular gramophone listener by the sound of the blues. All of Larkin's overt jazz poems are, on the most basic level, about listening to music, all but one ("Reasons for Attendance") about listening to phonograph records.

To uncover what is difficult to read in the poem, it is important to note that its opening imagery is dictated not by the content of a particular blues—that is, not by the *text*, the blues as artifact—but by the listener's re-creation of its *performance*. This is also true of the other jazz poems, and it involves an interesting difference between traditional art's privileging of the artifact—the poem, the painting, the symphony—and the privileging of the performance in jazz and the blues. (The distinction will also be significant in "For Sidney Bechet" and "Reference Back.") In *The Jazz Scene* Hobsbawm (writing as Francis Newton) notes this difference between jazz and other arts:

The fundamental unit of the orthodox arts is the "work of art" which, once created, lives its life independently of all but its creator. . . . The "work of art" which is particularly appreciated we call a masterpiece, a category wholly independent of performance. . . . Now jazz simply does not function this way. Its art is not reproduced, but created, and exists only at the moment of creation.[8]

The music of American blacks, Dave Laing notes, is "indifferent to the making of artefacts,"[9] an observation that enables us to see that Larkin's first "Guitar Piece" is a significant departure from the traditional poem about art—Keats's "On First Looking into Chapman's Homer," say, or Auden's "Musée des Beaux Arts." Traditionally such poems celebrate

---

8. Francis Newton, *The Jazz Scene* (New York, 1960), 137.
9. Laing, *Sound of Our Time*, 188.

the genius of the artifact or of the artist who produced it, its effect on the reader or viewer, its interpretation of life. Whatever the focus, the assumption is that the work of art can be separated from its moment of creation and exhibited as an object for contemplation or interpretation. "Musée des Beaux Arts," for example, makes sense only if we concede that the artifact, the Breughel painting, has meaning that is permanently available in its artistic form. Its composition or treatment of space states its meaning—the lack of connection between human events.

Auden's "In Praise of Limestone" says of music as an art that it "can be made anywhere, is invisible, / And does not smell," suggesting a traditional distinction between art and life to which the jazz critic Nat Hentoff responds, "But music is made by men who are insistently visible, especially, as in jazz, when the players *are* their music."[10] Hentoff's jazz aesthetic is, it appears, the aesthetic of Larkin's "Guitar Piece," which equates the players and their music and directs the focus to the moment of the performance of the music, the insistently visible reality behind the invisible artifact. "Behind the blues," Larkin writes in *All What Jazz*, "spreads the half-glimpsed, depressing vista of the life of the American Negro" (*AWJ*, 234). The poem is not a celebration of the blues as artifact, but of the blues as reality, the blues as an expression of the experience from which they derive, and in this respect it exhibits the convention that has always defined the blues.

"Although they call it the blues today, the original name given to this kind of music was 'reals,' " Henry Townsend, the St. Louis bluesman, explained to William Barlow. "And it was real because it made the truth available to the people in the songs." The one aesthetic standard for all of the early blues, David Evans writes, "is telling the truth." For the knowledgeable blues fan the question of the difference between good and bad blues is meaningless; the proper question is between the simulation and the "real thing." As Richard Middleton puts it, "bad blues is not blues." Invoking this principle, Larkin writes, "In this country we

10. W. H. Auden, *Collected Shorter Poems, 1927–1957* (London, 1966), 240; Hentoff is quoted in Arthur Knight, *"Jammin' the Blues*, or the Sight of Jazz, 1944," in *Representing Jazz*, ed. Krin Gabbard (Durham, 1995), 11.

have had to wait a long time for direct access to the real thing," which he characterizes as "vocal music, by Negroes for Negroes, in which is recorded nearly every facet of their lives" (*AWJ*, 36). Although it ultimately fails, Larkin's "Guitar Piece" can be read as a highly stylized form of blues honesty. Its theme is a blues convention taken to another level. It will attempt to be brutally honest about the bluesman's world and the illusion of his attempt to escape it. It develops what Middleton calls the "double-bind" to which the blues respond—a situation in which the American black "cannot win, but from which he cannot escape."[11] (More than thirty years later a Larkin poem, "Aubade," will have another go at this persistent blues motif, this time more successfully.) Now, after visualizing a world composed of a tin-roofed shack by the tracks, dust, sun, work, and boredom, the speaker considers the escape from these conditions the blues has traditionally promised and dismisses it as a deception in the manner of the later "Poetry of Departures," which addresses our fantasies about walking out on our unhappy lives.

The blues do not sing only of unhappiness, and blues commentators have always recognized the mixed tone traditional blues convey, a combination of resignation and escapism. In his Foreword to Oliver's *Blues Fell This Morning*, Richard Wright points out that "the most astonishing aspect of the blues is that, though replete with a sense of defeat and down-heartedness, they are not intrinsically pessimistic." Middleton speaks of the "sad-happy" spirit of the blues; Lawrence Levine characterizes them as "a blend of despair and hope." The poem's version of this mixture is "Contentedly discontent." In his later commentary on blues records in *All What Jazz* Larkin can get no closer to the feeling the blues convey than this paradoxical construction in such phrases as "desperate serenity" (*AWJ*, 228) and "despairing placidity" (*AWJ*, 244). It is easy to locate the source of discontent but why "*contentedly* discontent"? It

---

11. William Barlow, *"Looking Up at Down": The Emergence of Blues Culture* (Philadelphia, 1989), 326; David Evans, *Big Road Blues: Tradition and Creativity in the Folk Blues* (New York, 1987), 53–54; Richard Middleton, *Pop Music and the Blues: A Study of the Relationship and its Significance* (London, 1972), 51, 26.

is because the performance of the blues is itself thought to provide relief in various ways, not only in the catharsis of the very act of singing but in the escape promised by what is sung. These lines popularized by Muddy Waters suggest the blend of present despair and potential escape:

> If I feel tomorrow, the way I feel today,
> I'm gonna pack my bags and make my getaway.[12]

The most famous symbol of escape in the blues is the railroad. Albert Murray notes that the preoccupation with railroad imagery in blues titles and lyrics suggests that its function was mythological as well as pragmatic, and its value as an image in the storehouse of blues imagery was, Oliver argues, as "a symbol of power, of freedom, and of escape":

> When a woman gets the blues, she goes to her room and hides,
> When a man gets the blues, he catches a freight train and
> rides.[13]

Blues fans will recognize immediately the central place of the railroad in Larkin's "Guitar Piece." It is introduced in the first line, and in the final four lines the poem returns to it with an honesty that does the blues one better. It acknowledges that this famous blues image of escape *is* merely conventional; in truth, there is no escape:

> Though the tracks
> Burn to steel cities, they are taking
> No one from these parts. Anyone could tell
> Not even the wagon aims to go anywhere.

12. Paul Oliver, *Blues Fell This Morning: Meaning in the Blues,* 2nd ed., foreword by Richard Wright (Cambridge, 1990), xv; Middleton, *Pop Music and the Blues,* 53; Lawrence Levine, *Black Culture and Black Consciousness: Afro-American Folk Thought from Slavery to Freedom* (New York, 1977), 237; Muddy Waters's blues lyrics are quoted in James C. Cobb, *The Most Southern Place on Earth: The Mississippi Delta and the Roots of Regional Identity* (New York, 1992), 284.

13. Murray, *Stomping the Blues,* 118; Oliver, *Blues Fell This Morning,* 58. The centrality of the railroad to the very essence of the blues, its sound and rhythm, is argued by both Murray (124) and Houston Baker in *Blues, Ideology, and Afro-American Literature: A Vernacular Theory* (Chicago, 1984), 8.

The poem sees through the illusory promise of "leaving" so central to the spirit of the blues,[14] a convention later appropriated as one of Larkin's own figures for self-deception in "Poetry of Departures" (*CP*, 85):

Sometimes you hear, fifth-hand,
As epitaph:
He chucked up everything
And just cleared off,
And always the voice will sound
Certain you approve
This audacious, purifying,
Elemental move.

Oliver's analysis of this blues convention clarifies what the "Guitar Piece" hints at and "Poetry of Departures" says outright:

Any analysis of blues lyrics reveals that verses which state the singer's intention to "leave" figure prominently. He is "going to leave this town," to "walk down the dirt road" or to "catch the next thing smokin'." Often the singer has "a mind to ramble"—but it *is* a mind, a dream of escape. . . . [S]uch a man might never summon the nerve to make so bold a move. Instead he might content himself with the resolution that he would leave if "he still feels the same way, to-morrow."[15]

"I'd go today," the persona of "Poetry of Departures" declares, "if / It weren't so artificial, / Such a deliberate step backwards," and the earlier "Guitar Piece" shows a move—somewhat ill-defined—toward a version of the less deceived persona who exposes the illusions by which the rest of us live our lives. This early unmasking of the blues convention of "leaving," that is, remains in the Larkin canon and reappears in a nonblues form.

But while its attitude of honesty and its conventions may derive

14. In *Mystery Train: Images of America in Rock 'n' Roll Music*, revised ed. (New York, 1982), Greil Marcus nominates these two lines from "Milkcow Blues Boogie" as "two of the most perfect lines in blues": "If you don't believe I'm leavin' / You can count the days I'm gone" (180).

15. Oliver, *Blues Fell This Morning*, 45.

ultimately from the blues, the *voice* of the concluding lines of the first "Guitar Piece" is foreign to the blues. It is in fact an Audenesque voice that can, by chance, be identified. "In much of Larkin's early work," A. T. Tolley writes, "it is possible to point to the particular poem by Auden that is being imitated," and that is the case here. The voice Larkin's "Guitar Piece" has absorbed is that of Auden's "No Change of Place," which Larkin included in *The Oxford Book of Twentieth-Century English Verse:* "Metals run, / Burnished or rusty in the sun, / From town to town, / . . . Yet nothing passes." Auden and the blues exist uneasily together in the poem, and the speaker's detachment works against the normally personal and intimate voice of the blues singer. "A blues singer seldom considered his themes apart from himself, seldom narrated incidents in which he had not actively participated, or projected himself," Oliver notes. "He did not view his subject as an objective outsider but rather from within."[16] It is the blues tone that the poem is unable or unwilling to capture, so that it gives, finally, the effect of what an early jazz critic like Hugues Panassié might call a "straight" version of a hot number—Guy Lombardo playing "Tiger Rag." It will be some time before a Larkin poem can successfully create the *effect* of jazz or the blues, as opposed simply to characterizing it from a distance.

The pattern of the first poem of "Two Guitar Pieces," however, will become the pattern in Larkin's overt jazz poems; that is, for the reader the music is an absence around which the poem is built—the jazz trumpet in "Reasons for Attendance," Oliver's "Riverside Blues" in "Reference Back," Bechet's saxophone in "For Sidney Bechet." Although the later poems will be much more successful in evoking the music to which they respond, the confluence of music and poetry in these poems produces one of the perplexing ironies of intertextuality: the musical text essential to the poem is not recoverable for most of the poem's readers. Does this mean that these are lesser poems for readers who cannot supply the musical texts that would complete them? Cedric Watt believes that this is the case with "For Sidney Bechet":

16. Tolley, *My Proper Ground,* 4; *The Oxford Book of Twentieth-Century English Verse* chosen by Philip Larkin (London, 1973), 404; Oliver, *Blues Fell This Morning,* 276–77.

[T]o the jazz fan who knows Bechet's solos and the legends of New Orleans . . . the poem's allusions will be clear and its enthusiasm for the music will need no vindication; whereas readers who lack this knowledge will encounter not only a more difficult poem but also one which is hollow at the core: for the poem's centre is provided by memories of that busy, urgent, questing and finally soaring tone of Bechet's saxophone, with its distinctive vibrato and majestic lyricism.[17]

It is not, however, simply *memories* of Bechet's saxophone that are at the poem's center. The convention of the poem is that Bechet's saxophone is sounding beneath the lines of the poem even as we read it, as is made clear when the narrator interrupts the poem to respond directly to the musician: "Oh, play that thing!" (*CP*, 83). This makes Watts's issue of the reader's knowledge of Bechet's saxophone style even more pertinent. Is the poem hollow at the core for readers who are ignorant of its musical intertext? I will return to "For Sidney Bechet," but for the moment I will take up the larger issue of jazz as an intertext in Larkin's poetry and some of the implications that arise when we recognize that the significance of a poem like "For Sidney Bechet" or "Reference Back"—the poem's means of signifying—depends on its relationship to a piece of music that theoretically inhabits the text but (for the majority of readers) is nowhere to be seen or heard.

To place this issue in a larger context it should be acknowledged that the reader's relationship to the text and intertext of "For Sidney Bechet" is only an emphatic instance of what is true in reading any poem. A good portion of contemporary theory has devoted itself to demonstrating the intertextual nature of all reading, based on the premise that literary texts, far from being the self-contained creations of individual and unique imaginations, are a part of a larger network of texts. All texts have their meaning in relation to other texts, using the term in its broadest sense to include both identifiable works that are a part of a culture's storehouse of ideas and concepts and what Jonathan Culler calls "anonymous discursive practices, codes whose origins are lost, that make possible the signifying practices of later texts." Poststruc-

---

17. Watts, "Larkin and Jazz," 27.

turalist critics for the most part agree that there is an intertextual dimension to all reading, and in the most basic sense—in Culler's assumption that any text is intelligible only in relation to a prior body of discourse[18]—this is obviously true. What these critics disagree about is the extent to which the work's significance depends on the reader's identification of the intertext.

Michael Riffaterre, whose practice I follow here, assumes that all reading is intertextual, whether or not the intertext is identified, but that it is in principle identifiable. The relationship between a text and its intertext is opened when the reader's attention is drawn to anomalies or obscurities that cannot be accounted for by the context—Riffaterre's "ungrammaticalities," which he regards as "traces left by the absent intertext, signs of an incompleteness to be completed elsewhere." It is these textual clues that set in motion an intertextual reading, "even if the intertext is not yet known or has been lost with the tradition it reflected." It should also be noted that intertextual theory is concerned primarily with the *reading* of texts, and not their composition. Intertextuality, Riffaterre points out, "refers to an operation of the reader's mind," and an intertext he defines as "the corpus of texts the reader may legitimately connect with the one before his eyes" or "the texts brought to mind by what he is reading." Whether the intertext is an anonymous cultural system, the conventions, say, of thirties dance band lyrics, or an identifiable work, a song by George and Ira Gershwin, Riffaterre argues that the text's significance depends on the absent intertext: "even while the hypogram remains unidentified, the text's troublesomeness keeps pointing to this need: the hypogram must be found, a solution outside the text must be found, in the intertext."[19]

And one may speculate that these are the two varieties of jazz

18. Jonathan Culler, *The Pursuit of Signs: Semiotics, Literature, Deconstruction* (Ithaca, 1981), 103, 101.

19. See Michael Riffaterre, "Syllepsis," *Critical Inquiry,* VI (1980), 627, 626; "Intertextual Representation: On Mimesis as Interpretive Discourse," *Critical Inquiry,* XI (1984), 142; "Interview," *Diacritics,* XI (1981), 14.

intertexts in Larkin's poems. There are first those that are in principle identifiable and whose identity may or may not be of significance. Larkin raises this question about John O'Hara's *Appointment in Samarra*. Is it significant that his hero Julian English plays Whiteman and Goldkette rather than the more authentic Armstrong, Ellington, "or even the Chicago Rhythm Kings" before going out to the garage and killing himself? Was O'Hara, whose *Butterfield 8* showed he knew his jazz, being satiric? (*AWJ*, 146–47). Is it of any real importance to know *which* Bechet recording is playing in "For Sidney Bechet"? Perhaps not. Is Oliver's "Riverside Blues" of any significance in "Reference Back" other than simply as a colorful jazz title? In fact, it appears to be, just as the identity of the popular songs contained in "Reasons for Attendance" may influence our reading. But there is a second category of musical intertexts in Larkin that raise different issues. These are anonymous intertexts that may point simply to a set of cultural conventions—those of the blues, say, as in the first poem of "Two Guitar Pieces"—and that are both more pervasive in Larkin's poems and more troublesome for the reader since their significance is seldom obvious.

"Reasons for Attendance" (*CP*, 80) from *The Less Deceived* is Larkin's first successful jazz poem, successful at least in engaging readers, attracting a body of commentary, inviting the kind of misreadings that attest to its complexity. Like "Places, Loved Ones" from the same volume, which may be read as a companion piece, it is ostensibly a defense of individualism—ultimately, bachelorhood—against the claims of community, attachment, or what the poem calls the "happiness … found by couples." It develops its defense through a series of antitheses—outside/inside, detachment/engagement, the individual/the couple, and (oddly) the aesthetic/the sensual. The crucial distinction, however, is one that Larkin carries over from his jazz life, listening/dancing: jazz is not properly a music for *dancing;* it is for appreciative *listening,* as the jazz aficionado understands. Alan Sinfield notes this distinction in support of his view that the poem "sets serious aspirations in the jazz scene against its more popular aspects." Here is Francis Newton's explanation of the jazz lover's attitude toward dancing:

The true-blue jazz lover, who looks down with contempt on commercial pop music, and would not dream of actually dancing to his favourite music unless his girl insisted on it—and then only as a concession to cultural backwardness—is a late phenomenon. As a type he has emerged out of the mass of swaying couples who did not look for creative art in the places where jazz was played, and whose main reason for liking jazz was that it was good to dance to.

Both Larkin and his narrator in "Reasons for Attendance" fit the type Newton describes. When asked by an interviewer if he danced as well as listened to jazz, Larkin responds, "Dance, you mean dance? Dancing was very much more formal in those days. Not a jazz thing" (*RW*, 50–51). It is the difference between thinking of jazz as something close to an art form—"(Art, if you like)"—and jazz as an excuse for experiencing "[t]he wonderful feel of girls" that is the basis for the speaker's argument, and Newton has described it exactly in his portrait of the true jazz fan: "Jazz, for the fan, is therefore not simply a music to be enjoyed as one enjoys apples, or drinks, or girls, but one to be studied and absorbed in a spirit of dedication."[20] The link between the speaker's version of individualism—his refusal to give in to the attraction of the dancing couples—and his attitude toward jazz, however, has been misread.

David Timms reads the poem's appeal to art as a reference to Larkin's own art of poetry, as if being a poet were the speaker's justification for his isolation. "It is worth noting," Timms says, "that this is the only occasion on which Larkin mentions the fact that he is a poet in the whole of his mature work." Other readers have made the same leap. It is a poem about "the poet's calling," or "the lonely artist," or the poet's "life of individual fulfilment, the life of 'Art' " as an alternative to the "wonderful feel of girls."[21] But this is not quite the argument of the poem, since the speaker never makes an appeal to poetry or the poet as the basis for the debate. There is no evidence in the poem that the

20. Alan Sinfield, *Literature, Politics, and Culture in Postwar Britain* (Oxford, 1989), 166; Newton, *Jazz Scene*, 230, 232.

21. See David Timms, *Philip Larkin* (New York, 1973), 87; Stephen Regan, *Philip Larkin* (London, 1992), 95; Terry Whalen, *Philip Larkin and English Poetry* (London, 1986), 37; Graham Holderness, "Philip Larkin: The Limits of Experience," in *Critical Essays on Philip Larkin: The Poems*, ed. Linda Cookson and Bryan Loughrey (London, 1989), 110.

speaker *is* in fact a poet (and, as Timms suggests, if he is adopting the persona of the poet, it would be one of the rare moments in the Larkin canon when he does so). The poem's argument is based rather on two responses to jazz, two antithetical "reasons for attendance," and the speaker comes down on the side that offers what he regards as the more authentic reason.

He is drawn by the rough and authoritative sound of the jazz trumpet and stops for a moment outside the dance to watch through the lighted window in a scene reminiscent of a moment in Hermann Hesse's *Steppenwolf* where Harry Haller stands outside a jazz dance hall both attracted and repulsed by the sensuality of the music. Since Larkin's speaker is outside and alone and the couples move to "the beat of happiness" inside, his first impression is that they have found what he lacks, that he should be inside with them. "Face to flushed face" in the fourth line is a play on "cheek to cheek" and the 1935 Irving Berlin song of that title, which equates happiness and dancing:

> Heaven, I'm in Heaven.
> And my heart beats so that I can hardly speak.
> And I seem to find the happiness I seek
> [W]hen we're out together dancing cheek to cheek.[22]

Here is the poem's version of dancing and happiness, with the heart beat reappearing as a musical beat:

> The trumpet's voice, loud and authoritative,
> Draws me a moment to the lighted glass
> To watch the dancers—all under twenty-five—
> Shifting intently, face to flushed face,
> Solemnly on the beat of happiness.
>
> —Or so I fancy, sensing the smoke and sweat,
> The wonderful feel of girls. Why be out here?

It is a legitimate question for a man observing happiness from the outside, and the force of "Or so I fancy" indicates that it is the *speaker's*

---

22. Hermann Hesse, *Steppenwolf,* trans. Basil Creighton (New York, 1961), 41–42; Irving Berlin, *The Songs of Irving Berlin: Movie Songs* (Milwaukee, 1991), 22–23.

desire, *his* fantasy of dancing cheek to cheek that invests the scene with its sensuous appeal, which is to say that his dispute (with himself) is genuine.

His first attempt to justify his position outside is unconvincing:

> Why be out here?
> But then, why be in there? Sex, yes, but what
> Is sex? Surely, to think the lion's share
> Of happiness is found by couples—sheer
>
> Inaccuracy, as far as I'm concerned.

"Sheer inaccuracy" is bluster, and the request for a definition of sex sounds like a debater's trick. (When he later introduces art as his counterpoint to sex, he could as easily have asked, "Art, yes, but what is art?") Blake Morrison has pointed out that the asides here—"But then," "yes," "surely," "as far as I'm concerned"—attest to the speaker's lack of success in attempting to convince himself that he is on the right side of the glass.[23]

The reference to the happiness found by couples does, however, provide a link to a more convincing argument that depends on reversing the hierarchy the poem has set up between the dancing couples and the lone individual who can only listen from the outside:

> What calls me is that lifted, rough-tongued bell
> (Art, if you like) whose individual sound
> Insists I too am individual.
> It speaks; I hear; others may hear as well,
>
> But not for me, nor I for them; and so
> With happiness.

There is some play here with *tongue* and *bell*. Larkin's interpretation is that the bell "is the trumpet-bell, and is naturally lifted when being played" (*Letters*, 223). Both the bell and the jazz trumpet are "rough-tongued," the jazz trumpet both in the sense of being more roughly tongued than classical trumpet and in producing what could be regarded

---

23. Morrison, *The Movement*, 104.

as a cruder tongue or language. The jazz term for this sound is "dirty." In being summoned by the "individual sound" of the trumpet and not by the opportunity to dance, the speaker verifies the authenticity of his reason for attendance. He is there to appreciate the art (if you like) of jazz rather than to use the music merely as a background for sex. Thus the argument makes its subtle appeal to an unwritten law of attendance at jazz concerts. The convention that the true appreciation of jazz *as an art* precludes dancing is a (missing) link between his scorn for the dancing couples and his defense of individualism.

In regard to the poem's defense, it should be noted that in the fifties psychological and sociological profiles of the jazz fan emphasized a correlation between jazz and individuality. In an early essay called "Listening to Popular Music" the sociologist David Riesman develops the paradox that hot jazz lovers are "individualists who reject contemporary majority conformities" but who, in the process, move into a new peer group and "adopt a new conformity under the banner of nonconformity." In his 1951 Freudian study of jazz Aaron Esman finds that the jazz audience "consists of individuals who, consciously or unconsciously, regard themselves as outside the accepted cultural framework and as unbound by many of its conventions." Jazz is thus "a music for those who seek liberation and individuality." Jazz, in short, has always been identified as what Frederick Garber calls an "individualist's art,"[24] an identification that is so deeply ingrained in the poem's speaker that it does not occur to him that it needs explanation. The "individual sound" of the trumpet evokes another meaning as well: jazz is an individualist's art in Garber's sense in that its essence is improvisation, so that each trumpet solo is theoretically unique. The speaker's assumption is that the individual sound of jazz can be appreciated only by an individual response, while jazz as a stimulus to sex can be appreciated by a couple or a whole dance floor of couples in unison, all on the same "beat of happiness."

24. David Riesman, "Listening to Popular Music," *American Quarterly,* II (1950), 369; Esman, "Jazz—A Study in Cultural Conflict," 224–25; Frederick Garber, "Fabulating Jazz," in *Representing Jazz,* ed. Krin Gabbard (Durham, 1995), 70.

Why is the one response superior to the other? The poem's logic is something like this: the ability to appreciate the art of the music—*art* is the privileged term here—outweighs in value the dancers' subversion of art for something else, and this appreciation cannot be a group enterprise. That is, the hierarchy *art music/dance music* is fused with the hierarchy *individuality/conformity*. Further, happiness is assumed to obey the same law as art; what brings one happiness cannot be dictated by someone else. This is the logic also of the nonjazz version of the poem, "Places, Loved Ones" (*CP*, 99), where the postulate, crudely stated, is that marriage is a surrender of one's choices for happiness, depending on fate "to bear / You off irrevocably. . . ." The belief that giving up one's individuality in marriage is fated, the poem argues, is as absurd as the belief that the place in which one resides is fated—as if one were to say, pompously, *"This is my proper ground, / Here I shall stay."* In "Reasons for Attendance" the argument rests on a more positive analogy. The speaker's individual response to the trumpet is analogous to the principle that governs happiness: "It speaks; I hear; others may hear as well, // But not for me, nor I for them; and so / With happiness." In both poems, variations on the same theme, the final stanza undermines to a degree the conviction established by the argument.

But not for me. Larkin begins the final stanza of "Reasons for Attendance" by violating one of his own prohibitions, the use of the jazz quotation. In a review titled "They'll None of Them Be Missed" Larkin calls for a ban on two jazz practices, the bass solo and "that irritating habit of present-day jazz, the quotation":

You know what I mean: the soloist is giving out on some accepted vehicle or other, when all of a sudden he interpolates a phrase or two from something quite different—another tune, a nursery rhyme, a national anthem. . . . What should we think of the actor who interpolated a line of "Gunga Din" in "To be or not to be"? (*AWJ*, 129)

The problem with the quotation, as with the bass solo, Larkin writes, is that they "break the emotional flow between player and audience" so that the "tension, the interest, dies away and has to be worked for all over again" (*AWJ*, 129). This is not the case, however, with the quotation that begins the last stanza of "Reasons for Attendance"—the interpolation of the title of the 1930 Gershwin song "But Not for Me," one of the great standards of the jazz repertoire. In the poem the phrase manages to fit both the context—others may hear and interpret the trumpet for *themselves,* but not for me—and the intertext—"They're writing songs of love, / But not for me." The Gershwin intertext answers the first stanza's romantic illusions about "dancing cheek to cheek" with its less deceived lyrics (which also state the crux of "Places, Loved Ones"): "I never want to hear / From any cheerful Pollyannas, / Who tell you fate / Supplies a mate; / It's all bananas!"[25] Unlike one of the examples he cites in his call for a ban on the practice of quotation— "Charlie Parker playing 'Pop Goes the Weasel' in some context which till then had been a serious one" (*AWJ,* 128)—the four-note phrase breaks neither the mood nor the rhythm. Its melody is, if anything, iambic, and rather than interrupting the emotional flow of the passage it deepens it.

Interestingly, this is not the only occasion on which Larkin interpolated a phrase from the Gershwin song, and in the other instance it is equally unobtrusive. In "The Tenor Player with 50 Legs," Larkin reviews, among other things, John Coltrane's version of "But Not For Me." In his next review of a Coltrane recording a few months later he says simply, "The screeching dreariness of John Coltrane is not for me" (*AWJ,* 141, 150), a small joke for readers who are paying attention. In "Reasons for Attendance" the quotation is of more significance, for it opens the gap in the last stanza that allows readers to see a complication in the speaker's attitude and to supply a significance to the poem's final stanza that works against its contextual meaning. The phrase itself contains the complication since it gives (once we recognize it as a quotation) two different reasons for nonattendance. The contextual meaning is that the speaker is outside and alone because his response to the music is aesthetic and individual. The intertextual significance is that he is outside looking in because he knows (sadly) that love and

25. George Gershwin and Ira Gershwin, *The George and Ira Gershwin Song Book* (New York, 1960), 60–61.

songs of love are not for him, so that his appeal to art may be no more than a defense against his desire for the "wonderful feel of girls."

This interpretation relies admittedly on an intertext that readers might dispute, and it may also be objected that the Gershwin quotation is much too subtle to trust with the undermining of the poem's fragile argument. It is clear, however, that the poem is aware of the possible undoing of its argument; the stanza ends by saying more bluntly what the Gershwin text has already intimated. After offering his reasons for solitude over couples the speaker concludes,

> Therefore I stay outside,
> Believing this; and they maul to and fro,
> Believing that; and both are satisfied,
> If no one has misjudged himself. Or lied.

The last line warns us against trusting the surface text. The poem is richer and more wide-ranging in the subtexts it incorporates than is first apparent, but one of these is not, as has been assumed, Larkin's own vocation as poet. In recent studies Roger Day writes of the speaker's justification of his life of "self-expression through art," and James Booth refers to "the speaker's defence of his lonely vocation to 'attend' to the 'rough-tongued bell' of art, rather than join in the dance of the couples," assuming obviously that the "rough-tongued bell" of art is poetry. Booth adds, "When he refers to his artistic vocation the sulky argumentativeness gives way to a more confident tone."[26] That the poem attempts its resolution through an appeal to the poet's own art represents an almost universal misreading. All the evidence of the poem is that the persona speaks not as the artist but as the connoisseur, one who understands and appreciates the subtleties of an art, in this case the art of jazz and not the art of poetry. And the poem's apparent (though not real) difficulty may be attributed to the obstacles its jazz intertext sets up for some readers and to the circumstance that the literary critics who have established its interpretation have not made the connection

26. Roger Day, *Larkin* (Philadelphia, 1987), 36; James Booth, *Philip Larkin: Write.* (New York, 1992), 97.

between jazz and art that the poem makes. They presumably would not share Larkin's view that as a cultural figure Louis Armstrong is "more important than Picasso" (*Letters,* 443).

Booth also argues that while it is true Larkin focuses on his enthusiasm for jazz in a few poems (he mentions "For Sidney Bechet" and "Reference Back," two other poems I will look at here), the success of these works "does not depend in the slightest on the reader's complicity in his enthusiasm."[27] If the success of a poem could be separated from its being read, this might be true; and it *is* true that enthusiasm for jazz is not as essential as familiarity with the jazz intertexts of these poems. But without some sense of the missing jazz texts and conventions to which these works keep referring us, a reading of them remains incomplete, as Booth's own reading of "Reasons for Attendance" indicates.

Although it appears in a volume (*The Whitsun Weddings*) published more than eight years after the appearance of "Reasons for Attendance" in *The Less Deceived,* "For Sidney Bechet" (*CP,* 83) was written only a few weeks later, and it is instructive to read the two together. Both open with the sound of jazz, Bechet's soprano saxophone replacing the anonymous trumpet of "Reasons for Attendance," and both are built on the antithesis between the speaker's response to the music and the response of nameless others. One could argue in fact that "For Sidney Bechet" is one of the most useful commentaries on "Reasons for Attendance," since the later poem incorporates the earlier one. (And since intertextuality flows both ways, for the reader the later poem inhabits the earlier one.) This phenomenon of two passages by an author serving as "two variants of the same structure" Michael Riffaterre calls *intratextual intertextuality,* and a motive for reading the two poems as different versions of the same structure is that components of each subtext will "acquire a meaning other than what they convey in context" since each will now be modified by our rethinking it in light of the other version.[28]

To read the two poems together is to be made aware that almost

27. Booth, *Philip Larkin: Writer,* 71.

28. Michael Riffaterre, "The Intertextual Unconscious," *Critical Inquiry,* XIII (1987), 380–81.

the whole of "For Sidney Bechet" is a reworking of two lines of "Reasons for Attendance": "It speaks; I hear; others may hear as well, // But not for me, nor I for them. . . ." The later poem gives form to what remains unimagined in the earlier one, the listeners' individual responses to a piece of music. The possible lie of "Reasons for Attendance" also makes an appearance as the later poem's "appropriate falsehood." What is at first disturbing in "For Sidney Bechet" is that the speaker appears to push even further the antithesis (in "Reasons for Attendance") between his authentic response to jazz and others' inauthentic responses. Depicting several fantasies of New Orleans that Bechet's music arouses in others, the speaker says, "My Crescent City / Is where your speech alone is understood." One of the elements of the poem that an intratextual reading helps unravel is what appears to be the speaker's rather arrogant connoisseurship.

The last line of "Reasons for Attendance" introduces the possibility that both the dancers' and the speaker's responses to jazz may be instances of inauthenticity, the dancers in appropriating the music for sex, the speaker in insisting disingenuously that he responds to it purely as art. "For Sidney Bechet" opens by rethinking this notion. The speaker's assumption here is that every audience response is a "falsehood," and, more significantly, an "appropriate falsehood." The adjective contains the senses of a response that is fitted to each listener's own imagination or desire, a false response that nevertheless "may properly be indulged," as Hugh Underhill has it,[29] and a response that has been appropriated, taken as one's own without the authority of the music itself. The poem then proceeds to picture such falsehoods, centering on images of Bechet's New Orleans. These are given as others' appropriate falsehoods against which the speaker will later set his own:

> That note you hold, narrowing and rising, shakes
> Like New Orleans reflected on the water,
> And in all ears appropriate falsehood wakes,
>
> Building for some a legendary Quarter
> Of balconies, flower-baskets and quadrilles,

29. Underhill, "Poetry of Departures," 185.

Everyone making love and going shares—

Oh, play that thing! Mute glorious Storyvilles
Others may license, grouping round their chairs
Sporting-house girls like circus tigers (priced

Far above rubies) to pretend their fads,
While scholars *manqués* nod around unnoticed
Wrapped up in personnels like old plaids.

As in "Reasons for Attendance," others' appropriations of jazz involve sexual fantasies, both in the idealistic picture of the French Quarter as a close community—"Everyone making love and going shares"—and in the more licentious picture of Storyville, the brothel district, with sporting-house girls circled around the listener's chair like circus animals. The unnoticed scholars *manqués* may initially seem out of place here, but they are the sporting-house pianists, who were called "professors," perhaps because many of them gave piano lessons. "The sporting-houses needed professors," Jelly Roll Morton notes in explaining why New Orleans was the home of some of the greatest pianists in the country. Professor Longhair (Roy Bird), a New Orleans pianist, singer, and songwriter, combined in his stage name two of the musical conventions used in the poem (which refers to "long-haired grief" in the last line). The oddly plural "personnels" in which the professors are wrapped are the members of the band. ("From the time I started with Victor," Morton says, "using different personnels in the Red Hot Peppers Band, I was for years their number one hot orchestra.")[30]

The richness of the poem's range of allusions and subtexts can be seen most clearly in the Gray quotation, the "Mute glorious Storyvilles"

30. Alan Lomax, *Mister Jelly Roll: The Fortunes of Jelly Roll Morton, New Orleans Creole and "Inventor of Jazz,"* 2nd ed. (Berkeley, 1973), 42–43, 302. *Mister Jelly Roll,* first published in 1950, may well be another of the texts the poem has absorbed. Morton's account of Storyville is in accord with the poem's, including the notion of the district's early days as "one big happy family" (42), the image of the prostitutes as animals in the "animule dance" (128–29), a seven-page account of Bechet as the "golden boy of this golden generation" (94), and a description of "the unabashed emotional flowering of jazz in Sidney's playing" (94).

that some listeners of Bechet may "license." *License* here is both the permit that allows the Storyville prostitute to operate and the licentiousness with which the district was associated. But these are "Mute glorious Storyvilles," yoking together a cultural intertext (a descriptive system associated with the brothel district of New Orleans), two literary intertexts (Gray's "Elegy" and Gray's use of Milton as a type of the literary genius), and a jazz intertext that will be supplied by the reader familiar with jazz and blues recordings. Storyville is also the name of a record label that issued or reissued (licensed) traditional New Orleans jazz and the blues—among others, Emile Barnes's New Orleans Band, Big Joe Williams, Sonny Williams, and the "Sidney Bechet Sessions," reissued from sessions of 1946 and 1947.[31] Larkin reviewed the Storyville Bechet sessions in a piece whose title quotes from an Armstrong recording, "How Long This Has Been Going On": "to hear Bechet's soprano pealing out in open domination on 'Old Fashioned Love' is to experience a wave of emotion only the great players can evoke" (*AWJ*, 216).

The review was published four years after "For Sidney Bechet" appeared in *The Whitsun Weddings,* yet it is difficult not to incorporate it into a rereading of the poem. (Is it a subtle way of identifying the music that produced the wave of emotion the poem records? The poem, after all, achieves its resolution through an appeal to old-fashioned love.) To think of Storyvilles as jazz or blues recordings is to recover part of the original sense of the line from Gray's "Elegy": "Some mute inglorious Milton here may rest." Gray's mute poetic genius becomes the poem's mute jazz recording and by extension its artist (who may have used a

31. There were two Storyville labels. The best known was launched in Boston in 1951, and Bechet was among the artists it recorded. It was most active in 1953–1955 and had virtually ceased recording by the sixties. A second Storyville company began recording traditional jazz in Copenhagen in the early fifties and was shortly taken over by another company. The Danish Storyville label issued a five-disc set featuring Bechet and Mezz Mezzrow that Larkin reviewed in a 1965 jazz column. ("These sessions, made for love rather than money, must always have a powerful claim on the attention of any Bechet admirer" [*AWJ*, 140].) See also *The New Grove Dictionary of Jazz,* ed. Barry Kernfeld (London, 1988), II, 496.

mute to soften the sound of his instrument, although this association seems less rewarding). There is this distinction however: Gray's "mute *in*glorious Milton" is only the *potential* artist; he could never become a Milton because he is unlettered. Larkin's "mute *glorious* Storyvilles," in addition to being sexual fantasies and once-famous sites for jazz, are jazz recordings not heard *as music* (except by the speaker, as will become evident in the last two stanzas), and *mute* achieves a distinctive irony in its association with recorded music, suggesting yet another traditional intertext, Keats's unheard melodies. But the passage also provides another unspoken if not unheard melody, as Christopher Ricks has pointed out, since it drops the prefix in Gray's *inglorious* and asks us, on the basis of the familiarity of the intertext, to reinsert it in our reading of the line.[32] Or, in keeping with the musical performance of the poem, we could say that the line permits us to be aware simultaneously of the original melody from Gray and the new melody based on it, the poetic equivalent of jazz improvisation.

"For Sidney Bechet" has assimilated the music of Gray's "Elegy" in yet another manner, which it has almost successfully concealed. It appropriates and masks the familiar quatrain form of the "Elegy," making it look unfamiliar. William Harmon has noticed that the poem (of seventeen lines) amounts to four *abab* quatrains with an added line in the last stanza. But it appears on the page as five triplets with a final couplet, so that it hides its quatrains inside what looks like a form of terza rima:

> That note you hold, narrowing and rising, shakes
> Like New Orleans reflected on the water,
> And in all ears appropriate falsehood wakes,
>
> Building for some a legendary Quarter. . . .

Harmon writes, "This arrangement resembles a four-against-three musical rhythm, and it delivers a pleasant surprise by concealing the measure of Gray's 'Elegy' . . . inside a threefold-looking design."[33] One might

---

32. Ricks, "Like Something Almost Being Said," 129.
33. Harmon, "Larkin's Memory," 219.

almost conceive of Gray's "Elegy" as the "standard" on which the later poem improvises.

And it is not simply Gray's *music* that we hear in the poem. "For Sidney Bechet" is in one crucial respect a rewriting of "Elegy Written in a Country Churchyard"; both poems make claims for what might be called noncanonical art. In lines that have become a part of the storehouse of traditional poetic clichés Gray imagines illiterate Miltons, unseen blushing beauty, and unrefined gems among the unlettered poor. John Guillory has observed that the "Elegy" creates a scenario in which one "imagines the literary production of the unlettered as having the status of . . . what in our discourse is called the 'noncanonical.'" Such works—perhaps Bechet's Storyville recordings could be placed in this category—are seen as having "a kind of *unvalued* value."[34] It is of course the issue of Bechet's value as an artist that Larkin's poem addresses, and it ends by elevating Bechet's unlettered and noncanonical music— a music that does not exist in *notation* as European music does—to a position even higher than canonical "scored" classical music.

This is to say that just as Gray's melody becomes a source for Larkin's rhythmic improvisation, the *sense* of Gray's poem can be heard in Larkin's thematic variations. On the surface "For Sidney Bechet" is a description of appropriate fantasies that Bechet's music evokes, but the traces of Gray's "Elegy" indicate a more crucial distinction between others' *mute* Bechet (the marginalized Bechet of exotic New Orleans jazz) and the speaker's Bechet whose voice is heard as *music,* and who is therefore granted his place in the cultural canon. In both poems, interestingly enough, the elevation of the noncanonical is through a privileging of the natural over the cultural—Gray's unrefined gem in its natural state, his flower "born to blush unseen" set against "Ambition," "Grandeur," "Luxury," and "Pride"; Bechet's unwritten music, existing only in performance, as the "natural noise of good" set against "artificial" (written) classical music.

It should also be noted that Bechet attempted a task similar to

---

34. John Guillory, *Cultural Capital: The Problem of Literary Canon Formation* (Chicago, 1993), 86.

Larkin's, that is, to preserve the integrity of his noncanonical music *as music* against the most persistent of the "appropriate falsehoods" of its origins. In his autobiography *Treat It Gentle,* transcribed from tape recordings completed shortly before his death in 1959, Bechet addresses the Storyville legend in his own way:

People have got an idea that the music started in whorehouses. Well, there was a district there, you know, and the houses in it, they'd all have someone playing a guitar or a mandolin, or a piano . . . someone singing maybe; but they didn't have orchestras, and the musicians never played regular there. . . . So how can you say Jazz started in whorehouses when the musicians didn't have no real need for them? . . . No, it wasn't red-light districts were making ragtime. Musicians weren't *going* there to make it. The only thing that was holding them back from playing it for everyone was that same thing that was always holding it back.[35]

Bechet's text brings to the surface a defensiveness about jazz's cultural and artistic standing that is buried more deeply in "For Sidney Bechet."

The poem's elevation of Bechet's jazz depends on the subtleties of the written/unwritten debate, which has always been part of jazz tradition. The pianist for King Oliver's Creole Jazz Band, whose music is playing in Larkin's "Reference Back," was for a time Lil Hardin (later the wife of Louis Armstrong), the only member of the band who had not come from New Orleans. She had grown up in Memphis, where she had studied classical music, and, as Graham Vulliamy reports, she was astonished to discover that Oliver's band, one of the most accomplished of its time, not only didn't play from musical notation but couldn't answer when asked what key they were playing in. Yet the unwritten nature of jazz may be turned to advantage, as is the case in "For Sidney Bechet." Dave Laing has emphasized the importance of the phonograph record in jazz history in that it reproduces "the *sound* of a *performance*," which is crucially different from the preservation of classical music, "whose notation is based upon a series of (ultimately) arbitrary decisions about how music is to be measured and classified."

35. Sidney Bechet, *Treat It Gentle* (New York, 1960), 53–54.

In a musical culture ignorant of notation, "there can be no clear division between composition and performance," as there is in music that exists as notation.[36] In Larkin's terms, jazz exists as "natural noise," while the feelings of classical music are "scored."

Laing's argument is that the phonograph record "made possible the preservation of 'non-written' music in its own terms." In jazz the relationship between the music and the record is exactly that between "a Beethoven concerto and Western musical notation," and the significance of the different means of preservation is that jazz and blues may be "faithfully recorded in the form in which their negro originators conceived and played them, rather than being dismantled and distorted in order to conform to the notation system." One of the features of early jazz such as that played by King Oliver's band was "collective improvisation," in which all the musicians improvised together within a framework of chords and rhythms. The importance of nonwritten recorded jazz, Laing argues, was that it was able to capture in a way notation could not "the polyphonic character of the ensemble playing": "Musical notation might have been able to cope with the details of this, but it could never have captured the totality."[37] This is another version of the implied argument of "For Sidney Bechet," the superiority of the sound of the actual performance—natural, improvised—to scored music.

The improvisational quality of the poem itself is emphasized in line seven when the speaker interrupts his account of others' appropriations of Bechet to yell directly to the solo musician, "Oh, play that thing!" This is one of those uncanny moments in Larkin's verse when the fictional world opens to reveal what appears to be a real world lying behind it (like the unnoticed leaves and hidden flowering weeds of "Here" and the world of locked-up offices of "Aubade.") What (for the reader) is an absence, the actual sound of Bechet's saxophone, is suddenly more authentically present than what is on the page, since the

36. Graham Vulliamy, *Jazz and Blues* (London, 1982), 43–44: Laing, *Sound of Our Time,* 35.

37. Laing, *Sound of Our Time,* 36–37.

speaker's response to the music is direct and natural—"Oh play that thing!" gives the impression of an unplanned interpolation from the conventional stock of jazz audience responses—and what surrounds it is necessarily contrived (written or "scored"). Cedric Watts's criticism that the poem is "hollow at the core" for readers who lack a knowledge of Bechet's music is thus, from this perspective, not altogether warranted. "For Sidney Bechet" succeeds in finding a way of representing not so much the music itself but someone *listening* to music at the very moment (conventionally) the poem is articulated. And "For Sidney Bechet" succeeds where "Reasons for Attendance" is only partially successful by realizing (rather than merely stating) the basic antithesis between the speaker's jazz and that of others. Further, in "Reasons for Attendance" the appeal to art gives the speaker a sense of superiority that he masks only through the irony of the final line ("If no one has misjudged himself. Or lied"). "For Sidney Bechet" appears at first to repeat this defensive posture, but the poem solves its dilemma without resorting to irony in what is almost a Yeatsian moment at the end.

Janice Rossen reads "For Sidney Bechet" as the closest Larkin ever came to the sort of transcendent vision he first admired in Yeats and later rejected. After devoting four stanzas to the appropriate fantasies awakened in others by Bechet's music, the speaker turns in the poem's last five lines to his own response:

> On me your voice falls as they say love should,
> Like an enormous yes. My Crescent City
> Is where your speech alone is understood,
>
> And greeted as the natural noise of good,
> Scattering long-haired grief and scored pity.

The privileged concept here is no longer art; it is now love. The speaker's Bechet is to the Bechet of other listeners what abiding love is to sporting-house love or mere sex. It is a version of the kind of Yeatsian sincerity—the depth of his feelings set against others' emotional shallowness—found in poems like "When You Are Old":

> How many loved your moments of glad grace,
> And loved your beauty with love false or true,

> But one man loved the pilgrim soul in you,
> And loved the sorrows of your changing face.[38]

Rossen observes that jazz is one of the few spheres in Larkin in which emotion is permitted without being smothered by irony,[39] and other readers have seen this as one of the rare ecstatic moments in the Larkin canon. It should be noted that the speaker still retains his advantage over other listeners, but it is now on the basis of an appeal whose legitimacy we are normally willing to grant, as we grant Yeats his superior claim to Maud Gonne's affections on the evidence that he loved her soul and her sorrows while others loved only her superficial beauty and her moments of happiness. Others love Bechet's music because it wakes appropriate falsehoods of a Crescent City free from sexual restraints. The speaker's Crescent City is where Bechet's "speech alone" is understood. The language is ambiguous; it appears first to say, *"My* Crescent City *alone* is where your music is understood," which is the connoisseur's argument of "Reasons for Attendance." A rereading recognizes the speaker's love/sex hierarchy: "Since I respond to your music as if it were the voice of a lover, my Crescent City is where your voice alone, your pure music on its own without the fantasies it wakes, is understood as something good in itself, a natural thing like love."

To conceive of jazz as itself the object of love for its devoted fans is, as we have seen, a jazz convention. To conceive of Bechet's saxophone as speech, a voice the speaker is able to identify and understand, is also conventional, since, as Simon Frith notes, "jazz critics describe players' unique 'voices' on their instruments." Graham Vulliamy points out that jazz musicians, unlike classical musicians, "use their instruments in imitation of the human voice": "They express themselves through their instruments and this is why all jazz musicians have styles and tones of their own, which are immediately recognisable." Interestingly it is Bechet himself that Vulliamy cites on this point. Giving advice to a pupil about

---

38. William Butler Yeats, *The Collected Works of W. B. Yeats,* Vol. I: *The Poems,* ed. Richard J. Finneran (New York, 1989), 41.

39. Rossen, *Philip Larkin: His Life's Work,* 49.

the different ways a single note might be played, Bechet concludes, "That's how you express your feelings in music. It's like talking."[40]

Cedric Watts finds the *scattering* of the last line ambiguous, since it can mean either "distributing in different directions" or "repelling in different directions." Both contextually and intertextually, however, only the second meaning can apply, since the "natural" (improvised, unscored) sound of Bechet's saxophone—a positive good—is set against (and disperses) the grief and pity of classical "scored" music ("long-hair" was a term applied to classical musicians in the fifties, and the pun on *scored* links it with both the markings of written music and the markings of pain or grief). Jazz as a natural music privileged over classical music as artifice is thus a version of the hierarchy of the speaker's natural love privileged over others' contrived sexual fantasies. And it is appropriate, finally, that the rhythm of the line in which jazz routs scored music—"Scattering long-haired grief and scored pity"—is syncopated. William Harmon, who says that Larkin's verse "will not remind anyone of the jazz most admired by Larkin," is himself reminded of jazz in reading the ending of "For Sidney Bechet," especially "the finely synco-pated rhythm in the last line—trochee, iamb, spondee, iamb, trochee—where the scazon [the substitution of a trochee for the concluding iamb] delivers the final rhyme a syllable sooner than our ear expects." Harmon guesses that "Larkin, who was something of a drummer, got a big kick out of writing a line at once so complex and so real-sounding."[41] And, he might have added, so closely in touch with the music to which the poem is responding and which it has obviously incorporated.

Reading "Reasons for Attendance" and "For Sidney Bechet" together underscores the extent to which they are versions of the same structure. Each is built on the experience of responding to jazz, and each is shaped by the narrator's setting his response against that of others and inventing an argument or trope by which his response may be privileged. Larkin's

---

40. Simon Frith, *The Sociology of Rock* (London, 1978), 179; Vulliamy, *Jazz and Blues*, 46, 140.

41. Watts, "Larkin and Jazz," 27; Harmon, "Larkin's Memory," 219.

third variation on the theme, "Reference Back" (*CP*, 106) from *The Whitsun Weddings*, begins as if it were to be a repetition of this structure but ends by departing significantly from it. The poem is complicated from the start by the fact that the inauthentic view of jazz is no longer anonymous—it is that of the speaker's mother—and by the self-consciousness of the speaker's examination of their two widely separated perspectives. In "Reference Back" the two antithetical responses to jazz produce a poem that is not so much about listening to jazz as it is about "the long perspectives / Open at each instant of our lives." Its *occasion*, however, is listening to King Oliver's "Riverside Blues":

> *That was a pretty one*, I heard you call
> From the unsatisfactory hall
> To the unsatisfactory room where I
> Played record after record, idly,
> Wasting my time at home, that you
> Looked so much forward to.
> Oliver's *Riverside Blues*, it was. And now
> I shall, I suppose, always remember how
> The flock of notes those antique negroes blew
> Out of Chicago air into
> A huge remembering pre-electric horn
> The year after I was born
> Three decades later made this sudden bridge
> From your unsatisfactory age
> To my unsatisfactory prime.

"*That was a pretty one*," called out by one's mother, is so obviously an inappropriate response to jazz (as opposed to, say, "Oh, play that thing!") that the speaker feels no requirement here to establish his jazz credentials. ("Pretty," as applied to jazz, usually had pejorative connotations.)[42] More than that, any jazz recording that one's mother finds pretty is rendered suspect. "Listen-with-mother" is a tag Larkin uses in jazz reviews (*AWJ*, 157, 231, 242) to categorize a kind of bland, unadventurous music that wouldn't offend one's mother. (An album

---

42. See Robert S. Gold, *Jazz Talk* (New York, 1975), 208.

called "Country Roads and Other Places," for example, is reviewed as "Gary Burton's latest listen-with-mother for flower children. The pieces are melodious and inoffensive" [*AWJ*, 242].)

Although the poem has been read as a tribute to King Oliver, it is also interesting to note that, for Larkin, Oliver was dangerously close to the "listen-with-mother" category. Larkin admits that he is "something of a heretic about Oliver" (*AWJ*, 190), one of the giants of traditional jazz; wonders aloud if Oliver "was all he was cracked up to be" (*AWJ*, 145); and finally confesses, "I don't care for Oliver," whose trumpet solos Larkin characterizes as "full of that childish wa-wa stuff" (*AWJ*, 248). This is to say that the jazz intertext here is not what it first appears to be—a tribute to Oliver, as Watts reads it, or, as Bruce Martin reads it, a case of a favorite record forever marred by its association with the speaker's mother.[43] If the record had been, for example, Bechet's "Old Fashioned Love," the mother's remark might have produced a different poem. But since the speaker is freed of the obligation of defending the art of the music in question, the motive in the two previous poems, he turns instead to the perspective suddenly opened by the confluence of the music and the mother's attempt to make some connection with the world it represents, what the speaker calls "this sudden bridge," a term that itself enters the poem by way of jazz.

The bridge, that is, exists both in the experience of listening to the music and in the music itself. In early jazz such as that of King Oliver, the bridge is a short section of four or eight bars that links the separate strains of a composition. In reviewing the set of recordings that includes Oliver's "Riverside Blues," Larry Gushee calls attention to the brilliance of Johnny Dodds's clarinet bridges, his ability "to place the final note of his own phrase on the beginning of a trumpet phrase."[44]

The function of Oliver's "Riverside Blues" differs from that of the two other jazz intertexts in that it represents not the speaker's love for

43. Watts, "Larkin and Jazz," 26; Bruce K. Martin, *Philip Larkin* (Boston, 1978), 72.

44. On the bridge in early jazz, see *The New Grove Dictionary of Jazz*, I, 150; Larry Gushee, "King Oliver's Creole Jazz Band," in *The Art of Jazz: Essays on the Nature and Development of Jazz,* ed. Martin T. Williams (New York, 1959), 46.

the music (the poem indicates no attitude toward the music itself) nor the art of jazz, but a theme—a concern with time—that is conventionally associated with art. Since King Oliver is synonymous with the beginnings of jazz, its dispersal from New Orleans, he serves Larkin as a marker for a moment in time, as he does in a much later remark to Kingsley Amis: "Christ, 27 years since [*Lucky Jim*]. That shakes me. Longer than between Oliver's first record and Basie's" (*Letters*, 638). "Riverside Blues" is one of thirty-seven titles recorded in Chicago in 1923 by King Oliver's Creole Jazz Band, and these are among the most famous recordings in jazz history, since they preserve what is thought to be, in spite of Larkin's reservations, the high point of the New Orleans jazz style.[45] "Riverside Blues" is thus important as an intertext not for what it says as artifact but for what it represents as a historical moment in time. As the title indicates, the music of the record is a reference back to the moment the record was cut, a "sudden bridge" the music constructs. The speaker focuses not on some feeling or mood conveyed by the music itself but on his re-creation of "those antique negroes [blowing] / . . . into / A huge remembering pre-electric horn," the music's actual performance. "Reference Back," it turns out, is in the long tradition of lyric poems that focus on a scene or object that serves as an occasion for meditating on the nature of time; the closest ancestor to the "flock of notes" that opens the perspective on time in the poem is perhaps Yeats's flock of swans in "The Wild Swans at Coole."

The narrator's specificity about the name of the record the mother responds to, the date of its recording (the year after he was born), and his own age (three decades) follows the pattern of "The Wild Swans at Coole," which "Reference Back" incorporates. The effect of Yeats's poem depends heavily on the exactness of the number of the nine-and-fifty swans and the nineteen autumns that have elapsed since his persona first made his count. These objects by which he has measured his own change over two decades, like the "antique" musicians of "Reference Back," give only the illusion of timelessness. In "Reference Back" the momentary bridge between mother and son and the gulf it reveals

45. See, for example, Vulliamy, *Jazz and Blues*, 43–44.

depends on the son's knowledge that he and Oliver's "Riverside Blues" are approximately the same age. A. T. Tolley has also noted that the Oliver recording was chosen because of its coincidence with the birth of the speaker: "The primitive 'pre-electric' sound seems as 'antique' as the faded, posed photographs of the Oliver orchestra make them look, suggesting how distant Larkin's own beginnings seem to him, as does the closeness he once had with his mother."[46] Looking forward from the perspective the recording opens, he sees himself in his "unsatisfactory prime" and the young woman who gave birth to him now in her "unsatisfactory age" while the "flock of notes" Oliver's band blew, like the "brilliant" and "Unwearied" swans, are "Blindingly undiminished":

> Truly, though our element is time,
> We are not suited to the long perspectives
> Open at each instant of our lives.
> They link us to our losses: worse,
> They show us what we have as it once was,
> Blindingly undiminished, just as though
> By acting differently we could have kept it so.

Larkin's rewriting of what is perhaps the most conventional of all lyric themes depends, as did "For Sidney Bechet," on jazz's distinction between the work as artifact and the work as performance. Unlike Keats's Grecian urn or Shakespeare's gilded monuments or powerful rhyme, which are, conventionally, outside of time, the recording of "Riverside Blues" is a "reference back" to a moment in time, Chicago in 1923, which has been lost. But the record has also preserved "undiminished" what has been lost, a particular performance that took place about the time the speaker was born. (The more immediate loss is the mother-son relationship that the record has momentarily bridged.) The jazz recording is thus a more complex figure for the perspective on time than the conventional artifact or even Yeats's swans since it simultaneously "link[s] us to our losses"—exhibits the past we have lost—and "show[s] us what we have as it once was"—authenticates the lost moment by

---

46. Tolley, *My Proper Ground*, 86–87.

preserving the *performance* (not simply the invisible music) exactly as it was. The phonograph (like the photograph in "Lines on a Young Lady's Photograph Album") provides the occasion for a perspective we normally find unsuitable precisely because it is able to preserve a moment of the past that, as the earlier poem says, "no one now can share" (*CP*, 72). Frederick Garber makes a similar argument in discussing the "semblance of authenticity" in sound recordings. The case in point is the Bix Beiderbecke and Frankie Trumbauer recording of "Singin' the Blues": "In the Bix and Trum recording we listen to the sounds of a scene at which Beiderbecke *had been* present, and what we listen to repeatedly is the reproduced sound of that past participial presence, precisely the sort of anteriority we see in photographs." Garber concludes that the phonograph record brings us as close as we can get to the "moment of making and the sounds of that moment."[47]

The contribution of "Reference Back" to the poetic conventions of temporality is to replace the artifact as existing outside of time with the work of art, the jazz recording, as a past moment *in time* authenticated. The latter, the poem says, is the more poignant reminder of time because it is simultaneously dead and "Blindingly undiminished." It is particularly painful to the son because it momentarily recreates a relationship between mother and son that has been lost and fosters the illusion that the bridge, like King Oliver's performance, could have been preserved— "By acting differently we could have kept it so." "Reference Back" differs from the other jazz poems in using jazz as a trope in a poem that is not directly about music or art, and in this sense it is closer than its two precursors to other Larkin texts not directly about jazz but inhabited by jazz and other popular music in much more elusive ways.

47. Garber, "Fabulating Jazz," 74.

4

GOOD MORNIN', BLUES

[Y]ou don't have to be black to have the blues. You can be white and wake up
in the morning and something is blue on you. You understand what I'm talking
about, around your bed, and you done got blue.

—Robert Shaw in William R. Ferris,
Blues from the Delta

Somebody said they'd heard Doc had died and asked [Armstrong] what was
wrong with him. Louis looked at them with a kinda sad face and finally he
says, "What was wrong with Doc? Man, when you die, *everything* is wrong with
you."

—Bill Crow, *Jazz Anecdotes*

ONCE we become aware of the common ground occupied by
Larkin's jazz aesthetic and his poetics, points of convergence appear
everywhere, yet there is still the problem of knowing how to read them.
Take for an example the distinction between jazz performance and
traditional poetic notation by which jazz "lives and dies in the moment
of performance," as Ted Gioia puts it,[1] while the poem's existence is

---

1. Gioia, *Imperfect Art*, 83.

atemporal, forever on the page and unaltered by a particular reading. I have argued that this distinction figures crucially in our reading of poems like "For Sidney Bechet" and "Reference Back," but how does it play out in Larkin's own ideology of poetic and musical relations? He is very much aware of the distinction and its implications, yet he reads it in a manner that may at first seem surprising.

In a 1979 interview Larkin wonders aloud whether certain of his assumptions about poetry—the way it rhymes and scans—came from listening to dance music (*RW*, 50), and William Pritchard believes that the influence of dance lyrics can indeed be heard "not merely in the fact that Larkin's poems rhyme and scan, but in how they sound, the way—line by line—they swing."[2] What constitutes *swing* in music has been notoriously difficult for jazz critics to define, but, quite apart from that, if Pritchard is correct in transferring an essential quality of jazz to Larkin's poetry ("It don't mean a thing if it ain't got that swing"), then, one assumes, it should be in performance that this sound comes through. If Larkin's poetry has absorbed jazz, dance lyrics, and blues, these should be heard best in the poems being spoken, when we can hear the *way* they rhyme and scan. They can "swing" once they escape the page, their existence as notation. Larkin has argued, to the contrary, that poems in general and his poems in particular do not find their authentic existence in performance, in how they *sound* when spoken, but on the page and, moreover, that performance is detrimental to the poem. The argument alerts us to a complexity in the manifold relations of music and poetry in Larkin that threatens our ability to read them.

In a 1962 piece on recorded poetry called "Masters' Voices" Larkin raises the question of poetry's relationship to musical performance: "Is the poem, as it were, the 'score' that must be brought to life by performance?" (*RW*, 136). The answer, it turns out, is no; the analogy is misleading. The poem read silently on the page has the advantage over the same poem read aloud, even by its author: "is spoken poetry—poems read by their authors in a way that lets us listen to them without

---

2. William H. Pritchard, "Larkin's Presence," in *Philip Larkin: The Man and His Work*, ed. Dale Salwak (London, 1989), 76.

distraction—a good thing? Is it better than reading? I still can't believe it is" (*RW*, 139). Twenty years later, in his *Paris Review* interview, he repeats the argument: "poetry readings grew up on a false analogy with music: the text is the 'score' that doesn't 'come to life' until it's 'performed.' " It's a false analogy because "people can read words, whereas they can't read music." Here is Larkin's case against the poem as performance:

Hearing a poem, as opposed to reading it on the page, means you miss so much—the shape, the punctuation, the italics, even knowing how far you are from the end. Reading it on the page means you can go your own pace, taking it in properly; hearing it means you're dragged along at the speaker's own rate, missing things, not taking it in, confusing 'there' and 'their' and things like that. And the speaker may interpose his own personality between you and the poem, for better or worse. (*RW*, 61)

This is not the position we might expect of a jazz enthusiast but the stance of the traditionalist holding the line against an illegitimate linking of music and poetry, of "someone hopelessly enslaved by an out-of-date reading technique," as Larkin characterizes himself in "Masters' Voices" (*RW*, 139). The argument takes one further turn, however, that readmits performance into the equation, even privileges it.

Larkin's justification for the page over the performance has as its basis the assumption that the poem on the page is already a kind of performance that a second performance, speaking the poem aloud, can never duplicate:

When you write a poem, you put everything into it that's needed: the reader should "hear" it just as clearly as if you were in the room saying it to him. And of course this fashion for poetry readings has led to a kind of poetry that you *can* understand first go: easy rhythms, easy emotions, easy syntax. I don't think it stands up on the page. (*RW*, 61)

This is an unexpectedly complex argument, combining elements of modernism and jazz with perhaps a trace of an entirely personal and understandable defensiveness. To start with the personal, it is difficult to read Larkin's stand against poetry as performance without seeing in it vestiges of a poet's lifelong defense against a painful stammer that disqualified him in his early career from public readings. Larkin has admitted the connection to an interviewer: "Up to the age of 21 I was still asking for railway tickets by pushing written notes across the counter. This has conditioned me against reading in public—the dread that speech failure might come back again."[3] The stammer would be an extreme form of what Larkin now assumes is always the case—a reader's voice transforming the *ideal* performance of the poem on the page to a *particular* and idiosyncratic performance. In Larkin's version of the ideal performance it is as if the poet is in the room with the reader, speaking the poem aloud but without a trace of a stammer or any other idiosyncrasy. To make his case for the poem as the poet's ideal performance Larkin is forced to employ two crucial assumptions of modernism that we might expect him to scorn since they are a part of the aesthetic he attacked as elitist and irresponsible in the introduction to *All What Jazz.*

The first is his variation on Eliot's objective correlative (which itself anticipates formalism's postulation of the ideal reader). In a short essay called "Writing Poems" published almost twenty years earlier, Larkin's formulation of the process was close to Eliot's objective correlative: "Some years ago I came to the conclusion that to write a poem was to construct a verbal device that would preserve an experience indefinitely by reproducing it in whoever read the poem" (*RW*, 83). Larkin assumes that the reader will hear the poem exactly as the poet speaks it with no complications in transmission. In a 1977 BBC radio broadcast he said that he wrote poems to be read "by readers who can imagine the sound of what they're reading." The poem is, however, conceived not as a score to be performed by the reader, but as a performance by the poet that every reader will hear in the same way. Eliot thinks of this in terms of the poet's "formula" for a particular emotion that terminates in a sensory experience by which "the emotion is immediately evoked."[4]

---

3. Hamilton, "Four Conversations," 76.

4. The BBC broadcast is quoted in Neil Powell, *Carpenters of Light: Some Contemporary English Poets* (Manchester, U.K., 1979), 104; T. S. Eliot, "Hamlet," in *Selected Prose of T. S. Eliot,* ed. Frank Kermode (New York, 1975), 48.

Larkin substitutes for Eliot's silent formula the tone of voice of the poet. Whereas Eliot's figure allows the poet to become invisible in the transmission, Larkin's figure places the poet in the room with the reader, and instead of finding the precise formula for an emotion he discovers a distinctive voice that the reader/listener cannot mistake. In an "auto interview" called "The True Voice of Feeling," the principle is stated more directly: "There's a book that argues that every poet writes for his own voice, and that if you listen carefully you can actually hear their voice in their poems—people like Milton and Shelley. Consequently they would be their own poems' ideal reader" (*RW*, 51). The formalist critic's ideal reader (whose nearest embodiment is the formalist critic) has here been displaced by a reader with a voice, the poet that formalism had sought to banish from the poem.

The second modernist principle, a variation of the first, is the notion of the poem as self-sufficient artifact containing within itself everything necessary for its own reading. But *reading*, again, suggests two distinct practices, interpreting and speaking aloud. Larkin is thinking of the poetic artifact not in the modernist's spatial analogy of painting or statuary—Cleanth Brooks's "well-wrought urn"—but in the temporal analogy of a performance to be heard: "the reader should 'hear' it just as clearly as if you were in the room saying it to him." In his figure the poem is not read (interpreted) or even experienced as formulated emotion but heard, or overheard.

Oddly, the implication of the argument is that the poem can be heard authentically (as spoken by its creator at the moment of its creation) only if it is not literally spoken aloud. Any actual performance of the poem interposes something between the poet's own performance and the reader/listener. Larkin's position against the performance of the poem on the poetry circuit is a version of the jazz fan's assumptions about authenticity. Reading a poem, in his analogy, is very much like listening to a definitive recording of a particular jazz classic, say Bechet's version of "Old Fashioned Love."[5] Joachim Berendt notes that in jazz

---

5. In Larkin's comments on the writing process there is an association between writing poems and listening to recorded music: "To write a poem is a pleasure: sometimes

the "once-improvised" is forever "linked to the man who created it." It cannot be "notated, and given to a second or third musician to play." In such a case "it loses its character, and nothing remains but the naked formula of notes."[6] A version by any other musician, even if played note for note, is inauthentic, since Berendt's conception of jazz, like Larkin's conception of the poem, is figured in terms of the "voice" of the artist in the originating performance.

There is another argument here borrowed from the confluence of poetry and popular music. A debate of the sixties was whether the lyrics of musicians like Bob Dylan and the Beatles were legitimate poetry; the argument against popular lyrics as poetry was that the words could not stand alone. They could exist only as performance. Larkin turns this argument against the fashion for poetry readings, which he says lead to a kind of poetry that is tailored *only* for performance—"easy rhythms, easy emotions, easy syntax." Such a thin poetry, separated from its actual performance, lacks the authentic voice of true poetry since its performance is not built into the structure and language of the poem itself: "I don't think it stands up on the page." Ironically, in this argument, poetry not written for performance gives a stronger and richer performance than poetry written to be performed. A more telling irony lies in the circumstance that to defend a traditional view of poetry Larkin resorts to a modernist argument he ridiculed in the introduction of *All What Jazz.* In his attack on modernism in the introduction he had parodied the modernist critic who recommended a poetry that was "more *complex,* that required you to *work hard at appreciating it,* that you *couldn't expect to understand first go*" (*AWJ,* 22). Now he argues that poetry written for performance lacks the complexities and subtleties of "notational" poetry, since the former is "a kind of poetry that you

---

I deliberately let it compete in the open market, so to speak, with other spare-time activities, ostensibly on the grounds that if a poem isn't more entertaining to write than listening to records or going out it won't be entertaining to read" (*RW,* 84). This is a version of Frost's "No tears in the writer, no tears in the reader," but it is significant that Larkin's association is not with strong emotion but with the entertainment of phonograph records.

6. Joachim Berendt, *The Jazz Book,* trans. Dan Morgenstern and Helmut and Barbara Bredigkeit (New York, 1975), 128.

can understand first go." It would appear that the relations among jazz, modernism, and poetry in Larkin do not yield easily to conventional readings.

The readings that Larkin's jazz has received thus far lay out a relatively uncomplicated kinship between the jazz and the poetry. William Pritchard, who hears the "swing" in Larkin's lines, also hears lines that sound like something "Fred Astaire sang . . . in some 1930s movie," lines that could have been delivered by Billie Holiday, and lines that "seem to have come out of some Golden Treasury of Popular Song." He detects a "distinctly Cole Porterish feeling" in a stanza of "Lines on a Young Lady's Photograph Album," and notes that "Larkin and Amis may have had better ears than any other recent English writers," a condition he attributes in part to "how much jazz, Pee Wee Russell and the rest, they listened to." The essay from which these observations are taken, "Larkin's Presence," reads the poet with great sensitivity; one must agree that Larkin was gifted with a fine ear, and a reader who cannot hear Cole Porter in some of his lines is deaf to the resonance of popular American music. Whether his ear came from listening to jazz is, however, a question that no amount of close reading or argument could answer. It is a kind of critical dead end, and there is something unsatisfactory about leaving the discussion of jazz and popular music in Larkin at that level. David Timms has similarly noted the sound of popular music in poems of *The North Ship:* one of them "reads like a rather uninventive popular song, and turns on just the sort of verbal trick that such songs so often do," and other poems from the volume "take the 'sophisticated,' world-weary, 'The Party's Over' kind of view." Michael Gearin-Tosh says of the last line of "An Arundel Tomb" ("What will survive of us is love") that it "might—in isolation—be from the Beatles."[7] It is encouraging to find other readers who recognize the presence of jazz and other forms of popular music in Larkin's verse, but so long as it remains at the level of "influence" it cannot be pursued very far or

7. Pritchard, "Larkin's Presence," 76–77; Timms, *Philip Larkin,* 30; Michael Gearin-Tosh, "Deprivation and Love in Larkin's Poetry," in *Critical Essays on Philip Larkin: The Poems,* ed. Linda Cookson and Bryan Loughrey (London, 1989), 37.

yield anything of consequence. It becomes merely a confirmation of what we already are willing to grant, Larkin's love of traditional jazz in all of its forms—blues, swing, popular standards—and the (occasional) presence of these in the poems.

There is a second level of inquiry in which readers have come closer to the question of how jazz helped shape the theory and practice of Larkin's own art. These readers' questions assume obvious parallels between Larkin's jazz and his poetry; their answers are unassailable but divorced from readings of particular poetic texts. David Timms's conclusions can stand in for several others:

Blues, the ethnic music of the American Negro, created spontaneously within the limits of a traditional but flexible form, and directly expressing the needs, complaints and aspirations of a suffering and oppressed people, is the staple and norm of authentic jazz, Larkin believes. . . . [T]here is a parallel between his beliefs about jazz and his poetic practice. He has said that poetry is "born of the tension between what [the poet] non-verbally feels and what can be got over in common word-usage to someone who hasn't had his experience or education or travel-grant." In common with Dr Johnson, Larkin sees in life "much . . . to be endured and little to be enjoyed"; and like the blues singer's art, Larkin's poetry mediates between this experience and his audience. His forms are "traditional" rather than "modern."[8]

Nothing Timms says here invites dissent; at the same time the kind of claims made—Larkin found life oppressive; his poetry mediates between his unhappy experience and his audience; like the blues, it is traditional—could be made even if Larkin had never heard the blues. There is, I agree, something of the blues singer's art in Larkin's poetry, but this claim would have more force if it were made in reading a particular text where the presence of the blues made itself felt in a manner that could be specified.

In "Larkin and Jazz" Cedric Watts does read briefly three texts in which jazz appears—"Reasons for Attendance," "Reference Back," and "For Sidney Bechet"—but his conclusion about jazz in Larkin is not derived from his readings and it plays no part in the way he approaches

8. Timms, *Philip Larkin*, 21.

these poems. It is taken from his reading of *All What Jazz*, and it develops a theme common to readers who have considered Larkin's jazz:

Philip Larkin's devotion to jazz had several large consequences. Melancholy and disillusionment came easily to Larkin; the works of Bechet, Armstrong, Bessie Smith and the other jazz-performers whom he admired provided sustenance and hope. They set him examples of creativity that seemed untainted by academia, by pedantry and snobbery. Repeatedly they must have encouraged him to produce poetry which, being both technically adept and emotionally frank (as good jazz is), would communicate itself more readily to readers and hearers than did much of the academically respectable poetry of modern times. Traditional jazz taught Larkin that despondency could be transmuted by art into affirmation.[9]

Jazz as a simple and emotionally honest art is set against the pedantry and snobbery of academic modernism. This of course is one of the themes of the introduction to *All What Jazz*, and there is little question that jazz provided Larkin a model for a kind of antimodernist popular art, as Watts suggests.

A. T. Tolley makes a similar argument. Jazz, he writes, epitomized "an art vital and immediate in its appeal, in contrast to the established 'classical' music, with its philosophical underpinnings, its high-toned sense of beauty and the assumption that one needed to have 'studied' music to respond to it properly." Both Janice Rossen and Andrew Swarbrick develop a variation on this theme, with which I also concur, drawing a connection between Larkin's love of jazz and his philistine pose. Jazz was a part of a larger "middlebrow" stance, Rossen says, "designed to create a self-protective image." For Swarbrick it was an "iconoclastic gesture," a part of a "defiant unpretentiousness" and a "rejection of the pieties associated with 'highbrow' arts."[10]

The theme of jazz as a weapon against highbrow modernist intellectualism is most clearly articulated in Clive James's insightful discussion of Larkin's jazz writing, "On His Wit": "The emphasis, in Larkin's admiration for all these [jazz] artists, is on the simplicity at the heart

---

9. Watts, "Larkin and Jazz," 27.

10. Tolley, *My Proper Ground*, 145; Rossen, *Philip Larkin: His Life's Work*, 99–100; Swarbrick, *Out of Reach*, 70.

of their creative endeavour. What they do would not have its infinite implications if it did not spring from elementary emotion." This jazz aesthetic, based on the privileging of emotion over intellect, "underlies his literary criticism and everything else he writes. Especially it underlies his poetry." It is more, however, than an aesthetic; "it is a world view, of the kind which invariably forms the basis of any great artistic personality." Against modernism as "intellectualized art" he proposes "not anti-intellectualism . . . but trust in the validity of emotion. What the true artist says from instinct, the true critic will hear by the same instinct." James's essay is one of a handful of essential discussions of Larkin's aesthetic. It is a view based on a (brilliant) reading of the reviews in *All What Jazz,* which James sees as "the best available expression by the author himself of what he believed art to be."[11] A convincing account of jazz in Larkin's poetry, however, should be required to go beyond Larkin's own expression of his aesthetic to the poems themselves, including poems not ostensibly about jazz or the blues. Ideally such an account should also go beyond "influence" and beyond simply hearing the sound of dance music or the blues in the lines of the poem. What would constitute a convincing account of jazz or other forms of popular music in Larkin would be a description, if that is possible, of the *significance* of a particular poem—the *way* it signifies—in relation to the musical intertexts and conventions it has absorbed.

"Aubade" (*CP,* 208), Larkin's last great poem—arguably the greatest and most terrifying poem he ever wrote—begins with a blues line: "I work all day, and get half-drunk at night." Larkin's friend Robert Conquest reports of his conversations with the poet that there was "talk . . . of a Blues version [of "Aubade"]—the first line coming in perfectly, perhaps the sign of a real 'influence.' "[12] If the line is only the sign of a blues influence then we can leave it at that, as Conquest does, and move on to other examples. There is good reason to believe, however, that what the line announces is that the poem is *already* a blues version,

11. James, "On His Wit," 103, 98.

12. Robert Conquest, "A Proper Sport," in *Larkin at Sixty,* ed. Anthony Thwaite (London, 1982), 35.

not a blues but a poem that has thoroughly absorbed the blues, some-thing new made out of the blues. Elvis Presley launched his career with "That's All Right (Mama)," the original version of which was by Mississippi blues singer Arthur "Big Boy" Crudup. Greil Marcus writes that "Elvis reduces the bluesman's original to a footnote." The result is not blues, but something new that owes its power to the blues: "Real white blues singers make something new out of the blues," Marcus argues, "or they sing out of a deep feeling for the blues, but in a musical style that is not blues—not formally anyway. But we can trace their strength to the blues."[13] "Aubade" is not a blues, but I will argue that we can trace its strength to the blues, although not as directly as with Elvis's first recording in Sam Phillips's studio in early 1954. The opening line of "Aubade" could be thought of as the visible tip of a much larger intertext beneath the poem's surface. Rather than a single identifiable text, it may be conceived of as a system of conventions, practices, and attitudes along with a large reservoir of lines and phrases, all of which we know as the blues, and to conceive "Aubade" as containing a blues intertext, I suggest, discloses elements of the poem otherwise invisible or at least more difficult to read.

Michael Riffaterre postulates that there are points in every text that signal the presence of such intertexts, and these sometimes take the form of an anomaly or obscurity, something out of keeping with the context, something that attracts attention or calls for explanation.[14] Before recognizing it as a blues line, the reader may be struck by the incongruity of the opening line of "Aubade," by the sense of its being out of place in the context of the first stanza:

> I work all day, and get half-drunk at night.
> Waking at four to soundless dark, I stare.
> In time the curtain-edges will grow light.
> Till then I see what's really always there:
> Unresting death, a whole day nearer now,
> Making all thought impossible but how

13. Marcus, *Mystery Train*, 174, 181.
14. Riffaterre, "Syllepsis," 626–27.

And where and when I shall myself die.
Arid interrogation: yet the dread
Of dying, and being dead,
Flashes afresh to hold and horrify.

This first of five ten-line stanzas seems to start on a wrong note. Something sounds odd, discordant, and it takes a moment to recognize that the first line doesn't quite fit with the rest of the stanza. Both the tone and the rhythm seem slightly off. While the rhythm and the syntax of the second line—"Waking at four to soundless dark, I stare"—are distinctly "literary," somewhat artificial, perfectly conventional for a poem called "Aubade," the first line appears to derive from another set of conventions. For one thing, its rhythm appears to be the poetic equivalent of syncopation. The basic rhythm of the line is iambic, but its two spondees shift the accents on *all* and *half* a syllable sooner than the iambic pattern calls for: "I work *àll dày*, and get *hàlf-drùnk* at night." In the words of *The New Grove Dictionary of Music and Musicians,* syncopation in music occurs when the phrasing is "shifted ahead of or behind the beat to create tension against the established pulse," as is the case in the last line of "For Sidney Bechet" when the substituted trochee delivers the rhyme a beat sooner than expected. Strictly speaking, the opening line of "Aubade" is *not* syncopation, since in musical syncopation the expected strong beat receives no articulation, but the feeling of syncopation, the tension between the articulation and the expected pattern, is certainly present. Philip Furia observes a similar effect in some of the lyrics of Irving Berlin, which are not true syncopation but the "lyrical equivalents" of syncopation, achieved by the "juxtaposition of words *against* music."[15] Syncopation is of course the signature of the blues, and we might not recognize Larkin's line as a blues line without it. Replace the spondees with two iambic feet and the blues begin to disappear: "I work by day and sit and drink at night."

Of course the comparison is unfair because my line (in addition to

15. *The New Grove Dictionary of Music and Musicians,* Vol. XVIII, ed. Stanley Sadie (London, 1980), 469; Philip Furia, *The Poets of Tin Pan Alley: A History of America's Great Lyricists* (New York, 1990), 54–55.

illustrating execrable poetry) also omits other qualities that identify this as the blues—the colloquial "half-drunk" stands out oddly against the poetic "soundless dark" of the second line. The directness of the opening clause—"I work all day"—is set against the "written" construction of the participial phrase that begins the second line, "Waking at four." The confessional quality of the first line and its almost embarrassing bluntness—its lack of aesthetic distance or disguise—also come from the blues. (One cannot imagine a lyric poet prior to Larkin referring to himself as customarily "get[ting] half-drunk at night.") Working and drinking are the common properties of the blues, drinking most often as a means of coping with despair, the defense of Blind James Cambell's "You know I'm sitting 'round here drinking, just to help me to forget" and Mississippi John Hurt's "Whiskey straight will drive the blues away." Working is an even more prevalent theme, in part because field hollers and work songs are deeply embedded in the blues. At times working and drinking may be found together, as in this Lonnie Johnson stanza that has incorporated the floating blues phrase appropriated by "Aubade":

> I work all day long for you, until the sun go down,
> I work all day long for you, baby, from sun-up until the sun go down,
> An' you take all my money and drink it up, and come home and want
> to fuss and clown.[16]

It is perhaps a measure of the resonance of the blues conventions in the first line of the poem that, even to a reader aware that he is beginning a poem by Philip Larkin, the work alluded to seems something more physical than what we would expect of a Larkin persona.

16. For the blues lyrics quoted here, see Paul Garon, *Blues and the Poetic Spirit* (New York, 1978), 92; Stefan Grossman, Stephen Calt, and Hal Grossman, *Country Blues Songbook* (New York, 1973), 101; Oliver, *Blues Fell This Morning*, 88. Many of the blues lines and stanzas I quote appear in variant forms and by different musicians in other collections, so my citation of a particular source and singer is at times arbitrary. As Paul Oliver has indicated, a blues verse may be "drawn upon by various artists as it suits a particular context." Often a single line—referred to as a "floating" line—or even a phrase will move from one blues to another, be given new rhymes and meaning and juxtaposed with new ideas (*Aspects of the Blues Tradition* [New York, 1968], 17–18). "I work all day" would be an example of a floating blues phrase.

In the typical three-line blues stanza, each line is a complete sentence or clause. As David Evans says, perhaps extravagantly, "Enjambment is unknown in the blues." "Aubade" 's opening stanza follows this pattern for its first half, making each line a complete clause, then moves into enjambed lines. The effect is as if the blues tone with which the poem begins gradually modulates into another form, submerging itself into the poem, where it remains present but more difficult to hear. This effect is also achieved by the fact that the second line continues the blues conventions begun in the first by alluding to one of the most common of all blues openings—"I woke up this morning"—but rephrasing it in nonblues language: "Waking at four." Bo Weavil Jackson's version is simply a variation (or a near repetition) of the way thousands of blues begin: "Now, I woke up this morning, mama / blues all around my bed." It is also customary for the blues to specify the hour, and four o'clock turns out to be the most popular blues time for waking: "It's four o'clock in the morning, and I can't close my eyes." Sunnyland Slim's "Train Time" begins, "It was early one morning, just about four o'clock," and Furry Lewis opens "Kassie Jones" with "I woke up this morning, four o'clock / Mister Kassie told his fireman get his boiler hot." The early morning, then—"In the wee midnight hour, not quite the break of day"—is the time of the blues, and the motif is so thoroughly conventional that no explanation or motivation is required. Muddy Waters sings, "Early in the morning before day, that's when my blues come falling down," and Son House greets the blues without apparent surprise: "Good mornin', blues, now gimme your right hand." Leroy Carr's 1934 "Blues Before Sunrise" is a late summation of a long tradition:

> I had the blues before sunrise, with tears standing in my eyes,
> I had the blues before sunrise, with tears standing in my eyes,
> It's such a miserable feeling, a feeling I do despise.[17]

---

17. Evans, *Big Road Blues,* 30; for the blues lyrics quoted here, see Jeff Todd Tilton, *Downhome Blues Lyrics,* 2nd ed. (Urbana, 1990), 150, 138; Samuel B. Charters, *The Poetry of the Blues* (New York, 1963), 45; Eric Sackheim, *The Blues Line: A Collection of Blues Lyrics* (New York, 1969), 258; Oliver, *Blues Fell This Morning,* 283; Charters, *Country*

"Blues Before Sunrise" displays the classic blues form, the twelve-bar three-line stanza, the first line repeated as the second line (with an occasional slight variation), and the different third line rhyming with the first two. Had Larkin written "Aubade" as a classic blues, it would have begun in a manner similar to this:

> I work all day, and get half-drunk at night.
> I work all day, and get half-drunk at night.
> In time the curtain-edges will grow light.

But of course the very fact that it is written means, for purists, that it cannot be an authentic blues. "If the blues are written down, the result is usually not blues," Richard Middleton has argued. For it is "precisely what is un-notatable" that constitutes the essence of the blues.[18] "Aubade" is *not* a blues and it does not aspire to be. It has incorporated an oral tradition within a written form, and the notational/non-notational distinction is not without its own implications. Because Larkin's blues line is written, for example, it need not be repeated. Traditionally, the repeated first line is attributed to the non-notational character of the blues; while repeating the first line the musician is giving himself time to come up with the rhyming third line that ends the stanza. It is this form that leads to the absence of enjambment in the blues. The first line must be a complete thought since it is to be repeated, and the third must be complete since it stands alone with nothing to follow.

These requirements lead to one other property of the blues that the poem alludes to in its first line. Because the *line*, complete in itself, is the basic unit of blues composition, it is customary for the blues singer to set one part of the line against another. These examples are given in Oliver's "Blues and the Binary Principle":

> Won't you iron my jumper starch my overalls.
>
> From St. Louis to the river river to the deep blue sea.

Blues, 252; Lawrence Cohn, *Nothing But the Blues* (New York, 1993), 131; Giles Oakley, *The Devil's Music: A History of the Blues* (New York, 1977), 176.

18. Middleton, *Pop Music and the Blues*, 53.

Babe if your heart ain't iron it must be marble stone.

I can tell from a little just what a whole lot means.

Sometime I b'lieve I will sometime I believe I won't.

Examples of this binary structure are endless; James Cobb cites several in *The Most Southern Place on Earth* including "Gotta mind to move, A mind to settle down" and "Sometimes I say I need you; Then again I don't."[19] From structuralist and poststructuralist perspectives *all* texts are built on binary opposition, but of course this is a theoretical binary, and the theorist is regularly forced to supply the antithetical term. The binary character of the blues is of another order in that it is consciously foregrounded as a matter of style, an expectation, and therefore conventional.

In "Blues and the Binary Principle" Oliver attempts to show that "the binary principle is deeply embedded in the structure and expression of the blues" and consequently that "the criteria used by the blues audience and by the artists themselves are directly related to it." The "perception of quality in the blues is bound up in its binary character."[20] Larkin's play with this blues motif in the first line amounts almost to parody, so heavy-handed and numerous are the instances—day against night, working against drinking, "*all* day" against "*half*-drunk." And the binary character of the line isolates it in the stanza since no other line uses opposition in so noticeable a way. Later in "Aubade" binary opposition does return in an emphatic manner, interestingly, in a manner that shows to what an extent the poem's significance depends on its blues intertext.

Put simply, "Aubade" is a poem about waking up at four o'clock and worrying about death. Its fear of death is traditional; its sensibility is radically untraditional. It is consciously untraditional in its rejection of its precursors' meditations on death. It is in a real sense a new poem, something not seen before, as new in its own way as Stevens's "Sunday

19. Paul Oliver, "Blues and the Binary Principle," in *Popular Music Perspectives,* ed. David Horn and Philip Tagg (Exeter, U.K., 1982), 168–71; Cobb, *Most Southern Place on Earth,* 285.

20. Oliver, "Blues and the Binary Principle," 172.

Morning," although it differs from the earlier poem in not attempting a resolution such as Stevens's "Death is the mother of beauty." Its novelty is in the opposite direction—not in coming to terms with death but in baring its utter defenselessness to a fate that has ceased to be an abstraction. The success of "Aubade" depends on an immediacy and honesty that derive from its blues intertext and a "double bind" situation that is also the property of the blues, expressed in its binary principle. In the last stanza, the speaker offers his version of the double bind that is the matrix around which the poem is constructed:

> Slowly light strengthens, and the room takes shape.
> It stands plain as a wardrobe, what we know,
> Have always known, *know that we can't escape,*
> *Yet can't accept.*

The poem's dilemma, underlined in my italics, is the dilemma from which the sensibility of the blues takes its character, the binary opposition in which neither pole is acceptable, the despair that arises from a situation for which there is no resolution. Since this is the sensibility that defines the poem, sets it against its predecessors in the poetry of transience, I want to trace it briefly in the binary character of the blues.

In *Big Road Blues,* David Evans has attempted heroically to define the feeling at the heart of the blues. Basing his definition on the testimony of blues singers, he concludes that it comes down to "worry," that the worry "is a feeling of being drawn in two or more different directions," and that it is reflected in the songs "by means of various tensions and contrasts." Quoting the singer Robert Curtis Smith, he concludes, "The blues feeling, then, is caused by a struggle to succeed combined with an awareness of overwhelming difficulties. The consequence is that in the long run 'there is no change,' so that 'there's nothin' else to do but what you doin' … and sing the blues.'" "The blues," Evans writes, "do not bring about solutions to problems" because the problems the blues sing of are not susceptible of solution. If the blues represent, as Richard Middleton says, a "strategy for living in an unlivable situation," then the alternatives they offer—"Gotta mind to move, a mind to settle down"—are of no real consequence, as the songs sometimes seem to recognize. James Cobb argues that the mixed feelings of the music reflect the ambivalence and uncertainty of the lives of the people who sang them: "Conflict and contradiction and the agony of making tough choices were apparent throughout the blues." And if there is no solution to the conditions the blues describe, then the only outlet for relief is in the singing. Lil Son Jackson recalls the conditions of his father's sharecropper life: "That was the onliest way he could get relief from it, by singin' them blues."[21]

The *therapeutic* value of the blues that all blues writers speak of (and to which I will return) follows from the acknowledgment that there is no solution other than the performance itself. Blues commentators speak of the "cathartic" role of the blues. Lawrence Levine tries to account for the strong tradition of disaster songs in black music by reference to the fact that in the blues tradition song could actually "be utilized to expunge difficulties." In *Urban Blues,* Charles Keil argues that catharsis is the primary function of the music: "a bluesman in the country or for the first time coming to grips with city life sings primarily to ease his worried mind, to get things out of his system, to feel better; it is of secondary importance whether or not others are present and deriving similar satisfactions from his music."[22]

These blues conventions may seem a great distance from an English poem about death, yet I want to show that the poem has absorbed them all, that "Aubade" is much closer to a blues tradition than to the long English tradition that preceded it. But this can be done convincingly only in looking at the significance of particular passages and conventions, and I want to begin by returning to the blues' double bind, which I take also as the center of the poem, from which every other feature of the poem derives. What is untraditional in the poem is its method of dealing with an anxiety that is both unacceptable and inescapable. Middleton has described this condition as the origin of the blues: "One

21. Evans, *Big Road Blues,* 18, 165; Middleton, *Pop Music and the Blues,* 49; Cobb, *Most Southern Place on Earth,* 285; Jackson is quoted in Levine, *Black Culture and Black Consciousness,* 257.

22. Levine, *Black Culture and Black Consciousness,* 257; Charles Keil, *Urban Blues* (Chicago, 1966), 76.

characteristic of the contradictions in Negro culture is that they are in general irresolvable. The Negro is in what has been called a 'double-bind' situation, a situation in which he cannot win, but from which he cannot escape." But the music produced by this situation "may also give unique insight." It may be an extreme form of "general developments in the West." Middleton argues that the blues provide the exemplary model for a response to a condition that is irresolvable: "Schizophrenic in musical make-up, therapeutic and cathartic in function, the blues are the most powerful weapon in the Negro's strategy for living. The blues-man sings out his troubles, purges himself (and his listeners, if any) and makes life livable."[23]

The function of the blues in this argument—and it is not eccentric by the standards of blues commentary—is to make an unbearable situation bearable not by resolving it but by laying it out nakedly and honestly, telling the truth, exposing (seemingly) every evasion. "Blues made the terrors of the world easier to endure," Greil Marcus writes in *Mystery Train*, "but blues also made those terrors more real."[24] The blues aesthetic, as we have seen, is that the blues tell the truth. They speak directly from experience, and the function of their truth-telling is a kind of mastery not unlike that suggested by the compulsion to repeat in Freud's "Beyond the Pleasure Principle."

The strategy of "Aubade" is to appear to face the truth about the fear of death as it has not been faced before in Western poetry. It will in the process expose the evasions of earlier treatments of the theme (such as Hamlet's soliloquy on that "undiscovered country, from whose bourn / No traveler returns," to which the poem clearly alludes). As Laurence Lerner has observed, the "vast silent context for this poem" is "all the great poetry of death," to which it responds as the first *truthful* poem of death. "How should we read 'Aubade'?" Lerner asks. "As if it were the only poem on death, so true that we don't need to waste our time thinking of the others? Or as an agonised reply to all those others, its careful elegance and its complicated rhymes a reminder of all that

23. Middleton, *Pop Music and the Blues*, 26–27.
24. Marcus, *Mystery Train*, 33.

poetry has done with the theme?"[25] In fact, the two readings are not at odds. The poem succeeds because it sets its "truth" against the quaint "literary" conventions of the vast silent context of earlier poems of death.

The second stanza begins by laying bare the most terrifying aspect of worrying about death. This is not the Romantic anxiety, easily defended against, of dying before one's life is completed—life as a page "Torn off unused," Keats's fear that he may cease to be "Before [his] pen has gleaned [his] teeming brain"—but an indefensible dread:

> The mind blanks at the glare. Not in remorse
> —The good not done, the love not given, time
> Torn off unused—nor wretchedly because
> An only life can take so long to climb
> Clear of its wrong beginnings, and may never;
> But at the total emptiness for ever,
> The sure extinction that we travel to
> And shall be lost in always. Not to be here,
> Not to be anywhere,
> And soon; nothing more terrible, nothing more true.

The first half of the stanza with its comfortable, clichéd attitude toward untimely death—"The good not done, the love not given"—is dismissed in favor of a more terrifying realization, a "total emptiness for ever." It is the "sure extinction" that we "shall be lost in always" that is the source of the poem's double bind since it is the ultimate anxiety and, in the poem's secular vision, the ultimate truth.

The phrase by which this is conveyed, however—"nothing more terrible, nothing more true"—has the effect, in my reading, of backing away from the immediacy of the speaker's realization. "Not to be here, / Not to be anywhere, / And soon" is successful in *realizing* the abstraction of eternal oblivion, of making it so real as to be inescapable. As Andrew Swarbrick has noted, the line contains a phrase from the early poem "Wires"—"Not here but anywhere"—in which "anywhere" was associ-

---

25. Laurence Lerner, "Larkin's Strategies," *Critical Survey,* I (1989), 119–20.

ated with the possibility of escape from one's present state.[26] The recognition of "Aubade" is the annihilation of "anywhere," the closing off of the possibility of escape. The final phrase is, however, quaint and distancing, and it shifts our attention from the terrible realization of total and eternal nothingness to its own odd and seemingly specious reasoning. "[N]othing more true," by being paired with "nothing more terrible," appears to be cunningly dragged in for our assent when it is not in fact a parallel assertion. One could agree that there is nothing more terrible than thinking of oneself as not existing forever, but in what sense is there nothing more true? If it is absolutely true then no other truth can be *more* true, but that is a logical quibble that has no real consequence. What the poem wants to convey in "nothing more true" is the *inescapable* nature of this truth—no truth is more difficult to evade. Some of our anxieties are groundless; some of the things we worry about at four o'clock may never come to pass. The extinction that we travel to, however, is "sure"; its approach is inexorable, "a whole day nearer now," and the reader of Motion's biography will now incorporate a later text into the poem: "Larkin had died at 1.24 a.m., turning to the nurse who was with him, squeezing her hand, and saying faintly: 'I am going to the inevitable' " (*Life,* 521). It is the inevitability that produces the poem's most frighteningly matter-of-fact line: "Most things may never happen: this one will." By the end of the second stanza, then, the speaker has uncovered the ultimate despair, a white English version of the predicament that gives rise to the Black American blues, a situation, in Middleton's terms, "in which he cannot win, but from which he cannot escape."

The poem's method of dealing with this form of despair is not to seek defenses but to remove, one by one, the defenses by which we customarily deal with it. Its attitude is the secular, "truthful" viewpoint of the blues that rejects every consideration but the here and now, that ridicules the intellectual and, especially, the pious. Like the blues, the poem dismisses matter-of-factly—without bothering even to argue the

26. Swarbrick, *Out of Reach,* 94.

case—the solution to despair offered by religion, "[t]hat vast moth-eaten musical brocade / Created to pretend we never die." The blues, David Evans writes, "are secular in the sense that they do not hold out hope for escape from one's problems through organized religion," and Greil Marcus notes that the "weight of [Robert] Johnson's blues was strong enough to make salvation a joke." This secular spirit is a part of a larger and more complex attitude—the blues singer is worldly-wise, lives in the present, recounts his despair with candor, and rejects any hope of outside help. It is this attitude that make the blues "sinful," the devil's music. Lil Son Jackson, who left the blues for religion, explains the difference between the blues and spiritual music:

If a man feel hurt within side and he sing a church song then he's askin' God for help. . . . [I]f a man sing the blues it's more or less out of himself. . . . He's not askin' no one for help. And he's not really clingin' to no-one. But he's expressin' how he feel. He's expressin' it to someone and that fact makes it a sin you know.[27]

The defiance that Jackson speaks of is crucial to the attitude we recognize in the blues. As Richard Wright has noted, the "theme of spirituality, of other-worldliness is banned." The blues are "purged of metaphysical implications, wedded to a frankly atheistic vision of life."[28] It may seem odd that the blues should be so uniformly secular, anti-Christian, but there is a good reason for it, and it is for the same reason that the third stanza of "Aubade" is so overtly anti-Christian. The banning of other-worldliness is in part a consequence of the blues' honesty—trouble is not so easily evaded as the church pretends—but secularism is also a necessary ingredient of the state of mind without which the blues could not exist. If religion could resolve the worry of which the bluesman sings, then the most fundamental of the blues' conventions and attitudes would be undermined. The third stanza of "Aubade" introduces this issue:

27. Evans, *Big Road Blues,* 28; Marcus, *Mystery Train,* 33; Jackson is quoted in Levine, *Black Culture and Black Consciousness,* 237.

28. Wright, Foreword to Oliver, *Blues Fell This Morning,* xiv.

This is a special way of being afraid
No trick dispels. Religion used to try,
That vast moth-eaten musical brocade
Created to pretend we never die,
And specious stuff that says *No rational being*
Can fear a thing it will not feel, not seeing
That this is what we fear—no sight, no sound,
No touch or taste or smell, nothing to think with,
Nothing to love or link with,
The anaesthetic from which none come round.

The method of the poem is an honesty so plain that religion and logic seem contrived against it, and with this tone we are returned to the most familiar signature of the blues.

The chief convention of the blues is that the blues are *not conventional but real.* The effect sought for in the blues, Middleton says, "depends not on 'beauty'—what the Western artist uses to discipline and channel his feeling—but on honesty." Dave Laing says of the country blues, "Expression of the natural, not creation of the beautiful was what counted," and he notes of the music that follows the blues tradition that it "represents the natural thing rather than the beautiful one." Following the "main impulse" of Black music, "it seems to be concerned less with producing finished artefacts than with expressing the feeling of the moment." The overriding aesthetic of the blues, Evans says simply, is "telling the truth." The bluesman Henry Townsend goes further to suggest that "[m]ost good blues is *about* telling the truth about things."[29] That is, truth-telling is not simply a matter of the style; it is what the blues are, *conventionally,* about.

It is important to recognize the conventionality of the blues' "truth" since it is also a convention of "Aubade." Neither the blues singer nor the poem has escaped artifice to arrive somehow in the domain of the real, the actual, but it is necessary for both to give that impression.

29. Middleton, *Pop Music and the Blues,* 51; Laing, *Sound of Our Time,* 6, 8; Evans, *Big Road Blues,* 53–54; Townsend is quoted in Barlow, *Looking Up at Down,* 326 (my italics).

"Music can not *be* true or false," Simon Frith writes, "it can only refer to *conventions* of truth and falsity." Larkin hints at this conventionality when he characterizes the blues as "a kind of jazz that calls forth a particular sincerity from the player" (*AWJ*, 224). That the sincerity or truthfulness called forth—the absence of artifice—is itself a device of artifice has not been frequently noted by blues commentators or performers. Albert Murray, writing against the grain of blues commentary, has wittily attacked the assumption "that blues music does not require artifice but is rather a species of direct emotional expression in the raw, the natural outpouring of personal anxiety and anguish." This widespread view of the blues "ignores what a blues performance so obviously is. It is precisely an artful contrivance, designed for entertainment and aesthetic gratification." When musicians announce that they are about to play the blues, they "do not mean that they are about to display their own raw emotions. . . . They mean that they are about to proceed in terms of a very specific technology of stylization."[30]

The stylization of truth is an important consideration in the reading of "Aubade." There is a sense in which the poem is as much about being *undeceived* as it is about death. The poem's success and its place in the canon of Western poems about death depend on the reader's impression of a candor so novel as to be unsettling. Its honesty is foregrounded by being set against the pretense of religion and the sophistical reasoning of logic (which says that since we will not *feel* oblivion we need not fear it). Against the intellectual and the contrived the poem displays its "truth," based on the immediacy of the here and now, on experience itself. What we fear in death is precisely the loss of immediacy, not dying but being dead, an eternal absence of sight, sound, touch, taste, and smell. It is a difficult argument to counter since what it appears to privilege is the truth of experience itself, the evidence of the five senses, whereas traditional attitudes toward death privilege mere abstractions—faith and logic.

This is to say that the "truth" so crucial to the tone of "Aubade"

---

30. Simon Frith, "The Real Thing—Bruce Springsteen," in *Music for Pleasure: Essays in the Sociology of Pop* (New York, 1988), 100; Murray, *Stomping the Blues*, 89–90.

is the result of contrivance and artifice; the poem is not somehow less artful, more true than other poems about death. Its truthfulness is entirely conventional and it derives from the blues intertext it has incorporated. This was evident from its first line, which appears to evade any attempt at aesthetic distance or disguise: "I work all day, and get half-drunk at night." The line reveals in a visibly stark form what then becomes submerged beneath the surface of the poem, the attitude that blues commentators have had so much difficulty in labeling; they speak of it most frequently as truth, honesty, reality, immediacy, or in Larkin's terms, "a particular sincerity." Whatever the characterization, it is this temperament that defines the view of life of the blues. Eric Hobsbawm (writing as Francis Newton) expresses it well: "behind the elementary, though remarkably effective, poetic apparatus of the blues, there lies a view of life, which that apparatus is designed to express with the utmost directness and economy of means. It is this which gives the blues their remarkable power, even when they are little more than doggerel." What characterizes this point of view? It is "adult, truthful, totally without illusions and humbug." It is, in short, "the truth": "Nobody beats about the bush in the blues; neither about life, death, drink, money or even love." In his essay on Robert Johnson, "When You Walk in the Room," Greil Marcus writes that to those who first heard a new music around the turn of the century, when, he argues, the blues really began, "the sound was strange, scary, confusing" because "the new blues singers were singing about things people had *never* wanted to talk about."[31]

For its effect, "Aubade" depends entirely on a view of life that is antiromantic, adult, truthful, without illusions or humbug, saying things people had never wanted to talk about. There is little progression of the argument as such, very little narrative or description, no conventional resolution. Each of its stanzas simply finds another way to become less deceived, to expose another illusion of our defenses against death, even the illusion of what appears to be the defense of the poem itself, the courage of standing up to death without traditional protections:

31. Newton, *Jazz Scene*, 158–59; Greil Marcus, "When You Walk in the Room," in *The Dustbin of History* (Cambridge, Mass., 1995), 149.

And so it stays just on the edge of vision,
A small unfocused blur, a standing chill
That slows each impulse down to indecision.
Most things may never happen: this one will,
And realisation of it rages out
In furnace-fear when we are caught without
People or drink. Courage is no good:
It means not scaring others. Being brave
Lets no one off the grave.
Death is no different whined at than withstood.

To this point we might have thought that one defense of the speaker was his courage to look death in the eye, but in the double bind that informs the poem he could just as well have whined. What makes this "a special way of being afraid" (and gives the poem its special form of terror) is the realization, pounded home in every stanza up to the last, that the anxiety at the poem's center is impervious to *any* cure.

The fourth stanza's binary of *being brave* versus *whining* is an interesting one because it forces the question of how to characterize the tone of "Aubade," which I have argued is essentially the tone of the blues. The speaker is clearly not "being brave"—he confesses, among other things, to "furnace-fear" when "caught without / People or drink"— but is he guilty of whining, and how can the blues be defended against the same charge? Moreover, why would we be drawn to a poetry or a music of whining? This has been a touchy subject for blues commentators, who are generally quick to acquit the blues of the charge of self-pity. In one of the earliest attempts to characterize the attitude of the blues Hugues Panassié notes in *The Real Jazz* the "plaintive quality" and the "often hopeless accent" of the music, yet he argues that "the blues, in spite of their nostalgic mood, have nothing to do with whining." And the reason is that when a bluesman sings the blues, "it is not to give way to his sadness, it is rather to free himself of it." Similarly, when Mary Ellison speaks of the themes of suffering, destitution, and disaster in the blues, she notes that the blues "never succumb" to their own pessimism. "The blues don't usually accept defeat." For Francis Newton, "self-pity and sentimentality are not in the blues," since their "fundamental assumption is that men and women must live [life] as it comes, or if they cannot stand that, that they must die. They laugh and cry because they are human, but they know it cannot help them."[32] The bluesman, then—and the same is true of the speaker of "Aubade"— can be defended against the charge of whining because he does not give in to the despair that he sings of. He is a realist, not a sentimentalist. And it may be, finally, that he speaks of his despair not to seek our pity—the motive of whining—but to find relief from it. This last, the cathartic function of the blues, is the most intriguing explanation of the bluesman's motives when applied to "Aubade," and it allows us to probe the significance of the poem's enigmatic final stanza.

Although it is held almost universally by those who have written on the blues, the idea that the blues have a cathartic function, that they "expunge difficulties" or ease the singer's "worried mind" or "get things out of his system" or "purge" him or "make life livable" is a difficult doctrine to endorse as a psychology of the blues culture since it has more to do with unresolvable issues that lie outside the text than with the words and music of the blues. Did Robert Johnson sing "Stones in My Passway" to ease his troubled mind? Perhaps he did, but that is another critical dead end. It is possible, on the other hand, to conceive of catharsis as simply another convention of the blues, in the same manner that one of the conventions of the pastoral elegy is that the poem itself provides a way for the poet to recover from his grief: "Tomorrow to fresh woods, and pastures new." Whether Milton actually felt better after composing "Lycidas" or Robert Johnson was soothed by a performance of "Stones in My Passway" is beside the point. The conclusion of "Aubade" is conventional in the same manner. Nothing in the speaker's argument prepares for it, but we accept it without protest, in part because of our sense that the speaker's fear has exhausted itself in its articulation and he is thus enabled to turn away from it. I am not the only reader to have heard this note at the end of the poem. "The fear is all too genuine," John Bayley writes of "Aubade," "but the

---

32. Hugues Panassié, *The Real Jazz*, revised ed. (New York, 1960), 24; Mary Ellison, *Extensions of the Blues* (New York, 1989), 12; Newton, *Jazz Scene*, 159.

fact of the poetry overcomes it—a very traditional feat."[33] Perhaps the blues simply share with all the arts of despair the convention of catharsis.

As "Aubade" comes to its final stanza it would appear to have set itself an impossible task. It is our expectation of a poem such as this that it will in some manner come to terms with the problem with which it has been struggling, yet the very essence of "Aubade" is its conviction that its struggle is with the one human problem that is both inescapable and unresolvable. To resolve it in the final stanza would be to undermine the entire poem since a part of its struggle is with the *conventional* resolutions of its predecessors. Its assumption is that it has gone beyond convention to the truth, although, as we have seen, this assumption is itself a convention of its blues intertext. The poem has cut itself off from any traditional answer, yet the final stanza gives the sense of having brought the poem's struggle to a successful end.

> Slowly light strengthens, and the room takes shape.
> It stands plain as a wardrobe, what we know,
> Have always known, know that we can't escape,
> Yet can't accept. One side will have to go.
> Meanwhile telephones crouch, getting ready to ring
> In locked-up offices, and all the uncaring
> Intricate rented world begins to rouse.
> The sky is white as clay, with no sun.
> Work has to be done.
> Postmen like doctors go from house to house.

It is a powerful ending that manages to give the impression of resolution, but does it betray its own assumption that there can be no resolution?

The stanza begins by returning to the opening scene—the bedroom now beginning to take shape in the earliest light—after thirty lines not tied to any locale except the mind. That is, the poem begins and ends with the simplicity and ordinariness of a familiar room; in between, it tries to capture, at a level far distanced from a particular setting, the movement of a mind worrying through a problem. Now the two come

---

33. John Bayley, "Philip Larkin's Inner World," in *Philip Larkin: The Man and His Work,* ed. Salwak, 161.

together, and the plainness of the room is made to stand for the plainness of the poem's thinking. The *it* of the second line that "we know, / Have always known" would logically and grammatically be the familiar bedroom, but by the end of the sentence it refers to our realization of the certainty of death, what we "know that we can't escape, / Yet can't accept." The argument is "plain as a wardrobe" both in the sense that it is obviously true and in the sense that it is free from embellishment. "One side will have to go," the speaker says simply of his double-bind binary, and he does not have to tell us which side that is.

If "Aubade" were a pastoral elegy, the last six lines would represent the turn, the point at which the speaker is, conventionally, purged of his despair and returned to the workaday world. Even if there is nothing in the poem's argument to prepare us for this conclusion, it seems as inevitable as the growing light in the room, and in a sense it is the coming of day that leads to the poem's way of dealing with death. At the end of "Aubade" the speaker has been purged of his anxiety, but not through any solution or resolve. The genius of the poem is to round back to its opening blues line for what small defense it offers against the fear of death. One cannot escape it or accept it, but one can be distracted from it. It is finally the world of work that comes with the dawn, the world of locked-up offices and crouched telephones getting ready to ring, that delivers the speaker from the terror of his realization of oblivion. How does one cope with a thought that is unacceptable and inescapable? By working all day and getting half-drunk at night. It was there from the beginning, the point from which the poem departs and to which it returns. It returns also in a more subtle way. The first stanza moves from the mode of the blues stanza, where each line is a single sentence or clause, to run-on lines. The last stanza reverses the pattern, moving from enjambment back to the three single-line sentences with which the poem ends: "The sky is white as clay with no sun. / Work has to be done. / Postmen like doctors go from house to house." In effect the poem begins with the form of the blues line, allows it to be absorbed into a more "poetic" line, then returns to it at the end.

The conclusion makes clear what we did not understand in the beginning: if there is a momentary cure for the fear of death it is simply that "[w]ork has to be done." "Aubade" begins and ends as a poem about work, fittingly since the blues began as work songs. In some ways the last stanza is the final rewriting of two earlier "work" poems in which work is figured as a toad. "Toads" (*CP*, 89) asks, "Why should I let the toad *work* / Squat on my life?" The answer is that "something sufficiently toad-like / Squats in me, too." In rewriting "Toads," "Toads Revisited" (*CP*, 147) takes a more positive attitude toward work. "What else can I answer, / When the lights come on at four / At the end of another year?" the speaker asks, and the answer, in a lighter tone, is that of "Aubade": "Give me your arm, old toad; / Help me down Cemetery Road." "Aubade" may acknowledge its rewriting of the toad poems with its crouching telephone as a figure for work, a more dignified and ominous version of the squatting toad. (In the same manner the "lobelias" of "Toads Revisited" is an acknowledgment of the play with that sound in the earlier "Toads": "Lecturers, lispers, / Losels, loblolly-men, louts.") Whatever the case, some readers will hear the earlier work poems in the final stanza, although the stanza has not been as accessible to readers as I have made it appear. Barbara Everett, one of Larkin's most attentive readers, speaks of the "true density" of the poem's final postman/doctor image, and what she says of it is more puzzling than the figure itself: "Poems perhaps are 'letters of exile.' . . carried by poet-postmen every day 'from house to house.' " These postmen are not carrying poems or "letters of exile" (a phrase from "Friday Night in the Royal Station Hotel") but letters of commerce. The sense of the last line depends on our recognizing that the delivery of the mail is a metonymic figure for the social intercourse, the exchanges of ideas and goods, buying and selling that constitute the work of the coming day. An early draft makes this reading more obvious: "Postmen go / From house to house like doctors to persuade / Life to resume."[34] The poem ends with the postmen performing the role of doctors making house calls, bringing a cure for the four o'clock blues.

34. Everett, "Art and Larkin," 139; the early draft is quoted in Swarbrick, *Out of Reach*, 152.

It would be possible, I suppose, to argue that "Aubade" undermines itself at the end, that it enacts a resolution only the absence of which makes the argument of the poem viable. Since, however, all texts theoretically deconstruct themselves and since it takes some wrenching to read the conclusion as having achieved any resolution that matters, this discrepancy is less compelling than the discrepancy between the tradition the poem consciously adopts—it announces itself as an *aubade*—and the tradition that underlies it. A French form originally, the aubade is a lyric about the coming of dawn, a morning song that is usually either a joyous celebration of the new day or a lament that two lovers must now part. Larkin's "Aubade" is of course written *against* the dictates of the form. It stands the form on its head, and this is made clear from the beginning when the elegant French title is followed immediately by a line from a more earthy tradition: "I work all day and get half-drunk at night." By the end of the first stanza it is apparent that the coming of dawn is not to be greeted with ritual celebration or romantic nostalgia but with honest despair, even horror. The formal intertext, a set of expectations of how a morning lyric greets the dawn, is referred to here only as a counter, a foil. Its function is to show the poem's departure from a traditional form, and in this way it reveals that "Aubade" has also absorbed the poetry of Auden.

Auden perfected the practice of writing against the expectations of the genre. It is his signature as much as syncopation is the signature of the blues. Auden's lullaby "Lay your sleeping head, my love" is sung to a sleeping lover rather than a child, and it says everything that a lullaby is supposed to suppress. (The lovers will be unfaithful; they are mortal, guilty; there *is* no certainty, no fidelity.) In the same manner "Now the leaves are falling fast" plays with the conventions of the nursery song, and "In Memory of W. B. Yeats" invokes the conventions of the pastoral elegy only to refute them, to suggest, as does "Aubade," that the conventional is the contrived response that will be corrected by the poem's honesty. "Aubade," however, takes Auden's method to another level, one in which Auden's "honesty" would be read as a bit quaint and romantic ("mad Ireland hurt you into poetry" or "Let the

Irish vessel lie / Emptied of its poetry").[35] What is Audenesque about "Aubade" is its method of setting up certain formal expectations against which the poem's own attitude will be measured, and it does this economically in its title and first line. The "official" attitude of the poem will be that of the aubade; its unofficial and operative attitude will be that of the blues. This does not mean that if we fail to hear the blues intertext we will misread the poem. The uncovering of "Aubade" 's blues conventions is not a necessary condition of its reading but a way of understanding its significance, of realizing the means by which it achieves a voice not heard before in English poetry.

35. Auden, *Collected Shorter Poems*, 142.

5

THE REAL WORLD AND THE
COLE PORTER SONG

Have I the right hunch or have I the wrong?
Will it be Bach I shall hear or just a Cole Porter song?
—Cole Porter, "At Long Last Love"

Strange how potent cheap music is.
—Noel Coward, *Private Lives*

THE most pervasive narrative in Larkin criticism, corresponding roughly to the account of Eliot's discovery of Jules Laforgue, is the story of Larkin's discovery of Thomas Hardy as the point of origin for the authentic Larkin of *The Less Deceived* and after. At the center of this narrative is the apprentice poet discarding one by one the masks of his strong precursors Dylan Thomas, Auden, and (principally) Yeats and, with the help of Hardy, discovering his true poetic self. The story incorporates enough detail of a seemingly offhand sort to be convincing: A Yeats volume stolen from a girls' school in Shropshire so entrances Larkin that he spends three years trying to write like Yeats. Hardy becomes his new master because Larkin's bedroom in Wellington happens to face east so that the sun awakens him early and he begins reading the book that he happens to keep at his bedside, *Chosen Poems of Thomas Hardy*. The discovery of Hardy frees him from the tyranny of Yeats, and the artificial, consciously poetic voice of *The North Ship* is replaced in the poems that follow by a real voice, one that speaks from life rather than literature.

The east-facing bedroom is a brilliant touch, Hardyesque in fact—the life-altering stroke of fate, the sense of happenstance, the convergence of random details that, separately, amount to nothing, but coming together launch the career of a new English poet. It is worthy of one of Hardy's own poems just as the Yeats reference is appropriately Yeatsian, the "Stolen Child" or "Lake Isle of Innisfree" Yeats of secret and exotic pleasures. Yeats's poems are not simply stolen, illicit, but stolen from the local girls' school, a comment on the kind of romantic sensibility they are now seen to reflect. The aptness of the details reminds us that this definitive narrative is not something painstakingly reconstructed by scholarship but a poet-novelist's own account of his career, offered principally in two texts, the introduction to a reissue of *The North Ship* in 1965 and a radio talk of 1968. Very much like Eliot, Larkin has been able to dictate the terms for our reading of his poems, since the early critics seized on his account of the move from Yeats to Hardy as the defining moment in his poetic transformation, and it has been only in the last few years, most notably after the publication of the *Collected Poems*, that readers have questioned the accuracy of this story or at least its usefulness as a description of Larkin's beginnings.

Perhaps the key passage in Larkin's account of the making of a poet is this one from the radio talk, one of the most frequently cited passages in all of Larkin:

When I came to Hardy it was with the sense of relief that I didn't have to try and jack myself up to a concept of poetry that lay outside my own life—this is perhaps what I felt Yeats was trying to make me do. One could simply relapse back into one's own life and write from it. Hardy taught one to feel rather than to write—of course one has to use one's own language and one's own jargon and one's own situation—and he taught one as well to have confidence in what one felt. (*RW*, 175–76)

Here is one of the controlling themes of Larkin criticism and one of the chief contradictions. The difference between the inauthentic Larkin of *The North Ship* and the authentic Larkin of *The Less Deceived* is that the latter writes from his own life and not from other poets' poems. "The capacity for setting down experience as he sees it, not as other people have held it to be, seems to be Larkin's true power," Philip Hobsbaum writes in 1988, suggesting the extent to which Larkin has established the basis for his evaluation. "Poems don't come from other poems, they come from being oneself, in life," Larkin told John Haffenden in an interview, and the antithesis of art and life, the theme of the apprenticeship narrative where Yeats is art and Hardy is real life, came to dominate the commentary on his verse. "Larkin is a poet of reality in the sense that the real world is never very far away in his work." He "writes his poetry not from a preconceived set of principles, but as a direct and personal response to particular experiences." "He learned from Thomas Hardy that his own life, with its often casual discoveries, could become poems, and that he could legitimately share such experience with his readers."[1]

Larkin has taken one further step to guide our reading of his poems, actually providing the text that we may use in charting his move from art to life. Larkin added a poem to the reissue of *The North Ship*, "written a year or so later, which, though not noticeably better than the rest," he says in the Introduction, "shows the Celtic fever abated and the patient sleeping soundly" (*RW*, 30). This is "Waiting for breakfast, while she brushed her hair," and Larkin's readers have dutifully followed his lead in their appraisal of it. The poem "shows that Larkin begins to form his own distinct poetic voice soon after he discovers Hardy," Salem Hassan writes. It is important "in showing a transition from the vague symbolism of many of the early poems to a style based on the concrete details of actual experience." For George Hartley, it is "a 'coda' to the

---

1. Philip Hobsbaum, foreword to Salem K. Hassan, *Philip Larkin and His Contemporaries: An Air of Authenticity* (London, 1988), x; John Haffenden, "Philip Larkin," in *Viewpoints: Poets in Conversation with John Haffenden* (London, 1981), 122; Whalen, *Philip Larkin and English Poetry*, 95; Timms, *Philip Larkin*, 19; Martin, *Philip Larkin*, 27.

others in *The North Ship* in the sense that it shows Larkin speaking in his authentic tone, abandoning those attitudes towards poetry and what is suitable for inclusion in it that marred the earlier work." "The poeticisms are gone," David Timms finds, and "Larkin shows that he is beginning to see himself in the context of the real world."[2]

Constructions of this kind are so thoroughly ingrained in Larkin criticism that any extended discussion of Larkin's poetry will have difficulty in avoiding them in one form or another, most recently in the form of attempted revisions or corrections. After the publication of the *Collected Poems* and in a few cases even before, readers began recognizing that Larkin's account of his poetic conversion and the accounts based on it were misleading. The first stanza of "Waiting for breakfast, while she brushed her hair," the poem which supposedly shows Larkin forming his own distinct poetic voice, "reads like a pastiche of early T. S. Eliot," Terry Whalen argues. The hitherto unpublished poems reveal that Auden and other poets of the Auden group had more to do with shaping Larkin's early poetry than either Yeats or Hardy, and the dismissal of Yeats for Hardy is clearly exaggerated; Yeats's music and mannerisms show up throughout the Larkin canon.[3] Such reassessments were inevitable—Barbara Everett's "Philip Larkin: After Symbolism" is a particularly persuasive revision of the early criticism—but it is not this aspect of the Yeats/Hardy narrative I wish to pursue further. My intent is not to propose an alternative reading for these early formulations of a poetry that transcends poetry—I have no account of Larkin's early career to put in their place—but to note some of their implications for my own project, which has to do with the presence in Larkin's texts of nonpoetic or at least nontraditional conventions and intertexts. And for my purposes I need only point to two obvious difficulties with the customary

2. See Hassan, *Philip Larkin and His Contemporaries,* 187; George Hartley, "Nothing to Be Said," in *Larkin at Sixty,* ed. Anthony Thwaite (London, 1982), 90–91; Timms, *Philip Larkin,* 34–35.

3. Whalen, *Philip Larkin and English Poetry,* 3; for the Auden influence see, for example, Regan, *Philip Larkin,* 66–77; for Larkin and Yeats, see Andrew Motion, *Philip Larkin* (London, 1982), 12–15, and Edna Longley, " 'Any-angled Light': Philip Larkin and Edward Thomas," in *Poetry in the Wars* (Newcastle upon Tyne, 1986), 113–39.

construction in which the opposition Yeats/Hardy becomes a coded form of contrived/authentic or poetic/real. It is, first of all, inherently contradictory, as Larkin himself seems to have recognized in midstatement, and it is of little value as a basis for reading Larkin's poems.

In his comments on the Yeats/Hardy theme Larkin finds himself entangled in a contradiction that threatens to expose its ideological function of naturalizing his poetic theory, and this contradiction has persisted in Larkin criticism. The swapping of Yeats for Hardy is at once a story of exchanging one model or set of conventions for another and a story of escaping poetic convention. Or, to put it another way, it is a story of evading the influence of precursor poets by adopting one of them as one's master. For the point of the story is not that Larkin stopped writing like Yeats and began writing like Hardy; it is that reading Hardy taught him to transcend the poetic and the literary. It led him to recognize that poems come "from being oneself, in life," from a "personal response to particular experiences." He begins "to form his own distinct poetic voice" and "to see himself in the context of the real world."

It is in suggesting just how Hardy was able to accomplish all this that Larkin unmasks the ideological base of his poetic, ideological in the sense that it attempts to disguise something artfully contrived—a social and cultural construct, a particular conception of poetry—as something natural, as if his conception of poetry were *not* in fact a conception but simply an ascent (or descent) into the real. Reading Hardy taught him, he says, that he did not have to conform to "a concept of poetry that lay outside [his] own life—this is perhaps what I felt Yeats was trying to make me do" (*RW*, 175). But how does Hardy's concept of poetry, as conventional in its own way as that of Yeats, escape the charge of lying outside his own life? Larkin sees the problem immediately. "[O]f course," he says, attempting to cover the gap he has opened, "one has to use one's own language and one's own jargon and one's own situations" (*RW*, 175–76). But in that case, we may then ask, what has Hardy contributed? Larkin's answer is revealing: *"Hardy taught one to feel rather than to write"* (*RW*, 175). Any aesthetic that privileges something called the "real world" over something else called "art" arrives at this point sooner or later. We have seen it already in the blues aesthetic. In opposition to the artifice of other types of music the blues are honest, real, authentic. They express real feelings rather than musical conventions. In a variation of the blues aesthetic Larkin removes Hardy from the realm of writing and relocates him in the realm of feeling. His influence, unlike that of Yeats, is thus not "literary" or "poetic" but real. And in following Hardy, Larkin moves from the world of the contrived and the conventional to the world of actual experience and real feeling. Faced with the identical argument in blues commentary, that is, that "blues music does not require artifice but is rather a species of direct emotional expression," Albert Murray has demonstrated in *Stomping the Blues* the degree to which the blues obey the rules of stylization and convention (87, 90). And long ago Roman Jakobson noted that "verisimilitude in a verbal expression or in a literary description obviously makes no sense whatever. Can the question be raised about a higher degree of verisimilitude of this or that poetic trope?" Larkin's account of his conversion to the real world and the many variations on it in Larkin criticism may accurately reflect the sense of the ordinary and the real that readers, including Larkin himself, have received from his poems, but they are of no value in *accounting* for this effect because they ignore the status of the poems as written texts. They imply that the power of Larkin's poetry derives from the poems' incorporation of "actual experience," from the unmediated expression of the facts of the poet's own life. Lolette Kuby thus repeats (and endorses) Larkin's claim "never to have written a poem (with the exception of 'Faith Healing') on a situation that he has not experienced at first hand."[4] This sounds suspiciously like the claim that one can't sing the blues unless one has experienced the blues.[5] In both cases the

4. See the discussion of Murray's argument in chapter 4; Roman Jakobson, "On Realism in Art," in *Readings in Russian Poetics: Formalist and Structuralist Views*, ed. Ladislav Matejka and Krystyna Pomorska (Ann Arbor, 1978), 39; Lolette Kuby, *An Uncommon Poet for the Common Man: A Study of Philip Larkin's Poetry* (The Hague, 1974), 135.

5. In *The Sociology of Rock* Simon Frith writes, "In the mid-sixties heyday of the white use of R & B and soul, letter writers to the *Melody Maker* agonised over a difficult question: can white men sing the blues?" (181).

assumption is that the works have somehow escaped their status as artifacts, that they are not artful but "true."

Responding to the same confusion in the commentary on popular music, Simon Frith notes, "Music can not *be* true or false, it can only refer to *conventions* of truth and falsity," and he is able to specify the practices of the musicians in question (Bruce Springsteen and the E Street Band) by which the *effect* of authenticity is achieved. "To be authentic and to sound authentic is in the rock context the same thing":

The E Street Band makes music as a group, but a group in which we can hear every instrumentalist. Our attention is drawn, that is, not to a finished sound but to music-in-the-making. This is partly done by the refusal to make any instrument the "lead." ... And partly by a specific musical busy-ness—the group is "tight," everyone is aiming for the same rhythmic end, but "loose," each player makes their own decision as to how to get there.... Springsteen himself is a rock and roll star, not a crooner or singer/songwriter. His voice *strains* to be heard, he has to shout against the instruments that both support and compete with him. However many times he's rehearsed his lines they always sound as if they're being forged on the spot.[6]

To pursue a version of Frith's argument here, we may note that Larkin's poetry cannot *be* real; it can only refer to *conventions* we associate with what we name the real. If his poems sometimes give the *effect* of ordinary experience, it is not because they have escaped the conventional; it is because they employ conventions that readers identify with something other than the classical tradition of European poetry.

David Lodge has located one such practice in Larkin's poems, and I offer his description as exemplary of the kind of reading I am pursuing. In "Philip Larkin: The Metonymic Muse," Lodge attempts to describe the "realist" mode of Larkin's poetry by examining the poems' tendency toward metonymy as a substitute for the expected metaphor:

Poetry, especially lyric poetry, is an inherently metaphoric mode, and to displace it towards the metonymic pole is (whether Larkin likes it or not) an "experimental" literary gesture. Such poetry makes its impact by appearing daringly, even

6. Frith, "Real Thing," 100.

shockingly unpoetic, particularly when the accepted poetic mode is elaborately metaphoric.

Thus in "The Whitsun Weddings" the sparse metaphors "are foregrounded against a predominantly metonymic background, which is in turn foregrounded against the background of the (metaphoric) poetic tradition." The opening of the poem "has a characteristically casual, colloquial tone, and the near-redundant specificity . . . of a personal anecdote, a 'true story.' " The scenery and the description of the wedding parties are "evoked by metonymic and synecdochic detail." There are few metaphors; "appearance, clothing, behaviour, are observed with the eye of a novelist or documentary writer and allowed to stand, untransformed by metaphor, as indices of a certain recognisable way of life." When a conspicuous metaphor does appear (as in the "arrow-shower" at the poem's conclusion), it is particularly powerful "partly because it is so different from anything else in the poem."[7] Lodge's discussion of "The Whitsun Weddings" and a number of other Larkin poems is convincing, I believe, because he is able to identify modes of expression by which a semblance of the real is achieved. I am less interested in the substance of this argument—the metonymy-metaphor antithesis—than in its implication that an explanation for the appeal of Larkin's voice is more likely to be found in the formal properties of his texts than in personal anecdotes. I also share Lodge's assumption that Larkin's texts appear unpoetic (early critics translated this too readily as "real") because they go against our expectations of what a conventional poem should look and sound like.

There is no one set of conventions to be identified in Larkin's poems just as there is no one Larkin poem. One of the impressions generated by the early criticism is that Larkin's poems share a common style, the sad plain style of "Deceptions," say, or "Places, Loved Ones." In fact, it is difficult to think of a poet who has produced a greater variety of

---

7. David Lodge, "Philip Larkin: The Metonymic Muse," in *Philip Larkin: The Man and His Work,* ed. Dale Salwak (London, 1989), 120, 124–25. The essay is taken from Lodge's *The Modes of Modern Writing,* which is based on Jakobson's distinction between metaphor and metonymy as the two poles of all discourse.

poems. "In terms of works of art, Larkin's harvest was quite remarkable," Barbara Everett correctly notes in "Art and Larkin"; "few lyric poets have achieved eighty or ninety poems, all autonomous, all essentially different from each other."[8] The reader who wishes to account for the appeal of Larkin's poems is faced not simply with one set of conventions (Lodge's study is a bit misleading in this respect) but with a wide range of styles and forms and techniques, not all of which aspire toward the gritty ordinariness of "Mr. Bleaney" or "Home Is So Sad." Since I am interested in the way Larkin's texts have incorporated the conventions and practices of blues, jazz, and popular songs, I also want to look at the way these musical intertexts have contributed to what Lodge calls the "shockingly unpoetic" quality of Larkin's poems. I am not concerned simply with the assumed "realism" of these texts but with a wide range of effects that can be traced to the presence of musical intertexts. Thus far I have concentrated on jazz and blues intertexts, but I want to broaden the field in this and the following chapters to include other forms of popular music.

Before Larkin knew there was such a thing as American jazz, he listened to dance bands, "anything with four beats to the bar." "I must have learned dozens of dance lyrics simply by listening to dance music," he told an interviewer, and added that although some of them were pretty awful, "some of them were quite sophisticated" (*RW*, 50). Among the most sophisticated were those of the theater composer Cole Porter, who has been called (in an obituary Larkin cites) "the supreme sophisticate of American song" (*RW*, 227). I will focus on Cole Porter not because he is conspicuously present in Larkin's poems but because he can be made to represent a particular set of musical conventions that *does* surface at times and because Larkin uses him to represent the essence of a quality he admires in thirties song lyrics.

"Lines on a Young Lady's Photograph Album" (*CP*, 71) is the opening poem of *The Less Deceived,* and its positioning has been taken as evidence that it announces Larkin's realist aesthetic. "Larkin is a declared realist," David Lodge writes. " 'Lines on a Young Lady's Photograph

---

8. Everett, "Art and Larkin," 132.

Album,' strategically placed at the beginning of his first important collection . . . is his 'Musée des Beaux Arts,' taking not Flemish painting but snapshots as the exemplary art form."[9] And it is true that the poem is, or purports to be, about the unforgiving realism of photography:

> But o, photography! as no art is,
> Faithful and disappointing! that records
> Dull days as dull, and hold-it smiles as frauds,
> And will not censor blemishes
> Like washing-lines, and Hall's-Distemper boards,
>
> But shows the cat as disinclined, and shades
> A chin as doubled when it is, what grace
> Your candour thus confers upon this face!
> How overwhelmingly persuades
> That this is a real girl in a real place,
>
> In every sense empirically true!

It is easy to see how the language of these lines as well as the poem's opposition of art and life might lead a reader to Lodge's conclusion that it takes its aesthetic from the verisimilitude of photography rather than the contrivance of art. Yet it is impossible, finally, to read the poem in this fashion. Its voice and attitude come not from the documentary but from the most artificial and contrived (the customary term is "sophisticated") branch of American popular music, one that has over the years acquired the adjective "Cole Porterish."

I am not the first, I should point out, to have heard this note in the poem. Two of the most careful readings of the poem, those of William Pritchard and (most recently) James Booth evoke the name of Cole Porter in attempting to describe the poem's complex tone. Booth is correct, I think, in observing that the poem projects the sexual relationship it develops through "playfully comic social stereotypes." The speaker and the young woman whose photographs he eyes hungrily "from pose to pose" are represented as stock figures—he is the self-consciously lecherous older man, she the "sweet girl-graduate" in pigtails

9. Lodge, "Philip Larkin: The Metonymic Muse," 122.

or a trilby hat. Or as Andrew Swarbrick has it, the strategy of the poem is "self-mockery," the speaker depicting himself as "the dirty old man leering at the girl's photos."[10] This is to say that far from projecting a slice-of-life realism, the poem is unabashedly conventional in its effects. It aspires to a kind of detached sophistication in tone, to acrobatics of rhyme, and to memorable individual lines that readers (at least some readers) may identify not with traditional poetry but with American popular song.

Pritchard culls as examples of the effect of popular song the lines "From every side you strike at my control" and "Not quite your class, I'd say, dear, on the whole," and both Pritchard and Booth note that the feeling of the sixth stanza is Cole Porter–like. What that may mean is difficult to articulate. Musicians are accustomed to relying on the ear and scorning definition—thus the legendary response to the question *what is jazz?* attributed to several musicians (Larkin attributes it to Fats Waller [*AWJ*, 260]): "Lady, if you has to ask you'll never know."

Here is the relevant passage from the sixth stanza. The speaker has reached the point in his meditation where he recognizes that what he has thought of as the empirical truth of photography may be something closer to a sense of the past, *"what was,"* from which we are now excluded:

> Or is it just *the past?* Those flowers, that gate,
> These misty parks and motors, lacerate
> Simply by being over; you
> Contract my heart by looking out of date.

It may be possible to approach a definition of what is Cole Porterish in these lines (and others in Larkin's verse), although it requires an excursion into what Larkin calls "the 'Cole Porter song' " (*RW*, 227), as if it comprised a genre of its own.

Another Hardyesque coincidence—it is to Larkin we may turn for a description of the "Cole Porter song." In 1972 Larkin reviewed *Cole: A Biographical Essay*, edited by Robert Kimball, a book made up primar-

---

10. Booth, *Philip Larkin: Writer*, 128; Swarbrick, *Out of Reach*, 48.

ily of photographs and song lyrics. Titled "Supreme Sophisticate" in *Required Writing* (the designation Larkin took from one of Porter's obituaries), the review is essentially an inquiry into Cole Porter's appeal, which is in part defined by Larkin's title—in both his life and his songs Porter is the embodiment of sophistication:

Several strands of appeal can be disentangled. The simplest is that Cole Porter was smart, a rich boy . . . who made good. We all (Americans especially) are sneakingly impressed by the character in faultless clothes who can talk to French waiters and is with the best bunch on the beach, and in a way Cole was all that ever went with evening dress. (*RW,* 225)

He is the romanticized opposite of the typical Larkin persona, who is all that *doesn't* go with evening dress, the persona of "The Dance," for example, who is contemptuous of his own appearance in evening clothes ("The shame of evening trousers, evening tie") and leery of his colleagues at the dance "sitting dressed like this" (*CP,* 154–55). In Larkin's review, Cole Porter is thus the antithesis of what Hardy has earlier been made to represent. He is an emblem of a style and a manner that lie outside one's own life, and his suspected presence in a poem about "a real girl in a real place" is a complication that a reading of the poem might well take into account.

It was not simply his lifestyle, however, that was the basis for Porter's appeal: "above all," Larkin writes, "Cole was a great song writer." Larkin divides his songs into two kinds, "word-dominated and tune-dominated" (*RW,* 226), and it was the former that acquired the appellation "Cole Porterish." In *American Popular Song,* the songwriter-composer Alec Wilder notes the irony that although Cole Porter was the most thoroughly trained musician of all the great theater composers—including Jerome Kern, Irving Berlin, George Gershwin, and Richard Rodgers—he is better known and more highly esteemed for his lyrics than his music. And it is for this reason that it is easier to characterize a Cole Porter song than, say, an Irving Berlin song. Wilder describes it as "high fashion, witty to a markedly sophisticated degree, turned out, oftentimes it seemed, for the special amusement of his social set." The lyrics seldom indulged in tenderness, and even when concerned with emotion, "they often managed to keep at a polite distance from true sentiment by means of a gloss, a patina of social poise." They frequently resorted to cliché, and they relied heavily on the "light touch, the mordant turn of phrase, the finger-tip kiss, the *double entendre,* the awareness of the bone-deep fatigue of urban gaiety, the exquisite, and the lacy lists of cosmopolitan superlatives."[11]

Larkin's characterization of the Cole Porter lyric goes in a slightly different direction. He places Porter in a nineteenth-century comic tradition, emphasizing his skill, his range of reference, and especially his gift with rhyme. In what seems almost a parody of Eliot's praise of the metaphysical poets for uniting thought and feeling, Larkin suggests that those who were "exposed daily" to songwriters like Porter might come to see that "songs (and perhaps even poems) were skilfully made things, requiring thought as well as feeling" (*RW*, 227). Larkin's focus is on the *literacy* of the Cole Porter song, perhaps defensively so, as if to erase a distinction between the literary and the merely popular:

As a lyricist, therefore, Cole Porter was well within the comic song/drawing-room ballad tradition that persisted into the Thirties from the previous century. Whether he influenced it is doubtful; the "Cole Porter song," that feat of rhyme and reference, was rarely copied, and for the rest one must remember that it was a highly literate decade, compared at least with much of what followed. (*RW*, 227)

It is odd that Larkin's example of what is distinctively Cole Porterish—the literacy, the feat of rhyme and reference—is not in fact by Porter. Perhaps he perceives that it is more easily isolated and displayed in a heavy-handed form:

> The Venus de Milo
> Was noted for her charms,
> But, strictly between us,
> You're cuter than Venus,
> And—what's more—you've got arms.

11. Alec Wilder, *American Popular Song,* ed. James T. Maher (New York, 1972), 223.

And to suggest the falling off in popular music since the thirties, he adds, "I have tried, without much success, to imagine Mick Jagger singing this" (*RW*, 227). Larkin was apparently much taken with this verse (from Leo Robin's and Lewis Gensler's "Love Is Just Around the Corner") and the Mick Jagger reference. He repeated them both in a 1979 interview, in which he argues that such lyrics constituted "a kind of folk poetry" and wonders if his assumptions about the way poems are supposed to sound came from listening to them (*RW*, 50).

Whatever his assumptions, it is possible to show that some of his texts have absorbed conventions of American popular song, and I offer one clear example from the "Cole Porter song." What Wilder calls the "lacy lists of cosmopolitan superlatives"—other commentators refer to it as the "catalog" song or the "list" song—was an especially pronounced convention of the Porter lyric. Wilder is apparently thinking of "You're the Top," whose chief appeal is its wit and range of reference over a hundred lines of such superlatives as an Arrow collar, a Coolidge dollar, the feet of Fred Astaire, Camembert, an O'Neill drama, Whistler's mama, Dante, and the nose on the great Durante (all of these from one of its seven refrains). Larkin notes that this kind of word-dominated song "reads like a single idea repeated (with the aid of a rhyming dictionary) virtually *ad infinitum.*" The list song represents Porter's "Gilbertian side" since, as Larkin reminds us, "he was Gilbert as well as Sullivan," the lyricist as well as the composer. The Gilbertian list song "is highly amusing at a party or in a theatre, but inevitably seems artificial on repeated acquaintance" (*RW*, 226). Larkin's example of the list song is "Let's Do It," which manages to repeat through sixty-odd lines variations on the pattern of "Locusts in trees do it, bees do it, / Even highly educated fleas do it, / Let's do it, let's fall in love."[12] An even better example, one that Larkin appears to suppress in his review, is "At Long Last Love," which occupies an unusual niche in the Cole Porter canon.

Brendan Gill writes in the American edition of *Cole* that "Cole's accident . . . is the central episode of his life—not the most important

---

12. Robert Kimball, ed., *Cole*, introduction by Brendan Gill (New York, 1971), 89.

one but the one that everything else stands in relation to." Larkin tells the story in his review:

From being the expatriate playboy-composer, he came back to America and conquered first Broadway and then Hollywood; then at the height of his success he had a terrible accident, a horse falling on him and smashing both his legs. For the rest of his life he was crippled and in great pain, but it made no difference to his work. Even when awaiting the ambulance he went on with the lyrics of "You Never Know." (*RW*, 226)

Larkin is technically correct here, but he goes out of his way to avoid mentioning the name of the song Porter was working on while he awaited medical assistance—*You Never Know* is the name of the show in which the song eventually appeared. Here is what Larkin read in the book under review: "When this horse fell on me, I was too stunned to be conscious of great pain, but until help came I worked on the lyrics for a song called *At Long Last Love*."[13] Larkin's circumvention is of no consequence in itself, but still we may raise the question of why he avoids the title of a well-known song that both Porter and Brendan Gill (in his introduction to *Cole*) name in their accounts of the accident—to be a good story it requires the title of the song—and substitutes the title of a now-forgotten Broadway show (which neither mentions).[14] Rather than answering the question directly by attributing a particular motive to Larkin I will substitute another Hardy-like coincidence. The song Porter reports he worked on as he lay terribly injured awaiting help is, so far as I can tell, the one clearly identifiable Cole Porter intertext in the Larkin canon.

"At Long Last Love" is another list song, but an interesting variation on the type in which the wit of the seemingly endless catalog and the absurdity of the rhymes are used in a tender ballad. Wilder points out

13. Ibid., xvi, 150.

14. Ibid., xvii. It *is* a good story as Brendan Gill tells it. He holds back the name of the song until the end of the climactic sentence: "As Cole later told the story—and he liked a good story—lying there, he took out a pencil and notebook and set to work on the lyrics of a song that became *At Long Last Love*."

how extraordinary it is that one "accepts the wry, bumptious lyric in juxtaposition to the languorous, romantic melody," especially since, as he notes, "the high point of the melody is accompanied by the words 'is it Granada I see or only Asbury Park?' " The line gives the pattern for the list—is it *x* or is it *y?*—one the real thing, the other a lesser version:

> Is it an earthquake or simply a shock?
> Is it the good turtle soup or merely the mock?
> Is it a cocktail—this feeling of joy,
> Or is what I feel the real McCoy?
> Have I the right hunch or have I the wrong?
> Will it be Bach I shall hear or just a Cole Porter song?
> Is it a fancy not worth thinking of,
> Or is it at long last love?

And so on through four eight-line refrains, with the pattern alternating between the romantic ("Is it the rainbow or just a mirage?") and the comic (Porter's second sly reference to his own name, for example, in "Is it a real Porterhouse or only a steak?"), extending even to the slapstick ("Is it a kiss on the lips or just a kick in the pants?").[15]

The Larkin text that incorporates "At Long Last Love," "Is it for now or for always" from *The North Ship* (*CP*, 296), indicates by the banality of its language ("I take you now and for always, / For always is always now") and its seeming idealization of the "you" addressed that the effect to which it aspires is that of the popular song.[16] David Timms notes that it "reads like a rather uninventive popular song, and turns on just the sort of verbal trick that such songs so often do."[17] Had he recognized the Cole Porter intertext, he might have altered "uninventive." One could argue that it reads like a reply to a quite inventive popular song. It has absorbed the conventions of the catalog

15. Wilder, *American Popular Song*, 244–45 (in the published version Porter changed the line to "Is it the Lido I see or only Asbury Park?"); Kimball, ed., *Cole*, 150.

16. Larkin also alludes to the cliché of Porter's title in one of his own titles, "Long Last" (*CP*, 151), a poem about old age in which the Cole Porter song is not evident.

17. Timms, *Philip Larkin*, 30.

song, the particular "is it x or is it y?" pattern of "At Long Last Love," and even one of its pairs—the second refrain's "Is it the rainbow or just a mirage?" is clearly the intertextual reference for the poem's "Is it a mirage or miracle. . . ?" This is to say that Larkin's text contains "At Long Last Love," and what at first seems so very odd about the work's tone and construction in a serious "Yeatsian" volume of verse— what the context cannot explain—is a product of the poem's reference to its absent intertext. It is in effect the answer to a question that it does not display:

> Is it for now or for always,
> The world hangs on a stalk?
> Is it a trick or a trysting-place,
> The woods we have found to walk?
>
> Is it a mirage or miracle,
> Your lips that lift at mine:
> And the suns like a juggler's juggling-balls,
> Are they a sham or a sign?
>
> Shine out, my sudden angel,
> Break fear with breast and brow,
> I take you now and for always,
> For always is always now.

The poem responds to its intertext both figuratively and literally. The song poses the catalog question "is it x or is it y?" and leaves the answer in suspense; the poem introduces the question in the first line, with x being "now" and y "always," then answers it in the last two lines; the resolution is that "x is y"—"I take you now and for always, / For always is always now."

One might say of the poem what Larkin said of the Cole Porter list song; it is "amusing" but "inevitably seems artificial on repeated acquaintance." The poem's contrivance is in fact so pronounced that the reader will almost certainly have lost interest before reaching the final lines. The success of "At Long Last Love" depends on several devices that the poem fails to master. In his discussion of the song's lyrics Philip Furia notes in particular "the witty images that range from the European elegance of 'Bach' to the prosaically American 'Chevrolet,' the blend of elevated diction and brash slang in conversational phrasing, and the cleverly skewed rhymes of sh*ock*, m*ock*, *cock*tail, and Mc*Coy*."[18] The poem employs the bare conventions of its musical intertext without incorporating any of its saving graces, and the result is a kind of literary curiosity, a contrivance that is of interest primarily because it exposes so readily the intertextual process that resulted in its unfinished form. It may be that the poem's status as a poetic oddity lies in its inability to digest completely its intertextual material or to fuse material from widely separate traditions. After the popular song wit of "Are they a sham or a sign?" for example, come two lines that demand an entirely different set of responses: "Shine out, my sudden angel, / Break fear with breast and brow." This passage is clearly not Cole Porterish, and its incongruity is disastrous to the poem partly because it exposes its pieced-together construction. The difficulty with "Is it for now or for always" is that its intertexts lie too close to the surface, as is the case in several other poems from *The North Ship*—"To write one song, I said" (*CP*, 291), for example, where the Yeatsian intertext (from "The Fisherman") has been only partially absorbed.

This is not the case, however, with "Lines on a Young Lady's Photograph Album," to return now to the poem with which we began. The popular music intertext is so deeply buried in "Lines" that it can be detected only at a couple of points, and its significance is to complicate our response to the poem's attitude rather than serve as a distraction. The complication is this: on the surface the poem is in praise of the "candour," the empirical truth of a medium that is faithful "as no art is" to the real. It sets up a hierarchy familiar in the Larkin canon, the real privileged over the artificial. Yet its intertext, which dictates the voice of the speaker, reverses this hierarchy. The poem's tone is derived from conventions that make no pretense of documenting the real. Steve Coombes notes, "Writing for shows, thirties lyric writers were in both the best and worst senses of the word in the business of creating fictions. The moods of their lyrics do not reflect emotions they had actually felt

18. Furia, *Poets of Tin Pan Alley*, 175.

nor that they expected anyone to think that they had felt nor even that they expected anyone else to feel for that matter."[19]

To test this gap between the appeal to empirical truth and the appeal to emotions that occur in thirties music lyrics we may reread the speaker's description of the photographs in the sixth stanza of "Lines." He has just observed the special virtue of photography, that it "overwhelmingly persuades / That this is a real girl in a real place," and he has attributed this sense of the real to the fact that photography is always about something that is over, something from which we are excluded. Had the poem continued in this direction, that is, as a treatise on realism in art, its causes and conditions, it would have justified Lodge's position that it announces Larkin's documentary-like aesthetic. But when the poem offers its *own* description of the photographs in question, it does so in a manner that distinguishes the poem's medium of expression from photography's:

> Those flowers, that gate,
> These misty parks and motors, lacerate
> Simply by being over; you
> Contract my heart by looking out of date.

The technique here displays the opposite of the quality the speaker has praised in photography, which was essentially the faithfulness "that records / Dull days as dull," the transparency of a seemingly unself-conscious medium. It is precisely the self-consciousness of the poem's description of the photographs that strikes us in this passage, incorporating all of the show-off conventions we refer to as Cole Porterish: the short phrases, the frequent, unexpected, and clever rhymes (gate/lacerate/out of date), the pun on *contract,* the parallel between the scenes in the photographs "being over" and the woman "looking out of date," the wit displayed in the notion that looking out of date is a winning virtue, and the list or catalog that, as Philip Furia says of Porter's list, is used both to "hold off and indulge feeling."[20]

19. Quoted in Simon Frith, "Why Do Songs Have Words?" in *Music for Pleasure: Essays in the Sociology of Pop* (New York, 1988), 128n.

20. Furia, *Poets of Tin Pan Alley,* 179.

This last effect points us to another Cole Porterish quality in these lines, more difficult to define but contained in Dave Laing's discussion of thirties lyrics that display the qualities listed above. Laing argues that the "cult of sophistication" and the increasingly self-conscious lyrics of songwriters like Berlin, Kern, and Porter "provided a way of avoiding the system of sentimental phrases which was all the history of the popular ballad presented them with as examples." One feature of the pre–Cole Porter ballad was its attempt "to draw the listener into an immediate and total identification with the singer." The Cole Porter song rejects this effect, and "the 'self-conscious' writers used wit to get a distancing effect, which in a sense parallels the 'alienation-effect' that Bertolt Brecht sought to achieve in his plays." Furia notes Porter's "characteristic lyrical twist that registers romantic affect yet treats it with urbane, almost clinical, detachment." In discussing the distancing effect of Porter's "Every Time We Say Goodbye," Laing concludes that one of its results is "to make us aware that this is a love song we are listening to."[21]

The two chief effects of the sixth stanza of "Lines on a Young Lady's Photograph Album" are to distance us from the emotion being expressed and to remind us that this is art and not reality. The lines are *about* feeling strong emotions, but the rhyming of "lacerate" and the pun on "contract"—the two verbs that refer to the heart, the emotions—elevate the display of wit of a particularly contrived kind above the expression of feeling. The aesthetic that dictates the lines on the photographs does not itself derive from photography; it is the antithesis of the candid, the unposed. These lines do not attempt to persuade us that they are an expression of real emotion in a real place, and that is because the conventions of the thirties lyric they have absorbed go in the opposite direction. Steve Coombes writes,

Nothing would have disturbed the cosmopolitan Cole Porter more than the idea that people might think that he actually did sit and moon over lost love— that emphatically was not his style. The moods of thirties lyrics are about what you ought to have felt or more accurately what you might like to have felt given

21. Laing, *Sound of Our Time,* 54, 55; Furia, *Poets of Tin Pan Alley,* 163.

the chance to think about it. Paradoxically, then, the tone is at the same time extremely sophisticated yet highly idealised.[22]

But why should the coupling of sophistication and idealization be a paradox? The poem and the Cole Porter song both demonstrate that the two go together. The poem idealizes the subject of the photographs, the speaker, and the relationship of the two through its self-consciously witty tone (in the way that the thirties song lyric idealizes love by elevating it to the level of artifice), and it sets this idealization against the naïve realism of photography, whose chief feature is that it *refuses* to idealize—"will not censor blemishes" and "shades / A chin as doubled when it is." What realist readings of "Lines" fail to recognize is that, whether intentional or not, photography is the antithesis of the mode of expression the poem adopts, and the poem's peculiar tone is in part the result of a discrepancy between what it *claims* to value—the real— and what it in fact *does* value—the attitude Wilder characterizes as "a patina of social poise" that keeps one "at a polite distance from true sentiment."[23]

I have labeled this attitude Cole Porterish, but the intertextual relations in Larkin's poems are certainly more complicated than I have made them appear, and one of the complications is suggested in Graham Greene's reference to the "Audenesque charm" of Porter's "You're the Top." If Porter is Audenesque, Auden is clearly Cole Porterish, as Bernard Bergonzi has shown in his chapter on thirties lyrics in *Reading the Thirties*. When we hear the sound of popular music in a Larkin text, then, to alter one of Porter's lyrics, is it Cole Porter we hear or just a W. H. Auden song? The question is of particular relevance now that the informing texts of Larkin's early poems have been located in Auden, MacNeice, and other members of the Auden circle. Stephen Regan states the revisionist view bluntly: "What the unpublished poems reveal, importantly, is that the formative influences on Larkin's work had less to do with the presence of Yeats and Hardy than with the prevailing

22. Quoted in Frith, "Why Do Songs Have Words?" 128n.
23. Wilder, *American Popular Song,* 223.

attitudes and techniques of such poets as W. H. Auden and Louis MacNeice."[24]

Bergonzi has demonstrated that the attitudes and techniques of Auden and MacNeice include the incorporation of popular song lyrics into their verse, as Larkin himself recognized in a review of MacNeice not included in *Required Writing.* Larkin notes that MacNeice "displayed a sophisticated sentimentality about falling leaves and lipsticked cigarette stubs" and proposes that "he could have written the words of 'These Foolish Things.' " Larkin also associates MacNeice with a Cole Porter–like sophistication in an essay on poets' recorded readings of their poems, where he writes of one of MacNeice's recordings, "Here the voice is not the style—at least, not if you think of Mr MacNeice, as I do, as poetically a sophisticated, almost dressing-gowned figure, dropping epithets into place effortlessly and exactly" (*RW,* 140).

Bergonzi argues that the MacNeice persona, "balancing irony and sentimentality, cynicism and nostalgia, had affinities with the characteristic spirit of songs by Noel Coward or Ira Gershwin or Cole Porter." As one persuasive example, "The Sunlight on the Garden," perhaps MacNeice's best-known lyric, displays "great verbal dexterity, reminiscent of Cole Porter or Ira Gershwin."[25]

The conventions of popular music are easier to recognize in Auden, partly because they tend toward the techniques of the catalog or list song. Here is the Auden version of the "is it *x* or is it *y?*" intertext from "At Long Last Love":

> Does it howl like a hungry Alsatian,
> Or boom like a military band?
> Could one give a first-rate imitation
> On a saw or a Steinway Grand?
> Is its singing at parties a riot?

24. See Bernard Bergonzi, *Reading the Thirties: Texts and Contexts* (London, 1978), 112; I am indebted to Bergonzi's chapter "Supplying the Lyrics" for the discussion of the popular song in Auden and MacNeice; Regan, *Philip Larkin,* 66.

25. Larkin's review of MacNeice is quoted in Pritchard, "Larkin's Presence," 78; Bergonzi, *Reading the Thirties,* 114.

> Does it only like Classical stuff?
> Will it stop when one wants to be quiet?
> O tell me the truth about love.

Another catalog poem, "Stop all the clocks, cut off the telephone" (now more widely known for its presence in a popular movie), contains this Porter-like stanza:

> He was my North, my South, my East and West,
> My working week and my Sunday rest,
> My noon, my midnight, my talk, my song;
> I thought that love would last for ever: I was wrong.[26]

If we hear in this passage Porter's memorable line "The east, west, north, and the south of you" from "All of You," it reminds us of one of the oddities of intertextual reading, where a later text—"All of You" was written in 1953—may help to shape our reading of an earlier one. (That is, it seems legitimate to associate the feeling of Auden's poem with the Cole Porter song; however, the Porter song it most resembles was published a couple of decades later.) But this kind of reading is common, especially when we read the earlier production of poets or songwriters with their later texts in mind.

As Bergonzi points out, the Cole Porter catalog song was especially congenial to Auden and there are a number of examples of it in the Auden canon, particularly in the plays. Perhaps the most Cole Porterish of all Auden's catalog songs (in the kind of knowing contemporary references that now seem dated) is this example from *The Dog Beneath the Skin,* which has three choruses constructed on the following model:

> If Chanel gowns have a train this year,
> If Morris cars fit a self-changing gear,
> If Lord Peter Whimsey [*sic*]
> Misses an obvious clue,
> If Wallace Beery
> Should act a fairy
> And Chaplin the Wandering Jew;

26. Auden, "Twelve Songs," *Collected Shorter Poems,* 95, 92.

The reason is
Just simply this:
They're in the racket, too![27]

A demonstration of the Cole Porter song in Auden's verse (as well as speculation on its significance) could be extended, but my intent is to suggest that the presence of Cole Porter in Larkin's texts is not quite as exotic as it first appears (*exotic* in Larkin's definition—"botanical term meaning introduced from abroad" [*AWJ*, 197]), that it is a part of a larger system of intertextuality that includes texts from what is now called the Auden group. And once we recognize the incorporation of the thirties song lyric into the poem as Audenesque, it is not surprising that its presence in Larkin should be so frequently intertwined with texts from Auden or other poets of the Auden group. "Two Guitar Pieces (No. 1)," as we have seen, has digested a curious mixture of the blues and an Auden poem titled "No Change of Place." "Aubade" fuses a whole system of practices associated with Auden—primarily those involved in writing against the expectations of the genre—with conventions of the blues. What makes "Lines on a Young Lady's Photograph Album" a particularly interesting poem intertextually is that in addition to the thirties popular song lyric it is informed by another identifiable text from an Auden group poet, C. Day Lewis's "The Album," one of six poems by Day Lewis selected by Larkin for *The Oxford Book of Twentieth-Century English Verse.*

"Lines" has incorporated the situation of "The Album," its point of view, and its primary theme, although in the service of a very different kind of effect. David Timms, who has also noticed the link between the two poems, writes, "Both poems start from the experience of looking at snapshots in an album, both poems are addressed to the subject of the photographs, and both lead to a reflection on how the past affects us in the present." He adds that there "is no other similarity," but the Larkin text is so obviously a response to the Day Lewis poem that it is constantly present in our reading of "Lines" once we recognize its

27. W. H. Auden and Christopher Isherwood, *Plays and Other Dramatic Writings by W. H. Auden, 1928–1938,* ed. Edward Mendelson (Princeton, 1988), 211.

presence. The structure of "Lines," for example, its movement from stanza to stanza, is from "pose to pose." It uses the succession of photographs as a way through the poem, and this is the organizing principle of "The Album," each of the five stanzas beginning with a new photograph or a turning of the page: "I see you, a child / In a garden sheltered for buds and playtime . . ."; "Then I turn the page / To a girl who stands like a questioning iris / By the waterside . . ."; "Next you appear / As if garlands of wild felicity crowned you . . ."; "One picture is missing . . ."; "I close the book. . . ." The unease of the Larkin persona at the sight of "these disquieting chaps who loll / At ease about your earlier days" and his characterization of them—"Not quite your class, I'd say, dear, on the whole"—is the Cole Porter version of a more heavy-handed passage in the earlier poem:

> Courted, caressed, you wear
> Like immortelles the lovers and friends around you.
> 'They will not last you, rain or shine,
> They are but straws and shadows,'
> I cry: 'Give not to those charming desperadoes
> What was made to be mine.'[28]

The Larkin persona's threat to remove "this one of you bathing" is a witty version of the more serious missing photograph in "The Album." "Lines" is, in short, a rewriting of "The Album," although "Lines" is the more engaging poem.

Timms believes that a comparison of the two shows that the Day Lewis poem is artificial, the Larkin poem more real, shaped by actual experience. The Day Lewis poem "is unified by the metaphors and similes, and the objects of each photograph: the girl is always surrounded by flowers." And blossoms become the controlling metaphor, running through each stanza. "Day Lewis erects a scaffolding of metaphors to keep the poem together—it is artificial, though not in any pejorative sense of that word." With the Larkin poem, however, "[w]e are con-

28. Timms, *Philip Larkin*, 76; C. Day Lewis, *Poems of C. Day Lewis, 1925–1972*, chosen and with an introduction by Ian Parsons (London, 1977), 124–25.

vinced not that the poet has brought a mood to the experience, but that the experience is actively shaping his mood." Like other Larkin critics of the realist school, Timms needs to argue that the poem is not "literary." Referring to a poem written a few months later, he notes, "Like 'Lines on a Young Lady's Photograph Album,' 'I Remember, I Remember' has a literary antecedent—though both poems arise from experiences other than literary ones."[29]

The conclusion I draw from a comparison of the two poems is nearly the opposite. It is possible to specify some of the experiences from which Larkin's poem "arose." It was written for Winifred Arnott (later Bradshaw), who has described for Andrew Motion some of the differences between the albums Larkin saw and the details of the poem (*Life*, 233–34). The primary experiences that shape it, give it its finished form, are, however, literary and musical. If the poem seems less "literary" than its immediate precursor, C. Day Lewis's "The Album," its more distant precursor, Tennyson's *The Princess*, the text to which its "sweet girl-graduate" directs us, and a whole system of poetic conventions designated by its old-fashioned title, that is because it draws its tone, its speaking voice, in part from nonliterary texts, in brief, American popular music, although these popular texts are no closer to actual experience. "Poems don't come from other poems, they come from being oneself, in life," Larkin said. "Lines on a Young Lady's Photograph Album," the poem sometimes put forward as supporting this proposition, actually refutes it, although as we have seen in Simon Frith's characterization of rock music, "To be authentic and to sound authentic . . . is the same thing." "Lines" obviously does not *sound* like its more traditional precursor "The Album." To suggest, however, that its sound is that of real emotion or actual experience is to misread it altogether, to mistake the sophisticated and idealizing conventions of the Cole Porter song for the conventions of verisimilitude attributed to photography. This is not to say, however, that the incorporation of popular music will customarily lead the poem in the direction taken by "Lines." The Cole Porter song is a special case. The conventions of popular

29. Timms, *Philip Larkin*, 77, 79.

music on the whole move in a different direction, call for responses that are closer to the sense of the real that Larkin's speaker praises in the photograph, and I will look at a different set of expectations associated with popular music in the next chapter.

6

THE CLICHÉ AND THE POPULAR SONG

Bob Dylan's art does not traffic in clichés, but it travels far and near by the vehicle of cliché. For what could a popular song be which scorned or snubbed cliché?

—Christopher Ricks, "Clichés"

He bought Maeve a copy of "Yesterday" and played it over and over, the combination of the gin and Paul McCartney's voice turning the listeners to sentimental jellies. Gin and the ambience might also account for his claim that Bob Dylan's "Mr Tambourine Man" was the best song ever written.

—Jean Hartley, *Philip Larkin,*
the Marvell Press, and Me

To profess to hear snatches of jazz or blues or popular songs in Larkin's texts is not to claim to hear music playing but to note the presence of some mode of expression identified with a particular musical genre, say the hortatory language of "For Sidney Bechet" ("Oh, play that thing!") or the metrical equivalent of syncopation in the opening of "Aubade." But of course "For Sidney Bechet" is not jazz and "Aubade" is not a blues, even if it is possible to specify jazz and blues conventions that inform them. And "Lines on a Young Lady's Photograph Album" is not a popular song; it is unmistakably a Philip Larkin poem. Beyond the Cole Porter rhyming of one of its stanzas, however, it seems to obey some more pervasive and distinctive musical rule of expression that reminds readers of lines of popular song. When William Pritchard hears lines in the poem "that seem to have come out of some Golden Treasury of Popular Song,"[1] he does not say what prompts the association, but one cannot fault his ear, and if he and other readers are in fact responding to the presence of musical conventions in the verse, it should be possible to identify them.

One of the exemplary popular music lines Pritchard extracts from the poem is "Not quite your class, I'd say, dear, on the whole." It has the sound of a line from a thirties show tune, but what, specifically, gives it that feeling? I would suggest that in addition to its Cole Porter tone it (almost) qualifies as a line from a popular song because it sets cliché-ridden language to a distinctive rhythmic beat. If we take *cliché* in its broadest sense as stereotyped expression, we recognize that the line is in fact composed entirely of clichés. Including "dear," which has attained that status as a term of address in popular song ("baby" and "mama" are equivalent blues terms), the line is made up of four clichéd expressions, the other three consisting of a variation of "not in your class" and two examples of what Eric Partridge in his *Dictionary of Clichés* calls "formulas that have become mere counters"[2]—"I would say" and "on the whole." And the most banal of these, "on the whole," occupies the most prominent position, ending the line and furnishing the rhyme.

The line is unusual in its willingness to indulge in the naked cliché. In other passages in the poem the language suggests the triteness of

1. Pritchard, "Larkin's Presence," 77.

2. In *A Dictionary of Clichés* (London, 1978), Eric Partridge defines the cliché as "an outworn commonplace; a phrase, or short sentence, that has become so hackneyed that careful speakers and scrupulous writers shrink from it because they feel that its use is an insult to the intelligence of their audience or public" (2). Christopher Ricks notes wittily that Partridge's definition demonstrates that the "only way to speak of a cliché is with a cliché," and asks "what, as a metaphor, could be more hackneyed than *hackneyed*, more outworn than *outworn*?" ("Clichés," 54).

popular music slightly doctored. The conclusion of the sixth stanza—
"you / Contract my heart by looking out of date"—approaches the
hackneyed effect of the popular song but backs away from it with
contract, the word that more than any other dictates our reading of the
line (and is clearly not a part of the vocabulary of popular song). The
pun on "you contract my heart" is multileveled and intellectual, not
immediately accessible to the reader as it would be in song. It is the
poetic equivalent of the more banal "you make my heart stand still"
or "you touch my heart" (with a faint suggestion of infecting it, as one
might contract a disease), but it is also a way of saying "I pledge my
heart to you," *contract* now in the sense of *betroth*. One of its effects is
to maintain the sophisticated tone of the stanza—its cleverness keeps
the speaker at a certain distance from his heart—but the language is
also important in allowing the line both to allude to the cliché that
underlies it, "you break my heart" or one of its near equivalencies, and
to rise above it. The line, that is, establishes its significance by appealing
to the reader's associations with the underlying commonplace—the
matrix by which we understand the significance of "you / Contract my
heart," which would otherwise appear nonsensical—but the variation
on the cliché allows the poem to retain its literary status. A popular
song, however, one entitled "Old-Fashioned Girl" perhaps, might well
relish the line "You touch my heart by looking out of date," since it is
composed of not one but two clichés, and popular music has welcomed
what poetry traditionally has been taught to avoid or to disguise.

Once a poetic lover has uttered the word *heart*, he is already danger-
ously near the world of cliché even if his utterance is *heartfelt* or comes
from *the bottom of his heart* or is said with *all his heart* or to *his heart's
content* or with *heart and soul*, or even if *his heart is in the right place*
or *his heart is in his mouth* or *he has a heart of gold* or a *heart as big as
all outdoors*. "A cliché begins as heartfelt, and then its heart sinks,"
writes Christopher Ricks in his instructive essay on clichés, song lyrics,
and poetry. "But no song about lovers and their hearts can afford to
turn away from those truths which may never get old but whose turns
of phrase have got old and grey and full of sleep. The trouble with a
cliché like *take it to heart* is that by now it's almost impossible to take

it to heart." Ricks is examining the way popular songs, in particular the songs of Bob Dylan, take the cliché to heart, and it happens that Dylan does play on *take it to heart* in "I Threw It All Away":

> So if you find someone that gives you all of her love,
> Take it to your heart, don't let it stray. . . .

The slight alteration from "take it to heart" to "take it to *your* heart," Ricks notes, is just enough to make it "heartfelt." (Another demonstration of his perception that it is only with a cliché that one can speak of a cliché.) The *it* of the cliché is important because it replaces the expected *her* in the second line: "there is the tiny touching swerve from 'someone' in the previous line—you'd think it was going to be 'So if you find someone that gives you all of her love / Take *her* to your heart,' and take her in your arms."[3]

Ricks demonstrates the manner in which Dylan refreshes the cliché, makes it new, and I will return to that, but I want to begin with his recognition that clichés are essential to the lyrics of popular music; they could not exist without them. In Dylan's "I Threw It All Away," to stay with that example (and one example is almost as good as another in this clichéd embarrassment of riches), we find "I treated her like a fool," "I threw it all away," "I had [it] in the palm of my hand," "I never knew what I had," "Love . . . makes the world go 'round," and "Take a tip from one who's tried."[4] I am interested in the cliché as a mode of expression in popular music because it turns up so frequently in Larkin's texts with (I will argue) similar consequences. Larkin's poems share with the songs of Dylan—Dylan as a representative of pop music from the sixties on and as its presiding genius—an unabashed devotion to the cliché, unoriginal or stereotypical expression, phrases from which serious poets might be expected to shrink. I am not arguing that this tendency gives Larkin's poems the sound or rhythm of popular songs, although that is sometimes the result, as it is in "Lines on a Young

---

3. Ricks, "Clichés," 62–63; Bob Dylan, *The Songs of Bob Dylan* (New York, 1980), 116–17.

4. Dylan, *Songs of Bob Dylan,* 114–17.

Lady's Photograph Album." It is rather the *popular* aspect of the popular song that the cliché brings to the fore. The resulting poems are not in any real sense popular verse nor may they be properly read with the sort of attention customarily devoted to popular literature. Many of them, however, wear the guise of texts designed for popular appeal, and it is the disguise that interests me here.

Before turning to Larkin's texts it is useful to inquire into the performance of cliché in popular songs. What accounts for their devotion to the cliché? Is it simply that these texts are unaware of their banality? In his essay "Why Do Songs Have Words?" Simon Frith defends the apparent banality of pop music lyrics by arguing that they are in some sense *about* ordinary language. A general point "to make about all pop songs," he writes, is that "they work on ordinary language." In "putting words to music, songwriters give them a new sort of resonance and power." Sociologists of pop culture have been concerned with "lyrical content, truth and realism," but "they have neglected to analyse the ways in which songs are about themselves, about language." Frith contends that it has taken the modern literary artist—Auden, MacNeice, Graham Greene, Brecht—to recognize the resonance of pop lyrics. For Brecht, "the appeal of pop lyrics lay in their ability to open up language— Brecht used the rhymes and rhythms of popular clichés to say significant things *and* to expose the common-sense phrases in which such things are usually said."[5]

Frith's argument is that the effect of the clichéd language and slang of popular music lyrics is to "defamiliarize" the language of the everyday

---

5. Frith, "Why Do Songs Have Words?" 121. My discussion of the cliché in popular music is based in large part on the accounts given in Frith's essay and in Richard Middleton's *Studying Popular Music* (Philadelphia, 1990). Although the designations "pop music" and "popular music" are often used interchangeably, some music commentators would make the distinction that Middleton makes in *Pop Music and the Blues,* 144: Pop is "the popular music of adolescents—and post-adolescent sympathisers—from Rock 'n' Roll onwards, and is not to be confused with older, still continuing styles of popular music—though Pop itself does not always avoid such confusion." That is, pop music is a form of popular music, but popular music (the prerock style of popular music that continues to be written and played) is not pop music.

world, and this concept turns up frequently in the commentary on pop culture. In an essay cited by Frith, David Lodge writes, "Slang is the poetry of ordinary speech in a precise linguistic sense; it draws attention to itself *qua* language, by deviating from accepted linguistic norms, substituting figurative expressions for literal ones, and thus 'defamiliarizes' the concepts it signifies." Slang, Lodge concludes, "must answer some genuine linguistic need and possess some distinctive rhetorical appeal, which it would be worth trying to analyze and understand."[6]

In *Studying Popular Music* Richard Middleton makes the same argument about the language of popular song. "For the most part," he writes, "the language used is everyday language—clichéd, trite, familiar—though it may be reassembled into new combinations. The point is to 'defamiliarize the familiar,' to invest the banal with effective force and kinetic grace, to draw out of the concrete world of denotation some sense of those human generalities translated by musical processes." This strategy of defamiliarization Middleton traces back to British music hall lyrics and forward to the words of rap and reggae. It is also responsible, he argues, for much of the success of the early Beatles, whose lyrics depended on the "magical musicalization of the everyday," the cliché set to music—"with love from me to you," "I wanna hold your hand," "you know what I mean," "you know that can't be bad."[7]

Clive James, who writes of Larkin that he "has no special poetic voice" but simply brings out "the poetry that is already in the world," notes also that the genius of the Beatles was to "take a well-worn phrase and make it new again." The process is that of defamiliarization. "The sudden shift of weight to an unexpected place continually brought the listener's attention to the language itself, engendering a startled awareness of the essentially poetic nature of flat phrases he'd been living with for years." Far from displaying a lack of awareness of the banality of their words, James argues, the songwriter's art is to hear "the spoken

6. David Lodge, "Where It's At: California Language," in *The State of the Language*, ed. Leonard Michaels and Christopher Ricks (Berkeley, 1980), 506.

7. Middleton, *Studying Popular Music*, 229.

language as a poem," to value words "not for their sense alone but for their poise and balance."[8]

How do popular songs bring the listener's attention to the language itself? How do they "musicalize the everyday"? There is presumably no single process at work, but the effect must be a product of the exchange between ordinary language and extraordinary rhythms and melodies, which restress a familiar phrase or alter a commonplace expression so minutely that it takes on new life. "Writing poetry," Larkin said, "is playing off the natural rhythms and word-order of speech against the artificialities of rhyme and metre" (*RW*, 71). This could, with only slight alteration (adding the adjective "commonplace" to "speech"), stand as the formula for the success of the popular song, with the emphasis on the "playing off" of the natural, even the mundane, against the artificial.

In a lecture called "Fascinating Rhythm" Roy Fuller offers an instance of this process, the coming together of the banality of language and the sophistication of melody and rhythm, or, as he phrases it, an instance of music "discovering subtleties in the most commonplace of words." The trite phrase is "How long has this been going on?" and the musician is George Gershwin:

[W]hen he has to set that, a line of regular iambic tetrameter, surely he sees how banal it would be to emphasize the word "this" as the underlying stress pattern of the words requires: "How lòng has thìs been gòing òn?" What he does is to give the line three beats only—on "long," the first syllable of "going" and on "on." The three middle words, including the word "this," are unaccented, giving the effect of a little skip in the middle of the line—"How lòng has this been gòing òn?" It is the action itself and the action's duration that Gershwin brings out, and how right it seems when he does it.[9]

Oddly, Larkin also had his turn at exploring the subtleties of these commonplace words, although perhaps not so successfully as Gershwin. The title of a review in *All What Jazz* that features, among other

<hr/>

8. James, "On His Wit," 105; James's comments on the Beatles are quoted in Frith, "Why Do Songs Have Words?" 122.

9. Roy Fuller, "Fascinating Rhythm," in *Professors and Gods: Last Oxford Lectures on Poetry* (New York, 1973), 86.

recordings, Armstrong's rendition of the Gershwin song is "How Long This Has Been Going On!" The alteration is just enough to make us look at the words again and to hear their strange new beat against the more familiar older rhythm. This example reminds us also of the extent to which the titles of these reviews have so openly absorbed the cliché. The title of the collection itself, for example, manages to shift the original sense of the phrase "all that jazz," as well as its rhythm, with the substitution of one letter. Sometimes the titles allow the banality of the cliché to stand alone—"Having a Ball," "Don't Go 'Way Nobody," "Thundering Herds," "Wandering Minstrels," "How Do We Stand?" "Home Fires Burning," "Great Expectations," "Just Around the Corner," "Moment of Truth," "Founding Fathers." Sometimes the cliché is the basis for saying something new, and these titles provide a primitive set of examples of the way intertextuality functions, the phrase depending on the presence of the cliché it encloses for its significance (however small), as in "Survival of the Hottest" (Pee Wee Russell at fifty-six), "Horn in a Dilemma" (Bix Beiderbecke's bad career choices), "The Holy Growl" (James "Bubber" Miley as a growl trumpeter), and a host of others—"Bands Across the Sea," "Old Man Mainstream," "Twilight of Two Old Gods," "Record-Making History."

All What Jazz is of course a kind of journalism, and we might expect in these reviews an appeal to the language of the newspaper, but when we come to the poems, we will see that the openly displayed cliché is one of their most pervasive means of expression. The table of contents of the *Collected Poems* offers an abundance of examples—"Next, Please," "Born Yesterday," "Church Going," "First Sight," "Far Out," "As Bad as a Mile," "Take One Home for the Kiddies," "Wild Oats," "Send No Money," "Long Last."[10] Larkin's titles are particularly blatant in their

10. That Larkin's use of the title cliché was the common practice for Tin Pan Alley songs is perhaps obvious, but the point is made dramatically in Philip Furia's list of famous songs in which "the most banal colloquial idioms were lifted into the romantic space of a lyric": "I Guess I'll Have to Change My Plan," "I Can't Get Started," "What'll I Do?" "Sure Thing," "There'll Be Some Changes Made," "How About Me?" "How Long Has This Been Going On?" "It Never Entered My Mind," "It's All Right with Me," "Just One of Those Things," "You Took Advantage of Me," "I Didn't Know What Time It

dependence on commonplaces and clichés. In the poems these may be altered slightly, disguised, or shifted from their original contexts, as in "let the cluttered-up houses / Keep their thick lives to themselves" in "Arrival" (*CP*, 51); "where my childhood was unspent" in "I Remember, I Remember" (*CP*, 81); "Where bridal London bows [looks] the other way" in "Deceptions" (*CP*, 32); or the play on "wine, women, and song" in the opening line of "The Dance" (*CP*, 154), "Drink, sex, and jazz."

What is the appeal of the cliché for Larkin? Or, to put the question in a form in which it can be more easily addressed, how does the cliché function in Larkin's texts? What is its significance, its effect? Can we say, as Simon Frith says of musical cliché, that Larkin's texts are in some sense *about* this kind of language or at least about themselves as texts that use this kind of language? "In the best of songs," Christopher Ricks has written in an essay on Bob Dylan, "there is something which is partly about what it is to write a song, without in any way doing away with the fact that it is about things *other* than just the song."[11] Ricks is referring to the way Dylan's songs are about how they end— they keep asking how long one can go on doing something. But in another and larger sense one could say that a Dylan song is partly about what it is to write a particular *kind* of song or a song with a particular set of social and cultural references. Dylan's songs keep asking us to think of his songs and of him as a singer/songwriter in a particular way (which is why his fans kept feeling betrayed as his songs continued to redefine the Dylan song).

Any self-conscious text is partly about its own production, its choices, its struggles with the principles of expression it has adopted, the system

---

Was," "Say It with Music," "Say It Isn't So," "Don't Get Around Much Anymore," "I'm Beginning to See the Light," "You're Driving Me Crazy," "Ain't Misbehavin'," "I Should Care," "They Can't Take That Away From Me," "From This Moment On," "I Don't Stand a Ghost of a Chance," "Everything Happens to Me," "Day by Day," "Night and Day," "Day In—Day Out." The list, he notes, "could go, as a more recent song has it, 'On and On'" (*Poets of Tin Pan Alley*, 11).

11. Christopher Ricks, "Can This Really Be the End?" in *Conclusions on the Wall: New Essays on Bob Dylan*, ed. Elizabeth Thomson (Manchester, 1980), 48.

of references to which it appeals, but jazz, blues, and popular music are particularly self-referential, like countless musicals about staging musicals. How many blues are about singing the blues? Jazz typically "sang songs about itself," as Larkin remarks (*AWJ*, 260), and Middleton points out the degree to which rock lyrics may be "about nothing but the music"—in a song like "Jailhouse Rock," for example, or Bill Haley's "Rock Around the Clock," or "Shake, Rattle, and Roll."[12] To say that the clichéd language or slang of Larkin's texts is self-consciously *about* itself, that it calls attention to the way it differs from the language of more traditional poems is obviously true, so obvious as not to be particularly fruitful as a method of approaching Larkin's commonplaces. When a Larkin poem such as "High Windows" uses the word *fucking*, for example, it is in a real sense *about* the use of such language in a "serious" poem.

Beyond self-reference, however, another crucial set of references defines the world the song pretends to inhabit and establishes the basis for its reception. Dave Laing speaks of the "universe" of Buddy Holly's music as fixed by the "high school courting code" of Everly Brothers songs. Middleton argues that one of the sources of the vitality of ordinary language in the popular song is "the rootedness of the words in the concrete reality of the here-and-now," and he agrees with Laing that for a large segment of pop music it is the language of the high school courting culture, a set of references immediately available to the teenage audience, that "places the songs in a particular social setting, a 'human universe' first explored by Chuck Berry and the Coasters." That is to say that the very banality of pop song lyrics is perceived as a source of their "realism." The cliché is a part of their rootedness in the here-and-now because it is the language of the here-and-now (or, more exactly, the here-and-now is no more or less than the *language* of the here-and-now). As Michael Riffaterre has noted of poetry, a text is seen as "true" because "it conforms to a mythology that the reader carries within him, a mythology composed of clichés and commonplaces."[13]

12. Middleton, *Pop Music and the Blues,* 159–60.

13. Laing, *Sound of Our Time,* 101; Middleton, *Studying Popular Music,* 229; Riffaterre, *Text Production,* 185.

Pop songs may be *about* clichéd language, then, in more than one sense. In the sense that this language places the song in a particular social setting, conjures up a descriptive system of manners, customs, habitual behavior, forms of address, courting rituals, the language is inseparable from the world to which it refers its audience. And the principle at work here—the degree of "realism" is in proportion to the audience's ability to identify the song's intertext, its system of reference, with the language by which they know their world—would appear to apply equally well to Larkin's poetry. To stay at the level of titles, the differences between the texts conjured up by Larkin's cliché-dependent titles and those of, say, the titles of the sections of Eliot's *Waste Land* are immediately obvious. The texts by which we read titles like "Next, Please" or "Take One Home for the Kiddies" or "Send No Money" are the commonplaces of the everyday world of business and advertising. Eliot's titles refer us to a set of texts far removed from this world—the Anglican burial service, two plays by Thomas Middleton, the Buddha's Fire Sermon, and a Hindu fable.[14] A Middleton play is no less real than an advertising slogan, but the intertextual significance of *The Waste Land*'s titles is obviously inaccessible to the reader (even the competent reader) not in possession of the notes of the Eliot scholar or of Eliot's own notes. And even in possession of these notes the reader has no sense that the poem is, as Richard Middleton puts it, rooted in the here-and-now.

To acknowledge the distance between the cultural levels of Eliot's and Larkin's intertextual references is only to say in other terms what we already know. Larkin's poems display a commonplace "reality" that *The Waste Land* eschews; *The Waste Land* is hard going, while Larkin's texts are relatively accessible, and so on down a long list that details Larkin's departure from high modernism. A. T. Tolley frames the distinction between Larkin and the modernists in these terms: "Larkin does

---

14. Some of Eliot's rejected titles do, however, approach banality, "Wanna Go Home, Baby?" and "Who Killed the Archbishop?" for example. The most famous of these, "He Do the Police in Different Voices," preserves its literary status by serving as an allusion to *Our Mutual Friend*.

not find himself, like Yeats and Eliot, seeking to order things through an obscure and invented personal symbolism. The order that he finds is the momentary order that reveals itself in our everyday commerce with experience, and the objects of that everyday experience provide the readily apprehended images of his poetry."[15] In his attack on modernism in the introduction to *All What Jazz*, Larkin sees the issue as modernism's slackening or breaking of the bond between the artist and the audience. The result is "mystification," the obscurity of modern art (*AWJ*, 23), which suggests that one of the obvious motives for a poet to revert to commonplace expression is to reestablish this lost bond with the audience. I will return to the issue of the audience in the next chapter, although I am not as much concerned with the "real" audience, the people who buy and read these poems, as with the audience the poems conventionally assume for themselves. The questions I raise here have to do with the function of clichés in particular texts, and I begin with works by Bob Dylan and Larkin that are constructed on the same cliché.

Bob Dylan's "When the Ship Comes In" incorporates an expression more often spoken in the first person. In *The Dictionary of Clichés* James Rogers explains the American sense of the phrase in this way:

When My Ship Comes In. When I get rich; when I achieve success, thereby making a pile of money. Many investors ashore were likely to have a financial interest in the cargo carried by a merchant ship in the days of sail, when travel and communication were slow. Since it was uncertain when such a ship would arrive, the people with financial interest had to wait quite anxiously and to worry about "when the ship comes in."

The song and its refrain ("The hour when the ship comes in") depend on the listener's familiarity with the cliché and with its financial associations (there is a reference to the unrolling of a "carpet of gold" in the third verse), but the song shifts the expression to a religious or, more properly, apocalyptic context. The hour when the ship comes in is not the moment of long-awaited financial success but the moment when the ordinary

---

15. Tolley, *My Proper Ground,* 152.

world is disrupted in an apocalyptic vision, when "the fishes will laugh,"
and "the seagulls they'll be smiling," when "the chains of the sea" will
be broken and "the foes" will "be drowned in the tide / And like Goliath
they'll be conquered":

> Oh the time will come up
> When the winds will stop
> And the breeze will cease to be breathin'
> Like the stillness in the wind
> 'Fore the hurricane begins
> The hour when the ship comes in.
>
> Oh the seas will split
> And the ship will hit
> And the shoreline sands will be shaking
> Then the tide will sound
> And the wind will pound
> And the morning will be breaking.[16]

The song uses the same strategy as several others composed at the
time, in which a clichéd phrase refers to a moment of reckoning when
present wrongs will be righted—"The answer, my friend, is blowin' in
the wind" or "It's a hard rain's a gonna fall." In all three instances it
is the cliché line that appears to resolve the issue of the song, even if
we're never quite sure in "When the Ship Comes In" or "A Hard Rain's
A Gonna Fall" exactly what the issue is. In his review of Dylan's album
Highway 61 Revisited Larkin refers to the "enchanting tune and mysteri-
ous, possibly half-baked words" of "Desolation Row," and he admits
of the album (which he praises) that "much of it was unintelligible to
me" (*AWJ*, 151). One value of the cliché in a song such as "When the
Ship Comes In" is that, drawing its meaning from the cultural storehouse
rather than strictly from the song's context, it is accessible beyond the
song's cryptic use of it. We know that the phrase is associated with
long-awaited success and, even more pertinent to an apocalyptic text,
that it is associated with the dream of a triumph that may never come—

---

16. James Rogers, *The Dictionary of Clichés* (New York, 1985), 288; Bob Dylan, *Bob
Dylan Song Book* (New York, 1970), 86–87.

people who use the phrase are typically those whose ships will never come in. In his entry on the phrase James Rogers quotes Henry Mayhew in his *London Labour and the London Poor:* " 'One [customer] always says he'll give me a ton of taties [potatoes] when his ship comes home.' "[17] That is, the phrase brings with it a wish-fulfillment element that the song extends with its own fantasy language of laughing fishes and smiling gulls—one day all our troubles will be over, it says, but we need not be too specific about how or when this will take place. The cliché is gnomic enough to forestall literal interpretation but instantly accessible in its own terms. It is, as Lodge says of slang, a kind of common language poetry—poetic in that it calls attention to itself as language and to the concept it signifies.

"Dylan has a newly instinctive grasp of the age-old instincts which created a cliché in the first place," Ricks notes, "and this is manifest on all the occasions when he throws new light on an old cliché, or rotates a cliché so that a facet of it catches a new light." Transposing a cliché of materialism to an altogether different situation in "When the Ship Comes In," he gives it a new meaning—creates, paradoxically, a new cliché. It is the phrasing, the language of the cliché that Dylan's music typically celebrates, repeating it again and again at the most climactic moments of the song, appropriating it. "Don't think twice, it's all right" or "like a rolling stone" are no longer clichés but Bob Dylan lyrics. (The latter, which refers us to one of the most familiar and hackneyed of clichés, had already been rehabilitated in Muddy Waters's 1954 "Rollin' Stone," and had become attached to a rock group and a rock magazine.) As Ricks notes, Dylan's art travels "by the vehicle of cliché";[18] even if cliché is one of the essential qualities of all popular music, in Dylan it is redoubled, raised to another level.

In Larkin's texts as well the cliché appears to have been raised to another level. It achieves at the very least a position unprecedented in the verse of a major English poet. Given the chance to comment on the way the "common phrase" functions in his poems, however, Larkin

17. Dylan, *Bob Dylan Song Book,* 20, 23; Rogers, *Dictionary of Clichés,* 288.
18. Ricks, "Clichés," 61.

passed it up. *"You use a lot of idioms and very common phrases—for irony, I'd guess, or to bear more meaning than usual, never for shock value,"* the interviewer for the *Paris Review* ventures. *"Do these phrases come late, to add texture or whatever, or are they integral from the beginning?"* "They occur naturally," Larkin replies and does not elaborate further (*RW*, 70–71). His answer is presumably that they are there from the beginning, that they are not an artificial device but a natural quality of speech. Elsewhere, he admits that his use of slang in particular does have shock value: "I mean, these words are part of the palette. You use them when you want to shock." He adds, however, "I don't think I've shocked for the sake of shocking."[19]

Janice Rossen, who notes that Larkin's vulgar language is drawn from the "flat, uninventive pool of words held in common by the prototypical 'common man,'" finds it impossible to say whether the motive for Larkin's use of such language is the cultivation of "an adolescent sensibility in order to shock his readers" or an announcement of "his solidarity with the common man." Or perhaps it is neither. Perhaps "Larkin, in using this diction, means exactly what he says." Barbara Everett reads Larkin's poetic development as "a pursuit of truth which is also a flight from 'Art,'" and the commonplace phrase contributes to both ends. She says of one such expression (in "Livings 1") that it "half-ironically half-salutes that densely actual commonplace existence that all Larkin's poems 'invent' as their subject." Larkin would no doubt agree. He told John Haffenden, "I don't want to transcend the commonplace, I love the commonplace, I lead a very commonplace life. Everyday things are lovely to me."[20] This speaks to Larkin's sense of his motive in choosing a certain level of language, to evoke the commonplace, or to "invent" it, as Everett suggests, and that may well describe the general effect of Larkin's language. But is it possible to examine in closer detail the function or the effect of the common phrase in a particular text, a poem such as his own version of "When the Ship Comes In"?

19. Haffenden, *Viewpoints*, 128.

20. Rossen, *Philip Larkin: His Life's Work*, 95; Everett, "Art and Larkin," 130, 135; Haffenden, *Viewpoints*, 124.

Larkin's version, "Next, Please" (*CP*, 52), is not a rewriting of the Dylan song—the poem preceded the song—but both are rewritings of the cliché "when my ship comes in," or its British variant "when my ship comes home."[21] Although, interestingly, the cliché itself does not appear in the poem, it dictates almost every line, and it is the hypogram (in Riffaterre's term), the commonplace or conventional expression by which we understand the significance of lines and phrases ("Sparkling armada of promises," "unload / All good into our lives") and by which we understand the significance of the shift to the "black- / Sailed unfamiliar" in the last stanza. While Dylan's song uses the expression for its own purposes, exploring its language, altering its meaning, appropriating it, Larkin's poem is *about* the cliché. It is about the cliché in general, the unexamined commonplaces by which we live our lives, and about *this* cliché—not just its language or phrasing (which are not present) but the *meaning* of the expression "when my ship comes home" as it has become a part of a culture's collection of such phrases and concepts. The poem's ultimate motive is to expose the concept contained in the cliché, which may be one reason the cliché itself does not appear. The poem depends on the reader supplying what has been omitted, on being in possession of what the poem requires for its significance, since it is the *reader's* illusion, articulated by the cliché, that the poem examines. (Although he tactfully speaks in the first person plural—"we / Pick up bad habits"; "we say"—the speaker has already disabused himself of the view the poem considers.) The poem unmasks the cliché's illusory nature by literalizing it, requiring the reader to look again at what has been disguised by its figurative language. It does what Dylan's song could not afford to do lest it undermine itself, that is, to expose the wish-fulfillment associations of the phrase, its status as self-deception.

The poem is in fact constructed upon two clichés, not only "when my ship comes home" but also the "next, please" of the title. It turns the first cliché on its head, suggesting a meaning opposite to that the reader presumably holds, but as it does so, the reader may recognize that the significance of the cliché of the title has simultaneously shifted,

21. See Partridge, *Dictionary of Clichés*, 250.

having escaped the meaning the poem originally assigns to it ("what's next?") and being restored to its meaning outside the poem, the one the reader presumably holds ("who's next?"). The opening stanzas of the poem attach the commonplace expression "next, please" to our naïve belief in the future as the source of happiness:

> Always too eager for the future, we
> Pick up bad habits of expectancy.
> Something is always approaching; every day
> *Till then* we say,
>
> Watching from a bluff the tiny, clear,
> Sparkling armada of promises draw near.
> How slow they are! And how much time they waste,
> Refusing to make haste!
>
> Yet still they leave us holding wretched stalks
> Of disappointment, for, though nothing balks
> Each big approach, leaning with brasswork prinked,
> Each rope distinct,
>
> Flagged, and the figurehead with golden tits
> Arching our way, it never anchors; it's
> No sooner present than it turns to past.

It is, the poem at first suggests, *we* who are asking "what's next?" on the assumption that something new is always approaching. In a letter to Robert Conquest Larkin mistakenly cited the poem as "What next?" (*Letters*, 236), recalling Yeats's poem on the same subject "What Then?" one of its primary literary intertexts. "What Then?" is a poetic version of the conclusion of *Reveries over Childhood and Youth:* "all life . . . seems to me a preparation for something that never happens." "Next, Please" is, in its early stanzas, a poem about the eagerness for the future contained in the refrain of "What Then?" that concludes each phase of a seemingly successful life: " '*What then?*' sang Plato's ghost, '*what then?*' "[22] In Yeats's version not even death ends this assumption that

22. William Butler Yeats, *Autobiographies* (London, 1956), 106; Yeats, *The Collected Works of W. B. Yeats*, Vol. I: *The Poems*, 302.

meaning and happiness always lie ahead, that the present is preparation for a future that never happens. In Larkin's rewriting of this commonplace of looking to the future, however, something decisive *is* eventually going to happen—"Something is always approaching." Our ship *is* coming in, although not in the way that we have expected. The difficulty of associating happiness with the future is that it arrives as the present and immediately turns to past. Or in terms of the poem's manipulation of the cliché through which we read it, our ship comes in but "it never anchors." Only one ship, that of the last stanza, escapes the endless cycle of our "bad habits of expectancy."

Beginning with the second stanza the cliché "when my ship comes in" is the referent for our understanding of the poem. That is, to whatever extent we find the poem "true," it is a truth that amounts to conformity to (or disagreement with) a linguistic formulation, a cultural commonplace. Riffaterre argues that this is true of all poems. "No advantage is to be gained by comparing literary expression to reality or by evaluating a work of literature in terms of such a comparison," he writes in *Text Production.* "Everything in what we call the signified is perceived in relation to clichés—in relation, that is, to word combinations, to signifiers." This is a way of saying that what matters to us as readers is "what is encoded," and in decoding the poem "the reader has no need to refer to his own experience of reality (which may be an inadequate one), because all he needs in order to understand and see is to refer to a linguistic code."[23]

We do not read "Next, Please," that is, by referring its language to external reality but to what Riffaterre calls the sociolect, a "repository of the myths, traditions, ideological and esthetic stereotypes, commonplaces, and themes harbored by a society, a class or a social group." A literary text shapes its own usage "in conformity or in contradistinction to the sociolect," since the sociolect contains the descriptive models and narratives that reflect the society's consensus about reality.[24] If we accept as a premise Riffaterre's contention that texts signify not by referring

---

23. Riffaterre, *Text Production,* 15, 184–85.
24. Michael Riffaterre, *Fictional Truth* (Baltimore, 1990), 130.

to "reality" but by referring to other "texts," to use the term in its broadest possible sense to include cultural commonplaces, we see that what is unusual about "Next, Please" is that it makes visible what is typically hidden in other poets' texts. And this is true of the function of the cliché generally in Larkin's texts and what makes them the poetic analogues of popular songs. Intertextual critics of Riffaterre's school hold that all artful texts are variants of commonplaces from the sociolect shared by the author and the audience. However, these are deeply buried in the text, retrieved occasionally with great effort and often not at all. In the texts of Larkin and of popular music, however, these commonplaces lie on the surface or, as in "Next Please," so close to the surface that the reader's possession of them is not usually in question.

Some of the effects of this practice are obvious. Such a text, like popular music, seems immediately accessible. In comparison to traditional poetic texts it will appear to lack "depth," to be all surface, not to require interpretation. Here, for example, is the poem's conclusion, where the ship of the cliché is given a new identity, but one we immediately recognize since it too has its significance in reference to the common phrase that serves as the poem's principal intertext:

> Right to the last
>
> We think each one will heave to and unload
> All good into our lives, all we are owed
> For waiting so devoutly and so long.
> But we are wrong:
>
> Only one ship is seeking us, a black-
> Sailed unfamiliar, towing at her back
> A huge and birdless silence. In her wake
> No waters breed or break.

Outside of "Aubade" there is arguably no more terrifying passage in all of Larkin than the image of extinction in the last stanza, and part of its force is due to the poem's success in finding an image for it to which readers can respond. In "Aubade" death is abstract, difficult to visualize—"Unresting death, a whole day nearer now," "The sure extinction that we travel to." In "Next, Please," however, it is given a form that we instinctively know since the cliché for the arrival of happiness is simply redirected. And rather than our seeking this black-sailed unfamiliar, it is seeking us. At this point—the point where we see that the poem has redefined the cliché that informs it—we may also recognize that it has restored the cliché of its title to its proper context. "Next, please" is not typically spoken *by* us but *to* us. It is spoken by shopkeepers, tellers, barbers, clerks of various trades at the point where we have reached the head of the line. According to Larkin's sister, the phrase "next, please" is one "he dreaded hearing as a child whenever he reached the head of a queue at school or in shops: it meant he would shortly have to speak, which would be embarrassing because of his stammer" (*Life*, 208). The poem is somewhat duplicitous in initially assigning the phrase to *us* as we await our ship coming in. *Our* "next, please" is ineffectual, as the poem demonstrates. It is more properly and more effectively spoken by death, the realization to which we have been led in the final stanza. What is important to recognize is that this realization has been attained through the text's manipulation of the two principal clichés that provide its full significance. A reader not in possession of these commonplaces would presumably find the development of the poem puzzling and somewhat arbitrary. A. T. Tolley, who seems, against all odds, to have missed Larkin's play with the principal cliché, characterizes the poem as "iconoclastic," an argument "worked out in terms of the analogy between hopes or expectations and approaching or passing ships."[25]

The trope of the last stanza, death as the eternal silence of the ocean, the future's one certainty, leads us to another literary intertext by which the significance of "Next, Please" may be complicated to a degree. It is a passage from Nietzsche's *The Joyful Wisdom* called "The Thought of Death," the principal trope of which, ironically, is not our ship coming in but departing. Nietzsche's text depends on a different set of commonplaces related to ships, these associated with emigration—a new land, a new lease on life, sailing away:

---

25. Tolley, *My Proper Ground*, 58.

It is always as in the last moment before the departure of an emigrant-ship: people have more than ever to say to one another, the hour presses, the ocean with its lonely silence waits impatiently behind all the noise—so greedy, so certain of its prey! And all, all, suppose that the past has been nothing, or a small matter, that the near future is everything: hence this haste, this crying, this self-deafening and self-overreaching! Everyone wants to be foremost in this—and yet death and the stillness of death are the only things certain and common to all in this future! How strange that this sole thing that is certain and common to all, exercises almost no influence on men, and that they are the *furthest* from regarding themselves as the brotherhood of death![26]

In Nietzsche's text the "lonely silence" of the ocean waiting "impatiently" for those about to enter its domain—"so greedy, so certain of its prey"—modulates effortlessly into "the stillness of death," the one thing "certain and common to all in this future" because it is associated with the future to which the emigrant ship sails. The ocean's vast emptiness is, literally, the immediate future of those embarking and, figuratively (as death), their ultimate future. The ocean as a figure for death in "Next, Please," on the other hand, does not evolve naturally from the cliché on which the poem is built, and it has to be hauled into the poem by sheer force. It is in fact literally towed by the ship when it finally comes in, although it is no longer ocean but a "huge and birdless silence" in which "No waters breed or break." This is clearly an instance of a triumph produced by a text's agility in overcoming obstacles imposed by its intertexts, how to make the *arrival* of a ship associated with happiness synonymous with death in the way that Nietzsche's text emblematizes the ship's departure into the ocean's lonely silence.

The Nietzsche passage also brings to the surface a characteristic of the poem it shares with other Larkin texts, one of the most distinctive qualities of the volume (*The Less Deceived*) in which it appears. We may approach it by comparing the perspectives of the two texts toward the common insight they contain (we live as if the future were the bearer

---

26. Friedrich Nietzsche, *The Joyful Wisdom,* trans. Thomas Common, Vol. X of *The Complete Works of Friedrich Nietzsche,* ed. Oscar Levy (New York, 1964), 215.

of all happiness and ignore the certainty that it brings only death). Nietzsche finds this irony a source of great joy: "It makes me happy to see that men do not want to think at all of the idea of death! I would fain do something to make the idea of life even a hundred times *more worthy of their attention.*"[27] One might feel that this is a perfectly reasonable, life-affirming position to take. What would be the motive for a text that took the opposite position, whose strategy was to lead its readers to the realization that all their assumptions about happiness are illusions and that the only promise the future holds is eternal oblivion? The poem's stated motive is contained in yet another cliché, which may account for the fact that we accept it as legitimate without looking at it too carefully. The poem says that to adopt Nietzsche's perspective, to ignore the certainty of death as much as possible and to persist in our attempts to find happiness in life, is to "Pick up bad habits," in this case habits of "expectancy." The poem succeeds by exposing as fraudulent one of the commonplaces by which (it assumes) we live, but its success also depends on leaving another such commonplace unexamined.

Why is expectation a bad habit, and why is it better to dwell on the certainty of eternal extinction than on the possibility of happiness? It seems proper to inquire into the poem's assumptions since it tries so hard to mask them through the manipulation of clichés. Nobody wants to pick up bad habits, but what are they in this case? Waiting for one's ship to come in, thinking "next, please," and saying *"till then."* These expressions come ready-made with certain associations that predetermine our response. By defining the expectation of happiness with an expression from the sociolect that we all share, the poem maneuvers us into the "reality" posited by the cliché. To expect to be happy is to be deceived, it says, and to dwell on the future only as the bearer of death is to be less deceived, and this hierarchy is clearly at work throughout the volume in which the poem appears. Its title *The Less Deceived* itself depends for its full significance on a literary intertext, the reversal of Ophelia's "I was the more deceived," her response to Hamlet's "I loved

---

27. Ibid., 215–16.

you not." According to his friend Jean Hartley, Larkin "relished the thought of his readers hunting through *Hamlet* to find Ophelia's words" and felt "that if readers picked up the Hamlet context, it would give them an insight into his basic passivity as regards poetry and life." Despite his attack on modernism's veneration of " 'tradition' or a common myth-kitty or casual allusions in poems to other poems or poets" (*RW*, 79), Larkin's view of his title's significance is not so far away from Riffaterre's argument that such literary fragments, ready-made narratives, descriptive models, commonplaces, epigrams of various kinds "reflect a group's idea of or consensus about reality."[28]

Expectancy is a bad habit, to return to the poem, if it results in self-deception—being less deceived constitutes the privileged concept in the poem and in the volume—but the poem finesses the question of whether the speaker's denial of happiness and his fixation on extinction might not also be a form of self-deception, a way, for example, of defending himself against the possibility of disappointments in life and love, as in Ophelia's case. The question of who is more or less deceived is an open one, although the clichés in which the argument is framed will not allow us to think about it in any other terms. We could easily select commonplaces and ready-made descriptive systems in which the desire for happiness appears in a more favorable light, in which expectancy is not considered a bad habit, and the desire for change—"next, please"— is regarded as a virtue. In the poem, as in the popular song, one of the effects of openly displayed clichés is to provide a coating of verisimilitude whereby we accept readily what we might balk at were it stated in less familiar terms. To give one answer to the question with which we began—what is the function of the cliché in "Next, Please"?—we may say that it is to provide the "reality" to which the poem answers. Although he does not speak of the cliché, Tolley notes that Larkin's poems "are frequently structured so as to invite or assume agreement or complicity with attitudes that are implied by means of what is taken for granted in passing." These he calls "the images of everyday reality,"

---

28. Jean Hartley, *Philip Larkin, the Marvell Press, and Me* (Manchester, 1989), 74, 82–83; Riffaterre, *Fictional Truth*, 130.

and he argues that they are used "with the expectation of assent to a particular attitude that the images evoke for speaker and reader."[29] I am suggesting that in "Next, Please" (and elsewhere) it is not so much the images of reality but the language by which we ordinarily evoke a commonplace reality that invites assent. If we accede to the poem's argument, it is because we accept its given, that the phrase "when my ship comes in" is the universe in which the poem has its significance.

The cliché functioning as the (unstated) reality to which the poem conforms may also be found in "Wires" (*CP*, 48), written a few months earlier. The expression that chiefly informs it is "the grass is always greener on the other side," obviously another example of our "bad habits of expectancy," since it posits that happiness is always elsewhere:

> The widest prairies have electric fences,
> For though old cattle know they must not stray
> Young steers are always scenting purer water
> Not here but anywhere.

The cliché obviously furnishes the poem's fences. It is the other side *of the fence,* of course, but "of the fence" is understood in the expression, not normally spoken. (Because of its familiarity it is usually shortened, all the way down to "the grass is always greener," which makes no sense without the assumption that the phrase is universally shared, an assumption also made by the poem.) The poem, it will be noted, has electrified the fences, altering the cliché to suggest in the second stanza the means by which the less deceived experience (in another unstated cliché) the "shock of recognition." The literal shock of blundering against the wires makes what was external a part of the senses:

> Beyond the wires
>
> Leads them to blunder up against the wires
> Whose muscle-shredding violence gives no quarter.
> Young steers become old cattle from that day,
> Electric limits to their widest senses.

29. Tolley, *My Proper Ground,* 181.

"Wires," like "Next, Please," deliberately and almost perversely avoids the principal expression on which it depends in much the same way that "The Building" (*CP*, 191) withholds the one word that gives every line its significance. The building is a hospital, but through sixty-four lines the poem stubbornly refuses to name what is being described in such close detail. It is as if the suppression of the word that controls everything else in the text reenacted the meaning the poem assigns to this anonymous building: "That is what it means, / This clean-sliced cliff; a struggle to transcend / The thought of dying." A similar absence informs "Going" (*CP*, 3), the original clichéd title of which, "Dying Day," would have given the trick away (the moment of death disguised as the close of day). In these poems the reader's task is analogous to solving a riddle; once the right word or phrase is provided, what was opaque or mysterious is lucid, even ordinary, as "what keep drawing up / At the entrance are not taxis" or "all // Here to confess that something has gone wrong" in "The Building." "Wires" substitutes "purer water" for greener grass, but the alteration is transparent. What is "Beyond the wires" and what we experience from our desire for it arc both dictated by the expression held in common by readers of the poem.

This is not to say that the appeal of poems like "Wires" and "Next, Please" is only to the "common reader," to an audience that customarily traffics in commonplaces. "Wires" is a more intricate poem than it first appears, and a reading that stays at the level of cliché will miss a great deal. As James Booth has noticed, the rhyme scheme—abcd dcba—is unusual in that the second stanza is a mirror image of the first. Since there are no rhymes in the first stanza, it looks open, unfenced, tempting the reader like the steers to test its apparent lack of limits. Beginning with the first line of the second stanza—the point at which the steers "blunder up against the wires"—each line "closes" (in reverse order, dcba) a line from the first stanza, so that it is only when the last line of the poem rhymes with the first that it is completely enclosed. The fences were of course there from the beginning but, as the last line suggests, they have now become internalized. Or, to put it in terms of the poem's form, what appeared to be open-ended was always closed, but it is only with the last line (about the realization of limits) that one is completely disabused of this illusion.[30]

"Next, Please" could be regarded as a more successful rewriting of "Wires" with a different set of clichés, and any reading that uncovers its wit, its ironic play, its shifts in tone, its range of references must also exceed the kind of attention devoted to popular literature. The reference to the "golden tits" of the ship's figurehead, for example, rewards a reading that is able to encompass its complicated mixture of the idealized and the vulgar as well as its subtle shift from the gold of the fantasy of material success to sexual fantasy.

J. R. Watson has argued that the appeal of clichés for Larkin was "as evidence of the way in which people think, as examples of different kinds of ordinary human feeling." Watson observes that Larkin associates clichéd language with particular lifestyles or social positions and his poems "identify their speakers by this observation of the speech and manners of other people," as the speaker of "Mr. Bleaney," for example, "records the idiom of the landlady, and by so doing sets himself apart as a different voice." Larkin's use of clichés, Watson concludes, is "not unlike a certain use of photographs." In the same way that a newspaper offers images of the everyday world with photographs, captions, and commentaries, "Larkin's poems similarly take the clichés of ordinary life and ordinary speech, and notice them, wryly, with his own version of the editorial caption." While it is certainly true that many of Larkin's texts use the cliché to "place" their speakers sociolinguistically, caricaturing, as Andrew Swarbrick notes, "attitudes and social location in a representative phrase or cliché," the function of cliché in poems like "Wires" and "Next, Please" appears to go beyond caricature and beyond the commonplace expression as a revelation of feeling or character. Hugh Underhill writes that the cliché for Larkin embodies "the fictions and fantasies we cherish, but it also represents a kind of shared protective

30. See Booth's much more extensive discussion of the poem's technical wit in *Philip Larkin: Writer*, 84–87.

ritual—it is a token of a common humanity,"[31] a view that is closer to my own reading of the cliché in Larkin's verse and in the music to which he is drawn.

One popular explanation for Larkin's embrace of the cliché and of banality in general, as we will see, is that it is a part of his effort to reclaim the "common reader" modernism supposedly lost. "His use of stereotypes, of clichés, of the recognisable idioms and registers of particular voices, creates the representativeness of so many poems in *The Whitsun Weddings*," Swarbrick writes in his discussion of the volume. "By trading on the familiar, Larkin can seem to speak for the common man," even if his speaking "is always at one remove and Larkin is always the voyeur, observing from behind the window of his railway carriage." Barbara Everett has questioned the belief "that Larkin's work brought poetry back to ordinary people." What is misleading about this formulation, she writes, is that "people who read poetry are never ordinary people," at least not ordinary readers, since "the habit of reading at all differentiates a person." Everett notes further that questions about a poet's audience are always difficult because they are abstract, and that the more interesting question in Larkin's case has to do with what she calls "expectations of response." The idiom in which Larkin works is, like the "golden tits" of "Next, Please," a peculiar mixture of well-adjusted, temperate language on the one hand and slang, four-letter words, and clichés on the other. The result is predictably "complex and ironic," ironic because Larkin's anti-intellectual art may appear to contradict his own life and experiences as a poet and university librarian. Everett writes, "Larkin has come to make his own a field that one might well love especially in compensation for, or in contradiction to, a lifetime above all shut up in books, papers, words—the abstract appurtenances of literary intellect. The poet turns tenderly to the sweet middle ranges of 'philistine' experience."[32]

Does a poetry of philistine experience require a philistine audience? The question of audience seems of particular importance to Larkin, as

---

31. Watson, "Clichés and Common Speech in Philip Larkin's Poetry," 149, 150, 151; Swarbrick, *Out of Reach*, 3; Underhill, "Poetry of Departures," 189.

32. Swarbrick, *Out of Reach*, 121; Everett, "Art and Larkin," 132, 133.

it was to all the Movement writers. Blake Morrison devotes a chapter of *The Movement* to the issue of "the audience one writes for" among Movement writers, and he concludes that the "desire to reach two seemingly different audiences—one a small intellectual circle, the other a large body of 'Common Readers'—is one of the most important features of the group." The contradiction is contained in the use of the pronoun "we" in writers like Amis and Larkin. Morrison calculates that more than a third of Larkin's mature poems "profess to speak for their readers," that the "pronounced awareness of audience in Larkin's poetry may well have derived from his sense of belonging to a small intellectual group," but that, finally, the *effect* of Larkin's use of the pronoun "we" goes in the opposite direction—it gives the impression of taking in a much broader, more general audience.[33] The issue of the sense of an audience suggested by a Larkin poem and the relation between audience and cliché (and popular music) is complicated and interesting enough to merit more extended treatment, and I will look at it more closely in the next chapter.

33. Morrison, *The Movement*, 109, 124.

7

THE CLICHÉ AND THE COMMON READER

There is nothing like writing poems for realizing how low the level of critical understanding is; maybe the average reader can understand what I say, but the above-average often can't.

—Larkin, "Four Conversations"

The generalisations on Life, Love, Marriage, Sex, Woman, etc., which fill the popular novel, the magazine, and the magazine pages of the popular Press, provide film captions and headlines, and so form the popular mind, have set up a further barrier between a serious novelist and the reading public. To be understood by the majority he would have to employ the clichés by which they are accustomed to think and feel, or rather to have their thinking and feeling done for them.

—Q. D. Leavis, *Fiction and the Reading Public*

THE aesthetic appropriation of philistine experience—the irony of the poet-librarian who claims to write poems for people who believe that "[b]ooks are a load of crap" (*CP*, 131)—is central to Larkin's poetry, since one of its pretenses as popular verse, one of the conventions that inform it, is that it is to such people that the poems are directed.

These texts frequently associate cliché with the world of their hypothetical readers, as if their audience were identical to the audience for popular music and popular literature, the kind of reader surveyed in Richard Hoggart's study of the English working-class audience, *The Uses of Literacy,* which I intend to incorporate later in a discussion of the cliché and the conception of the common reader in Larkin.

In the first five lines of "A Study of Reading Habits" (the poem quoted above) the speaker, a former reader, refers to having his "nose in a book," of "keep[ing] cool," and "deal[ing] out the old right hook / To dirty dogs twice my size." "Fiction and the Reading Public" (*CP,* 34) is a particularly interesting example of the cliché-informed poem since it purports to characterize the sensibility of the general reader, and in the process exposes its own fiction of the reading public. One of the grounds for its disdain of its audience is that its stereotyped reader is incapable of thought or expression outside cliché:

> Give me a thrill, says the reader,
> Give me a kick;
> I don't care how you succeed, or
> What subject you pick.
> Choose something you know all about
> That'll sound like real life:
> Your childhood, your Dad pegging out,
> How you sleep with your wife.
>
> But that's not sufficient, unless
> You make me feel good—
> Whatever you're 'trying to express'
> Let it be understood
> That 'somehow' God plaits up the threads,
> Makes 'all for the best',
> That we may lie quiet in our beds
> And not be 'depressed'.
>
> For I call the tune in this racket:
> I pay your screw,
> Write reviews and the bull on the jacket—
> So stop looking blue

And start serving up your sensations
Before it's too late;
Just please me for two generations—
You'll be 'truly great'.

The poem's title alludes to Q. D. Leavis's survey of the British general reader through three centuries, *Fiction and the Reading Public,* which concludes that the "reading capacity of the general public . . . has never been so low as at the present time." The poem raises implicitly the central question of the book—"How does the reader of our own time compare with his predecessors?" Leavis argues that the principal difference between the modern best-seller and the best-seller of the eighteenth century is that earlier fiction "does not invite uncritical reading, it keeps the reader at arm's length, and does not encourage him to project himself into the life he reads by identifying himself with the hero or heroine." In the modern best-seller, "the author has poured his own day-dreams, hot and hot, into dramatic form, without bringing them to any such touchstone as the 'good sense, but not common-sense' of a cultivated society: the author is himself—or more usually herself—identified with the leading character, and the reader is invited to share the debauch."[1]

As does the poem, at least fictionally, Leavis relies heavily on the words of readers explaining what they want as well as the words of best-selling authors explaining what they *think* readers want (she had submitted questionnaires to sixty writers). The results are as predictable as the clichés of Larkin's fictional reader: "Writers like Thomas Hardy who have a dreary hopeless outlook on life are not welcomed in popular magazines, however deft their literary art." "To my mind an author can have no greater compliment paid to him or to her than to be told that his or her characters appear to the reader *real people.*" "The busy men and women who form the majority of the reading public, and who read fiction by way of relaxation and enjoyment, do not desire to have productions of literary 'art' supplied to them." "When I've got anything important to tell the public, I always tell it to them in clichés—because

1. Q. D. Leavis, *Fiction and the Reading Public* (London, 1939), 231, 205, 236.

that's the way they understand it best." The poem's attempt to parody the kind of philistine commentary that comprises the documentation of Leavis's *Fiction and the Reading Public* was perhaps destined to fall flat. It is easy to dismiss as itself the stock response of the failed or unread novelist—it was written soon after Larkin had abandoned his attempt to write a third novel—and the book's authentic statements are in most cases more outrageous (and funnier) than the poem's version of them: "The general public does not wish to think. This fact, probably more than any other, accounts for the success of my stories."[2]

Readers of Larkin's "Fiction and the Reading Public" who are also familiar with his view of the writer's necessary link to a "pleasure-seeking audience," the reading public supposedly lost by the moderns, may be puzzled by the poem's hostility toward the generalized reader. As this text's readers we have been placed in an awkward position. Is the poem an indictment of its own readers or have we, as readers of poetry, been exempted from the condemnation of the general reader? Do we exist for the poet only as caricatures or does the poem assume two classes of readers, the imaginary popular reader it parodies and the actual reader to whom it is directed? The poem answers the last question with its own publication; it appeared in the January 1954 issue of *Essays in Criticism* alongside essays on *Coriolanus,* Virginia Woolf's *The Waves,* Dryden's imagery, and Walter Pater, poems by Kingsley Amis and Donald Davie, a "Critical Forum" on "Reading Shelley," and a debate between I. A. Richards and F. W. Bateson on the meaning of Eliot's "A Cooking Egg." It is not likely that the poet would have confused the potential readers of *Essays in Criticism* with the kind of readers he conjures up in the poem and elsewhere, and I will argue that what is so obviously true of "Fiction and the Reading Public" applies in a general way to Larkin's poems—they assume the fiction of a popular audience but depend for what Larkin calls "successful reading" on the kind of elite audience that he habitually mocks. This conflict between the two audiences carries implications I want to pursue.

Larkin's essay on the reader, "The Pleasure Principle," begins with

2. Ibid., 28, 59, 65, 329n, 49.

the premise that if there is "no successful reading, the poem can hardly be said to exist in a practical sense at all" (*RW*, 80), but what would constitute successful reading, and could a reading by the audience portrayed in "Fiction and the Reading Public" be called successful? He notes further that the reader "seems no longer present in the poet's mind as he used to be, as someone who must understand and enjoy the finished product" (*RW*, 80). The old reader, who read for pleasure, was replaced by the academic reader, who reads from some other motive. "The cash customers of poetry, therefore, who used to put down their money in the sure and certain hope of enjoyment as if at a theatre or concert hall, were quick to move elsewhere. Poetry was no longer a pleasure" (*RW*, 81). The argument depends on Larkin's assumption that the poetry of Eliot or Stevens does not give pleasure, that the kind of enjoyment he speaks of is a common pleasure accessible to all, that of the radio or the concert hall—"I use 'enjoy' in the commonest of senses, the sense in which we leave a radio on or off" (*RW*, 82). It also depends on the assumption that the poem's highest aim is to give general readers the sort of pleasure to which they are accustomed: "at bottom poetry, like all art, is inextricably bound up with giving pleasure, and if a poet loses his pleasure-seeking audience he has lost the only audience worth having, for which the dutiful mob that signs on every September is no substitute" (*RW*, 82). Yet it is to this mob and their professors that a poem ridiculing the popular audience and published in *Essays in Criticism* would seem to have its appeal.

The opening lines of "Fiction and the Reading Public" ("Give me . . . / Give me . . .") announce the cliché that lies almost at its surface— "giving the reader what he wants." This adage is on the one hand the cynical prescription for success for writers of popular literature in Leavis's *Fiction and the Reading Public* and on the other the phrase that now means selling out for the uncompromising artist, although (Leavis points out) there may have been a time, Defoe's time for example, when giving the public what it wanted was not inimical to the production of art. Larkin's essay "The Pleasure Principle" is a version of giving the reader what he wants, since it argues that modernism's failure was to cease giving the audience what it wanted and therefore to lose the only audience that matters (the real "paying" audience as opposed to the artificial academic audience of *Essays in Criticism*). The poem is a way of asking "what *does* the reader want?" and it is difficult to reconcile the two texts published only a few years apart, since the poem suggests that what the reader wants is a hodgepodge of sensationalism, sentimentality, clichéd situations and responses, something that will "sound like real life," that will "make [him] feel good," have a happy ending, and show that everything is "for the best." Above all, it should not be depressing, since the chief prohibition of the how-to-get-published manuals Leavis surveys is the ban against stories that are depressing or pessimistic. Is this the reader whose loss Larkin regrets in "The Pleasure Principle"? And would we have any interest in a writer whose aim was to give such a reader what he wanted?

The reader caricatured here is not of course the reader of serious literature at all, the reader that the moderns were supposed to have lost. He is the reader of *popular* literature, an audience for Larkin's poems which, one would surmise, exists only conventionally, as the imagined recipient of the poems' voice or point of view. Larkin's texts at different times both idealize this audience and vulgarize it. It is both the potential salvation of literature and the instrument of its trivialization. This audience is also depicted in "Fiction and the Reading Public" as the repository of the cliché and of slang, as it is in Richard Hoggart's survey of the popular audience, *The Uses of Literacy*. Hoggart begins his chapter on "the newer mass art" by quoting a "popular musician": "I attribute my success to giving the people what the people want. I am not a snob." The market in popular literature "seems to be highly competitive," Hoggart writes, "and those who succeed . . . need to have an acute sense of what the public wants." Popular writers exhibit "a facility with thousands of stock phrases which will set the figures moving on the highly conventionalised stage of their readers' imaginations." The cliché is an essential convention of popular writers, in Hoggart's analysis, because their aim is to "intensify the daydreams of their readers." They do not attempt to create an "object-in-itself," he writes; "they act as picture-makers for what is behind the readers' daydream,"[3] and what is behind them turns out to be a collection of stock phrases and common-places such as those of Larkin's reader in "Fiction and the Reading Public."

Richard Hoggart was by chance one of Larkin's colleagues at Hull, and *The Uses of Literacy* was published two years after *The Less Deceived.* It is a study of English working-class culture with an emphasis on popular literature, music, and other forms of entertainment, and it is in some ways a sociological parallel to the poetry Larkin was writing at the same time. Both are interested in the language and habits of the "common reader" and what Barbara Everett calls the "densely actual commonplace existence" of ordinary people. Hoggart also holds the distinction of being, at least technically, the first official reader of *The Less Deceived;* he was the first person to reply when George Hartley decided to publish the collection by subscription (*Life,* 262). When Larkin published "Essential Beauty," a poem on contemporary advertis-ing, in the *Spectator* in 1962, he told Robert Conquest he would like to dedicate it to Hoggart, although, finally, he did not (*Letters,* 345). Larkin may have thought of him in connection with the poem because Hoggart had written on the clichéd appeals and devices of "compensatory" advertising in *The Uses of Literacy,* and the poem treats the billboard as an index of "how life should be" (*CP,* 144). "Advertising, like clichés, offers Larkin a lexicon of a community's deepest wishes," Andrew Swar-brick writes,[4] a view of the popular audience developed at length in *The Uses of Literacy.* The book throws some light on the relation of the cliché to the (presumed) general reader in Larkin's poems because Hoggart is interested in the stock phrase in a literate but unsophisticated audience. Although it was not his intent, what he has produced is as close as we can come to a handbook on the cliché in the popular audience at the time of *The Less Deceived.*

The Uses of Literacy reads like a celebration of the cliché among "the common people" because it is Hoggart's principal means of describing attitudes and ideas. Whenever he wishes to illustrate an attitude held

---

3. Richard Hoggart, *The Uses of Literacy* (London, 1957), 171, 172, 174.

4. Swarbrick, *Out of Reach,* 115.

by the mass audience, he offers a catalog of stock phrases. Here, for example, is his description of working-class take-life-as-it-comes stoicism:

At the lowest is the acceptance of life as hard, with nothing to be done about it: put up with it and don't aggravate the situation: "what is to be, will be"; "if y' don't like it, y' mun lump it"; "that's just the way things are"; "it's no good kicking against the pricks"; "what can't be mended must be made do with"; "y've got to tek life as it cums—day in, day out." In many of these is a note of dull fatalism; life is always like that for people like us. But the really flat ones are a minority among the phrases of roughly cognate type: in most the note is of a cheerful patience: "y've got to tek life as it cums," yes; but also "y've got to get on wi' it best way y' can"; "grin and bear it"; "ah well, least said, soonest mended"; "oh, it'll all be the same in a hundred years' time"; "all such things are sent to try us" (here, as in some others, the connection with religion is evident); "it isn't always dark at six"; "we're short o' nowt we've got"; "worse things 'appen at sea"; "ah well, we live in 'opes." It's all bound to be ups-and-downs, the rough with the smooth, roundabouts and swings: "it's no good moaning"; "mek the best of it . . . stick it . . . soldier on . . ."; "don't meet trouble 'alf-way." You may sort-of-hope for a windfall or a sudden, wonderful surprise, but not really; you've got to go on and "mek yer own life"; "keep yer end up"; "life is what y' mek it." "Mek shift and fadge" and you'll be "alright"—as private soldiers were when they knocked up something like a living-space out of the most unpromising conditions.[5]

Hoggart feels justified in using the cliché as his medium for imparting working-class attitudes since, as he also argues, the attitude is no more or less than the stock phrase that communicates it. People "may appear to have views on general matters—on religion, on politics, and so on," he writes, "but these views usually prove to be a bundle of largely unexamined and orally-transmitted tags, enshrining generalisations, prejudices and half-truths, and elevated by epigrammatic phrasing into the status of maxims." These maxims often contradict each other, "but they are not thought about, not intellectually considered. They have a hypnotic and final effect, the sound of revealed truth." The difference

---

5. Hoggart, *Uses of Literacy*, 78.

between contested ideas and clichés is that the "truth" of the latter is never in question since the phrase itself—"when my ship comes in," "the grass is always greener"—is never under scrutiny:

[I]t is important to remember that, in so far as ideas affect working-class people, they do not usually affect them as ideas, are not intellectually received and scrutinised. This is true even at a time when everyone is expected to have "views." The ideas seem to be adopted rather as received tags ("they say it's all relative nowadays"; "they say it's all a matter of your glands"), and are held on to when they seem comforting in much the same way as the older tags ("Ah well, it's all a matter of luck"; "Well, what is to be, will be").[6]

What Hoggart demonstrates through almost three hundred pages on the state of the stock phrase among less sophisticated readers is that clichés make up the language of popular song and popular literature primarily because they constitute the authentic world of their audiences. What he arrives at finally is the Nietzschean argument that for the lower end of common readers "truth" amounts to the interpretations contained in the reader's cultural store of stock phrases, tag lines, and enshrined clichés. Of course this may well be the case with all readers at whatever level of sophistication the reading takes place, as has been argued in recent theory.

What is distinctive about Hoggart's popular audience is that the effect of cliché is undisguised, brought to the surface, and the same distinction may be applied in setting Larkin's poems beside more conventional texts. What may be present indirectly in the latter will be unmasked in the Larkin text; sometimes, as in "Poetry of Departures" or "Places, Loved Ones," even italicized: *He walked out on the whole crowd,*" "*Take that you bastard,*" "*This is my proper ground / Here I shall stay*" (*CP*, 85, 99). In "Poetry of Departures" these italicized lines are something "you hear, fifth-hand"; the clichéd phrases are used here as shorthand to characterize a point of view in much the same way the cliché is employed in *The Uses of Literacy.* James Booth notes that the italicized phrases in "Poetry of Departures" "have something of the vivid

6. Ibid., 86, 87, 144.

force of cultural icons, like the isolated frames of comic strips in the pop-art paintings of Roy Lichtenstein." The comparison is suggestive—both artists appropriate and recontextualize the trappings of the popular audience—as is Booth's argument that elsewhere in the poem Larkin creates the artistic equivalent of the cliché. Phrases like "nut-strewn roads" and "Stubbly with goodness" sound vaguely familiar but are not the property of the common reader. They are, Booth suggests, "a poetic apotheosis of the cliché."[7]

Of course the concept of the common reader is itself a cliché of criticism, an unexamined stock phrase used as if there were a consensus on what constitutes this kind of reader. The common reader need not be simply the reader of popular literature, for example, the reader who reads purely for entertainment. That, however, appears to be Larkin's conception of the reader for whom he claims his poems are written, as is made reasonably clear in "The Pleasure Principle," where he speaks of readers as consumers, the "cash customers of poetry" who "put down their money in the sure and certain hope of enjoyment as if at a theatre or concert hall" (*RW*, 81). His opinion that poetry should be able to vie for the reader's attention with television and radio underscores this conception. In the essay "Writing Poems" he argues that poetry should be able to "compete in the open market," and although he is thinking of poetry from the poet's end, he also argues that it is essentially a matter of entertainment at both ends. Both the writing and the reading of poetry should be as pleasurable as "other spare-time activities" such as "listening to records or going out" (*RW*, 84). What I am suggesting is that although Leavis's and Hoggart's cliché-informed readers may not make up a significant share of the audience that actually reads Larkin's poems, they are very close to the readers who appear in poems like "A Study of Reading Habits" and "Fiction and the Reading Public" and in essays like "The Pleasure Principle" and "Writing Poems."

Larkin is, however, far from consistent on the subject of his audience. His earliest view, at Oxford, is that "a poet never thinks of his reader. Why should he? The reader doesn't come into the poem at all" (*Letters*,

---

7. Booth, *Philip Larkin: Writer*, 98, 99.

6). He has also said that "poets write for people with the same background and experiences as themselves" (*RW*, 69), but of course the fiction he toys with is that he is himself an ordinary reader. In the introduction to *All What Jazz* he imagines his readers for the jazz reviews not as a working-class audience (jazz never caught on with them) yet as the most ordinary and inarticulate of men:

My readers . . . sometimes I wonder whether they really exist. . . . Sometimes I imagine them, sullen fleshy inarticulate men, stockbrokers, sellers of goods, living in 30-year-old detached houses among the golf courses of Outer London, husbands of ageing and bitter wives they first seduced to Artie Shaw's "Begin the Beguine" or The Squadronaires' "The Nearness of You"; fathers of cold-eyed lascivious daughters on the pill . . . and cannabis-smoking jeans-and-bearded Stuart-haired sons whose oriental contempt for "bread" is equalled only by their insatiable demand for it; men in whom a pile of scratched coverless 78s in the attic can awaken memories of vomiting blindly from small Tudor windows to Muggsy Spanier's "Sister Kate," or winding up a gramophone in a punt to play Armstrong's "Body and Soul"; men whose first coronary is coming like Christmas; who drift, loaded helplessly with commitments and obligations and necessary observances, into the darkening avenues of age and incapacity, deserted by everything that once made life sweet. (*AWJ*, 28–29)

Grevel Lindrop argues that "Larkin wanted people to think that" these sullen inarticulate men "represent also his notion of the ideal readers of his poetry," and that appears to be the case, although wanting people to think it is not the same as believing it to be true. Are these sullen salesmen the readers to whom his brilliant passage is directed, for example, and would they appreciate it in the same way that it is savored by, say, Clive James? James says of *All What Jazz* that "no wittier book of criticism has ever been written";[8] would the wit of the reviews and the introduction be wasted on the dense helpless reader Larkin imagines for himself?

What is noteworthy about the gap between Larkin's fictitious inartic-

---

8. Grevel Lindrop, "Being Different from Yourself: Philip Larkin in the 1970s," in *British Poetry since 1970: A Critical Survey,* ed. Peter Jones and Michael Schmidt (New York, 1980), 47; James, "On His Wit," 98.

ulate reader and actual articulate Larkin readers such as James or Christopher Ricks or Barbara Everett is the manner in which the latter are positioned by poems that pretend to be written for someone else. Since the poet masquerades as a philistine and the poems masquerade as popular verse, a sophisticated reader or an academic reader—a reader who believes these are artful poems that reward scrutiny—is put in much the same position as Christopher Ricks listening to Bob Dylan or Larkin listening to the Beatles. Conventionally, the songs of these musicians are not directed to middle-class academic Englishmen, so that Ricks and Larkin are in effect eavesdropping, overhearing something written and performed for an entirely different level of listeners, the "authentic" audience, in the case of the Beatles a teenage audience. (The question of the audience to which Dylan's songs were hypothetically directed is more complicated, since he continued to alienate his audiences as he moved through stages of folk, rock, modified country, born-again Christian, etc.)

The classic case of what might be called the inauthentic audience, the audience that appropriates what was not originally intended for it and what (conventionally) continues to ignore it, is the English reception of Black American jazz and blues. In "Playing with Real Feeling—Jazz and Suburbia," Simon Frith considers the complications of the English appropriation of jazz, especially as it relates to the question of authenticity. One of the small ironies of the British response to what a 1933 reviewer characterized as "the music of the Harlem gin mills, the Georgia backyards and New Orleans street corners," Frith notes in his survey of the early reviews, was that it was embraced not by "ordinary people" but by "the slumming upper class," "the aspiring lower-middle class," the "chaps at Oxford and Cambridge":

"Real" jazz remained an elite taste into the 1930s. Constant Lambert took it for granted that Duke Ellington was only appreciated by "the high-brow public," while the restricted audience for Louis Armstrong's 1932 tour was reflected in both box-office takings and Fleet Street "shock horror." Gerald Moore concluded that Armstrong's music was "not for the general public for whom his enormously advanced work cannot possibly have any appeal," while Hannen Swaffer in the

Daily Herald described ordinary people walking out, leaving "excited young men of the pseudo-intellectual kind . . . bleating and blahing in ecstasy."

Jazz was considered "music for the connoisseur," and it involved, Frith writes, "painstaking passion, a yearning for sensuous, earthy experience equated now with solemnly earned excitement and the 'furtive' release of real feeling." The typical British jazz fan of the late thirties "was a swottish provincial school boy, a Philip Larkin, who later wondered what happened to his fellow enthusiasts."[9]

A "slumming" elitist audience appropriating what Peter Van Der Merwe contemptuously calls "American gutter music," the art of "the very dregs of its lowest classes," raises the question of the way this audience is positioned in relation to such music. One of the continuing debates of the early reviewers, Frith demonstrates, was the real/fake or authentic/inauthentic argument: "how could a white British audience be other than 'entertained' by noises made meaningful only in terms of their black American roots? How on earth could British *musicians* claim to play jazz for real?" He cites a 1937 review that tries to clarify the difference between authentic and inauthentic jazz. The only authentic jazz "was produced by black musicians for black audiences,"[10] which would mean not only that white musicians couldn't play it but that jazz by black musicians performed for a predominantly white audience was inauthentic. Nor was that likely to happen in any event since the British Ministry of Trade imposed a ban in 1935 that effectively denied the entry of American jazz musicians until 1954. The only truly authentic position for a typical British jazz fan, a Philip Larkin, was to *overhear* jazz (on the gramophone or the radio), in effect, to appropriate something essentially alien to his culture that, at the same time, appeared to speak directly to him.

Paradoxically, it is the alien character of the music that authenticates it, and Larkin acknowledges the paradox in the introduction to *All What*

9. Frith, "Playing with Real Feeling," 56, 59–60. The 1933 review Frith quotes is Spike Hughes's *Daily Herald* review of Duke Ellington's first British appearance.

10. Peter Van Der Merwe, *Origins of the Popular Style: The Antecedents of Twentieth-Century Popular Music* (Oxford, 1989), 213; Frith, "Playing with Real Feeling," 58, 57.

Jazz as he describes the experience of listening to the slurs of Americans with improbable names as he gazes across an English tennis court:

Sitting with a friend in his bedroom that overlooked the family tennis-court, I watched leaves drift down through long Sunday afternoons as we took it in turn to wind the portable HMV, and those white and coloured Americans, Bubber Miley, Frank Teschmacher, J. C. Higginbotham, spoke immediately to our understanding. Their rips, slurs and distortions were something we understood perfectly. This was something we had found for ourselves, that wasn't taught at school. (*AWJ*, 16)

The account underlines both the authenticity of the experience and its strangeness—the coming together of an English Sunday afternoon and the growl trumpeting of a Black American named Bubber whose specialty was what was called jungle music. The authenticity of the music clearly depends on the circumstance that it is not a part of the listener's culture or education, something "that wasn't taught at school" observed from the outside. Frith writes that "to understand the urge to 'authenticity' we have to understand the strange fear of being 'inauthentic.' In this world, American music—black American music—stands for a simple idea: that everything *real* is happening elsewhere."[11]

The sense of exclusion, the notion of authenticity, the use of the cliché, and the pretense of the popular audience are, I am suggesting, closely related in Larkin's poetry. In trying to determine the effect of the cliché in the verse we are led directly to the question of the popular audience, the reader for whom the cliché is not a literary curiosity, the "authentic" reader. Conventionally—and the cliché represents only one of many conventions directed toward this end—the poems give the impression, in Clive James's words (recalling the language at the conclusion of Larkin's "Bridge for the Living"), that they are "rebuilding the ruined bridge between poetry and the general reading public." Whether this is in fact the case is not what concerns me here; it is rather the effect of such an assumption on readers like James, who finds himself in the same position in relation to Larkin's art that Larkin occupied in

11. Frith, "Playing with Real Feeling," 61.

relation to American jazz, attempting to convince us that this *is* art even if it sounds like something ordinary or trivial: "His own criticism appeals so directly to the ear that he puts himself in danger of being thought trivial, especially by the mock-academic."[12] Larkin's texts, that is to say, reenact the conditions of his own enjoyment of jazz, blues, and popular music. One of the effects of the commonplaces and clichés of these texts on relatively sophisticated readers is to impart a sense of authenticity to the poems in the way that the middle-class English audience attributed authenticity to the American jazz from which they were effectively excluded.

William Harmon speaks of the "authenticating function" of Larkin's use of taboo words such as *piss* or *fuck,* but Joseph Bristow argues that the word *cunt* in "Love Again" has "no redeeming authenticity." Turned into poetry, he says, obscenity "betrays its force," becomes an empty gesture. "Once 'cunt,' 'fuck,' and 'piss' have become poetry they are, as Larkin's reputation proves, no longer obscene." His assumption is that obscenity can be authentic only so long as it resists being art, but I would argue that the effect of authenticity is maintained by the poems' pretense that they are not in fact art, that they are written for a popular audience. The principle is an extension of the effect of all "folk" music, as Frith explains: "folk songs were authentic fantasies because they sprang from the people themselves; they were not commodities." And stock phrases that recur in folk songs "are not clichés" but rather signify "the anonymous, spontaneous, communal process in which folk songs are made."[13] This is a version of Wordsworth's principle that the language of the lowest classes—"the language really used by men"—is more real than the language reserved for poetry or the language of his own class, which in turn is a variation of the principle Frith uses to explain the authenticity attributed to jazz by an English audience: "everything *real* is happening elsewhere."

Larkin was familiar with the principle and treats it directly in a poem

12. James, "On His Wit," 108, 104.

13. Harmon, "Larkin's Memory," 217; Bristow, "Obscenity of Philip Larkin," 179; Frith, "Why Do Songs Have Words?" 112.

from *The Whitsun Weddings* called "The Importance of Elsewhere" (*CP*, 104). The speaker says that in an alien environment (Ireland) his "strangeness," looking at life from the outside, worked to substantiate his existence, "To prove [him] separate."

> Living in England has no such excuse:
> These are my customs and establishments
> It would be much more serious to refuse.
> Here no elsewhere underwrites my existence.

John Goodby observes of the poem that it "provides a rationale for Larkin's characteristic isolated, onlooker persona," without which "the mature poetry is unthinkable," and Andrew Swarbrick notes that "the need for an 'elsewhere' " is essential to Larkin's imagination. Swarbrick's recent study of Larkin is shaped by the assumption that the poems "aspire to things 'out of reach,' " but he is mistaken, I believe, in his emphasis on the fantasy element of "elsewhere" in Larkin at the expense of its power of authentication. He argues that " 'elsewhere' stands for Larkin as an imaginative space, contiguous with experience but never actual," that it is "a realm of escape, of fulfilment, of fantasy."[14] While it is true that the "elsewhere" of Larkin's poetry may be associated with fantasy or escape (as in the case of New Orleans jazz in "For Sidney Bechet"), it is also true that the effect of absence or exclusion frequently has the opposite effect, sanctioning an experience or concept. In "Lines on a Young Lady's Photograph Album," for example, the speaker comes to see that it is in part his exclusion from the past the photographs depict—"a past that no one now can share" (*CP*, 72)—that validates it, and of course the speaker's perception in "The Importance of Elsewhere" is that the elsewhere of Ireland works to "prove" his separate being, "underwrites [his] existence."

It is significant in regard to Larkin's concept of "elsewhere" that all of his poems explicitly about jazz reenact in some form the listener's

14. John Goodby, " 'The Importance of Being Elsewhere,' or 'No Man Is an Ireland': Self, Selves, and Social Consensus in the Poetry of Philip Larkin," *Critical Survey,* I (1989), 133; Swarbrick, *Out of Reach,* 95, 1, 94.

own exclusion, which is directly linked to the poem's act of authentication. The clearest instance is "Reasons for Attendance," where the Larkin persona is outside the dance looking in, reflecting on the fact that his *not* being a part of the audience for whom the jazz is being played guarantees that his response is the more authentic—his jazz as art versus their jazz as dance music. In "For Sidney Bechet" the listener imagines the true scene of jazz, a New Orleans he will never see, and tells Bechet that his imaginary New Orleans, a version of elsewhere, is closest to the real spirit of the music and validates it: "My Crescent City / Is where your speech alone is understood. . ." (*CP*, 83). In "Reference Back" it is crucial that the performance of Oliver's "Riverside Blues" to which the speaker is now listening has taken place in Chicago three decades earlier. Like the photographs in "Lines on a Young Lady's Photograph Album," the music is made real by being "out of date," made inaccessible, removed from the speaker's present. Swarbrick comes close to violating his reading of "elsewhere" in Larkin when he says of "Lines" that "this remoteness is what the speaker finds moving about her photos," that "his nostalgia is possible only because the past he now observes is isolated from him."[15]

One of Larkin's pop music poems, "Annus Mirabilis" (*CP*, 167), is also a variation on the theme that real life is elsewhere. Whatever else it is about, "Annus Mirabilis" is about the sense of being excluded from the authentic audience of the Beatles' first LP:

> Sexual intercourse began
> In nineteen sixty-three
> (Which was rather late for me)—
> Between the end of the *Chatterley* ban
> And the Beatles' first LP.

I want to raise the issue of the speaker's relation to the Beatles' audience (and to Lawrence's), but I also want to raise the question of this poem's own audience, since the two appear to be related. To whom is the poem addressed—if not actually at least conventionally? By what signals or

---

15. Swarbrick, *Out of Reach*, 49–50.

signs may we reconstruct the hypothetical reader? To return to Blake Morrison's description of the Movement writers' two conflicting audiences, does the poem appear to be directed to a small intellectual or at least academic audience, one that would appreciate the *Chatterley* ban allusion, or a large popular audience, the audience of the Beatles' first LP to which, ironically, the speaker does not belong?

To ask about the poem's audience is another way of asking about its tone. How seriously are we to take the speaker's lament? Is the poem a parody of popular art, a piece of doggerel created for the amusement of the "slumming" academic reader, or an earnest appropriation of a popular style? Jonathan Raban has noted the complexities of tone the poem presents: " 'Annus Mirabilis' becomes a poem so promiscuous in its ironies that it turns into a maze, a stylistic labyrinth in which no directions are certain." It is "the Larkin poem to end all Larkin poems," and it "functions as a kind of criticism-by-self-parody of Larkin's entire work." Neil Powell, however, questions the self-parody, arguing that Raban takes the poem too seriously: "this is a poem in which the joke is very firmly on the reader. So it is not strictly speaking a self-parody: the poet seems to have set out to write not a parody of a Larkin poem but a poem which might be mistaken for a parody of a Larkin poem. I suppose it is therefore . . . a parody of a parody."[16]

Powell's reading involves us in an even more intricate maze, and neither reading appears to appreciate the extent to which "Annus Mirabilis" features one of the most successful artifices of Larkin's verse—the philistine style that authenticates the poem's voice, apparently removing it from the realm of artifice. Barbara Everett puts it this way: "Larkin's great art is to appear to achieve the literal while in fact doing something altogether other; his three volumes of major verse are the odd reticent triumph of a self-undercutting artist whose skills make him a 'secret poet' as some men are secret agents or secret drinkers."[17] By

---

16. Jonathan Raban, *The Society of the Poem* (London, 1971), 59; Powell, *Carpenters of Light,* 101.

17. Barbara Everett, "Larkin's Edens," in *Poets in Their Time: Essays on English Poetry from Donne to Larkin* (London, 1986), 245.

the same token Larkin's seeming appeal to the common reader may foster the secret elitist reader who recognizes the "something altogether other" of the poems and thus assumes the position of a Philip Larkin or a Christopher Ricks discovering the art of popular forms of music apparently directed toward a different audience altogether.

One sign that "Annus Mirabilis" (conventionally) assumes for itself a popular audience is that it borrows its most obvious conventions from popular music. Salem Hassan has pointed out that the poem takes from music the device of repeating with minor modification the entire first stanza as the final stanza of the poem:

> So life was never better than
> In nineteen sixty-three
> (Though just too late for me)—
> Between the end of the *Chatterley* ban
> And the Beatles' first LP.

"Annus Mirabilis" is, so far as I can tell, unique among Larkin's poems in using this structure, and its effect here is the sense of closure we may feel at the end of a song. In her study of poetic closure (as Hassan also notes) Barbara Herrnstein Smith explains why we respond as we do to this pattern: "at the most primitive level, it is effective because, as in music, it reproduces a familiar group of sounds." Since "the first stanza constituted an integral formal structure of its own," then "any part of it when it reappears, will cause the reader to expect the rest to follow; and when it does follow, closure will be strengthened."[18] The "pop music" feeling readers may pick up from the poem is thus easily accounted for; its overall structure and sense of closure are effects we associate with music rather than poetry. The poem is, moreover, about a moment in British culture epitomized by the music of the Beatles and the music's reception by the Beatles' audience, a moment from which the speaker is excluded. But there is another more common musical convention in the poem, one we have seen often in Larkin's texts.

---

18. Hassan, *Philip Larkin and His Contemporaries*, 119; Barbara Herrnstein Smith, *Poetic Closure: A Study of How Poems End* (Chicago, 1968), 66.

What is it that makes the *language* of the opening stanza of "Annus Mirabilis" at all interesting? The words are abstract, banal: "Sexual intercourse began / In nineteen sixty-three / (Which was rather late for me)." The effect, I suggest, is that of the popular song. It is difficult to think of a more uninteresting phrase than "fundamental things apply," and yet fitted perfectly to a melody it becomes memorable: "The fundamental things apply / As time goes by." The quality illustrated by both Larkin's opening stanza and Herman Hupfeld's phrase from "As Time Goes By" is what Dave Laing refers to as the "agility of the lyrics in following the contours of the melody," which "closes the gap between words and music." In popular music the interest is normally not in the words themselves but in the "interplay and intimacy between words, voice and music," and this is the effect the first stanza of "Annus Mirabilis" achieves. A phrase such as "*Chatterley* ban" or "Beatles' first LP" is mundane, journalistic; it is the agility of the phrases to fit into the shape of the poem's melody that reinvigorates them. Laing illustrates this agility with Cole Porter's "Ev'ry Time We Say Goodbye" and finds, interestingly, that "[s]ome of the same strategies were later used in the sixties by Lennon and McCartney in their compositions." Both Porter and the Beatles "were concerned to capture the idioms and movement of spoken language for their songs."[19] The success of "LP" is a case in point; it looks odd on the page but feels perfectly natural when spoken aloud or sung because it captures the movement of spoken language, although the departure of the long-playing record means that for a new generation of readers "LP" will carry a footnote as no longer idiomatic.

In *Poetic Closure* Smith points out that the repetition of an entire stanza "is not only a formal repetition but a thematic one as well; it is the reassertion of an utterance." Depending on the intervening material, it may shift the meaning of the original assertion or reconfirm it. Hassan proposes that the repetition in "Annus Mirabilis" shifts the tone "from the ironic, slightly envious tone of the outset of the poem to a sense of stability and confidence at the end of it." His argument is that the change conveys the poet's realization that life was never better *for him*

19. Laing, *Sound of Our Time*, 56, 98.

than in 1963 just because it *is* too late for him to be a part of the youth movement associated with the Beatles' music. Since he knows that happiness can never be achieved in life, he realizes as well that the sexual liberation that began in 1963 would be "boring."[20]

Hassan's is an interestingly perverse reading—most commentators find it hard to say anything about the poem that is not obvious—but it mistakes the poem's tone and does not take sufficient account of the theme of the outsider so persistent in Larkin's poems from "Reasons for Attendance" to "High Windows" (*CP*, 165), the latter another version of "Annus Mirabilis":

> When I see a couple of kids
> And guess he's fucking her and she's
> Taking pills or wearing a diaphragm,
> I know this is paradise
>
> Everyone old has dreamed of all their lives—
> Bonds and gestures pushed to one side
> Like an outdated combine harvester. . . .

Even if the speakers of these poems are mistaken in their inferences about the happiness of the young, both poems depend on their speakers' genuine sense of exclusion from a real life that is going on elsewhere. Hassan's more confident persona, who exposes the illusions of sexuality, seems to me foreign to the voice of "Annus Mirabilis" and the attitude of the speaker, especially in the middle stanzas that detail the implications of the sexual revolution as seen from the outside. The speaker is clearly more accurate about the "wrangle for a ring" and "shame that started at sixteen" of his own generation than the third stanza's idealized view of the youth culture as an "unlosable game." A game that is unlosable or a game where both sides cooperate for the same goal ceases to be a game. The speaker's exclusion from the Beatles' generation is suggested by his images of sexuality—a bargain, a wrangle, a quarrel, a game, something adversarial with one on a side—that are foreign to the mood

20. Smith, *Poetic Closure,* 66; Hassan, *Philip Larkin and His Contemporaries,* 119–20.

of the sixties. That is, the terms of his conception of sexual relations demonstrate his inability to think outside the old sexual paradigm.

> Up till then there'd only been
> A sort of bargaining,
> A wrangle for a ring,
> A shame that started at sixteen
> And spread to everything.
>
> Then all at once the quarrel sank:
> Everyone felt the same,
> And every life became
> A brilliant breaking of the bank,
> A quite unlosable game.

What is perhaps most revealing about the speaker's ambivalent attitude toward the popular audience from which he is excluded but which he pretends to address is the set of markers he uses to designate the point of origin of the new sexual paradigm. Both Lawrence and the Beatles represent public icons that the poem exploits, but they also epitomize the two audiences that the poem moves between. The Beatles hold a complicated set of associations for Larkin in *All What Jazz*, not least because they show what happened to the blues in England in the sixties. Larkin's view, which is widely shared, is that rock and roll stands in a direct line of descent from American blues, or, as Greil Marcus defines it, it is "black music altered in one way or another by white culture." In his history of rock Michael Bane calls it "a mutated form of black music, a white boy singing the blues"; the Beatles took it a step further, *"Englishmen* singing the blues."[21]

Before the Beatles, Larkin wrote in a 1961 review of a group of blues albums that "the blues are really with us today, the tradition extending from the pure form of these recordings to its infinite vulgarization by Elvis and his host of adored imitators" (*AWJ*, 38). In 1965 the Beatles'

---

21. Greil Marcus, "Introduction," in *Stranded: Rock and Roll for a Desert Island*, ed. Greil Marcus (New York, 1979), ix; Michael Bane, *White Boy Singin' the Blues* (New York, 1982), 17, 151.

album *Help* represented "the genuine blues overlaid with the hybrid and plangent romanticism that is the Lennon-McCartney hallmark" (*AWJ*, 146). But for Larkin the Beatles lost their early purity and reflected in microcosm what happened to jazz. By 1967 he was noting that a short history of their music from "She Loves You" to "Eleanor Rigby" would demonstrate "Marx's theory of artistic degeneration" (*AWJ*, 178). "How can one possibly rank 'A Day in the Life' with 'I Want to Hold Your Hand'?" (*AWJ*, 237). *Sergeant Pepper's Lonely Hearts Club Band* demonstrated "that the Beatles, having made their name in the narrow emotional and harmonic world of teenage pop, are now floating away on their own cloud." Larkin added, "I doubt whether their own fancies and imagination are strong enough to command an audience instead of collaborating with it" (*AWJ*, 186). The choice of "collaborating" to describe the Beatles' relation to their audience is indicative of Larkin's sense of exclusion from the youthful audience. Of an Armstrong recording he had earlier written that "it brought tears to my eyes. What it does for the teenagers I hardly dare hope" (*AWJ*, 119).

It is of course not simply for Larkin that the music of the Beatles is synonymous with the emergence of a new sexual ideology identified with the young—Elvis Presley holds the same distinction in American music. And while the poem's association of the Beatles with a fundamental change in human history has been read as a part of its wit, it is also a view held seriously by chroniclers of rock. In *Dead Elvis* Greil Marcus says of the Beatles' American counterpart that "Elvis did not simply change musical history. . . . He changed history as such, and in doing so he became history. He became part of it, irrevocably and specifically attached to it, as those of us who were changed by him, or who changed ourselves because of things we glimpsed in him, are not." In *The Sociology of Rock*, Simon Frith argues that although popular music has always idealized adolescence, what happened in the sixties was unique:

In the 1960s . . . this ideology of adolescence became something new, an ideology of youth; "The young ones" became "My generation." The significance of this change was that although adolescence had always been romanticised in song, although the teenage world had always had glamour, youth had been presented as a period of transition, a stage on the path to adulthood. The essence of the ideology of courtship, for example, was that a time would come, a marriage to the perfect partner, when all emotional and sexual needs would be fulfilled. In the 1960s this false suggestion was replaced by another—that youth was preferable to age and that no one need ever grow old. What was at issue was not chronology but ideology. If youth was the perfect social condition—glamorous, irresponsible, sexually vigorous, emotionally unrestrained; if to be young meant to be free from the narrow routines of maturity, then anyone who lived and thought right, regardless of age, could be "young." Teenage culture, in holding up "irregular, spontaneous, unpredictable, exhibitionist behaviour" as desirable became the basis for a more general ideology in which pleasure was a way of life.[22]

This is a version of what "Annus Mirabilis" recognizes as well, that the generation of the Beatles' first LP represents unrestrained pleasure as a way of life. The poem recognizes the degree to which the Beatles' music and its reception testify to a new ideology in place but balks at the second half of Frith's argument—the accessibility of this way of life to those who are not in fact a legitimate part of the audience for the Beatles' first LP.

The poem asserts that what is at issue *is* chronological, and the deeper irony is that Larkin's jazz has now come full circle. In the introduction to *All What Jazz* he argues that jazz was "the unique private excitement" of a select group of young people who "came to adolescence between the wars." Parents were suspicious of it, it had a bad reputation, and "[n]o one you knew liked it" (*AWJ*, 15). It was the music of *his* generation and belonged to no one else. And it is because he knows what it is to find his identity as a member of an audience that the speaker understands his present exclusion. He would have understood perfectly what a legitimate member of the Beatles' audience (Greil Marcus in 1969) says about exclusive possession of a music:

[R]ock 'n' roll has existed only since about 1954, and thus it's a sad fact that most of those over thirty cannot be a part of it, and it cannot be a part of them. I don't want to talk about the ability of adults to "enjoy the Beatles" or to

---

22. Greil Marcus, *Dead Elvis: A Chronicle of a Cultural Obsession* (New York, 1991), 7–8; Frith, *Sociology of Rock*, 188–89.

"think Dylan has something to say," but about the rock 'n' roll era as the exclusive possession of our generation, about what our love for it and our immersion in it might imply for our consciousness and vision.

"Rock 'n' roll has always had an awareness of its music as a special thing, reserved for a certain audience," Marcus writes,[23] and the poem conveys in a negative way, observing it from the outside, this sense of authenticity shared by the audience of the Beatles' first LP.

The album was *Please Please Me,* and the trial in which a jury decided that Lawrence's *Lady Chatterley's Lover* could be published in an unexpurgated edition took place three years earlier in 1960. The Lawrence allusion clearly functions in the poem as a sign of the easing of a sexual ban and so parallels the liberation associated with the youth culture. But the Lawrence associations are richer than that, since he is also identified in Larkin's texts with something *antithetical* to the Beatles, what might be called high art in contrast to the popular art of the Beatles. "Annus Mirabilis," that is, can be read in the light of Swarbrick's proposal that Larkin's verse reveals an "often unresolved conflict between a romantic, aspiring Larkin and the empirical, ironic Larkin, between the aesthete and the philistine." The passion for jazz and other forms of popular music was, as Swarbrick notes, an essential part of Larkin's unpretentiousness, his "irreverent rejection of the pieties associated with 'highbrow' arts,"[24] the art that the young idealist had found in Lawrence.

Lawrence was Larkin's first literary mentor, more revered than Hardy or Yeats. What Swarbrick calls "the high-minded art-for-art's-sake attitudes, the cultivation of artistic inspiration"[25] are associated with Larkin's discipleship to Lawrence recorded in his Oxford correspondence. He reported that he read Lawrence daily "(like the Bible) with great devotion" (*Letters,* 19). If one eliminates all of his books except *Sons and Lovers* and *Lady Chatterley's Lover,* "he is still England's greatest writer"

23. Greil Marcus, "Who Put the Bomp in the Bomp De-Bomp De-Bomp?" in *Rock and Roll Will Stand,* ed. Greil Marcus (Boston, 1969), 8–9, 18.

24. Swarbrick, *Out of Reach,* 19, 70.

25. Ibid., 4.

(*Letters*, 32). "To me, Lawrence is what Shakespeare was to Keats," Larkin said (*Letters*, 34), and he said of *Lady Chatterley's Lover*, which he reread several times at Oxford, that "it will live" (*Letters*, 144). There is some personal irony, then, in the move from Lawrence to the Beatles in the poem. The Larkin persona *is* an authentic member of the Lawrence audience. Lawrence in fact represents *his* generation's sexual liberation, which of course took a more academic and more elitist form, the difference between the private reading of a novel or an undergraduate argument about Mellors's morality on the one hand and the public and communal display of sexual freedom on the other, a Woodstock or a Beatles concert.

The poem seems to say that once the unexpurgated *Lady Chatterley* was available, once a liberated view of sexuality was in the air, then true sexual intercourse began, but there is an additional irony here. As Janice Rossen points out, the Lawrence allusion is also a private joke, "since Larkin and his fellow undergraduates had been reading Lawrence with admiration long before the 'ban' was removed."[26] Obviously, however, the elite audience associated with Lawrence did not undergo the same sexual conversion as the popular audience associated with the Beatles. As much as the Larkin persona would like to be a part of the popular audience, it is not accessible to him, in part because it represents the real life that is always elsewhere. The young Larkin wrote to his friend Jim Sutton, "I don't know about women & marriage. One thing I do think is that if we had known as many women as we have read books by D.H.L. we shd have a clearer idea of the situation" (*Letters*, 151). The sexual intercourse of the Beatles' generation was, however, not simply literary; it was the real thing, or at least that is the illusion of Larkin's speaker in "Annus Mirabilis." The *Chatterley* ban and the Beatles' first LP may on one level represent the same phenomenon, but on another they represent the two audiences for the poem, only one of which presumably would be interested in the poem's Latin title, its allusion to Dryden (and possibly Keats), and the false expectation the title sets up, immediately deflated by the first line. The wit of "Annus

---

26. Rossen, *Philip Larkin: His Life's Work*, 67.

Mirabilis" is easily accessible to the "literary" audience—the Lawrence audience—but the Beatles' audience came along "just too late" to read it as anything more than a popular poem about the sexual revolution.

The allusive literary title, this one referring us to Robert Louis Stevenson's "Requiem," set against the deflating first line, "sexual intercourse" now coarsened to "fuck you up," is one of the devices that makes "This Be the Verse" (*CP*, 180) appear a kind of companion poem to "Annus Mirabilis." Commentators tend to discuss the two together, as if sensing that they bear a close relationship although they are ostensibly on different subjects. In *A Writer's Life* Motion calls them "twin monuments" to Larkin's gift for describing "a drama of private feeling in 'commonplace' language." He also notes that although it was four years before he finished it, Larkin began "This Be the Verse" on the same evening he wrote "Annus Mirabilis" (*Life*, 373). This accounts for what we hear as the common voice of the two poems that helps pull them together. They serve perhaps as the two most extreme examples of a defining Larkin genre, the poem of entertainment that satisfies as well a more demanding reading.

"This Be the Verse" is more pointedly addressed to the popular audience than is "Annus Mirabilis"; as I read it, it pretends to be *literally* addressed to someone who could well be a member of the audience for the Beatles' first LP. The question of who is speaking and to whom the words are addressed is directly relevant to a reading of the poem:

> They fuck you up, your mum and dad.
> They may not mean to but they do.
> They fill you with the faults they had
> And add some extra, just for you.

It could be argued perhaps that the "you" in the poem is the colloquial "one" and that the speaker is a member of the youth culture complaining, "They fuck us up, our mums and dads." That reading accords with the first stanza, but not with the second and third, which take a broader view of the issue:

> But they were fucked up in their turn
> By fools in old style hats and coats,

Who half the time were soppy-stern
And half at one another's throats.

Man hands on misery to man.
It deepens like a coastal shelf.
Get out as early as you can,
And don't have any kids yourself.

The second stanza's suggestion that this is a universal condition and
the Housman-like magnificence of the first two lines of the third re-
move the poem from the perspective of the sixties audience and indicate
that it is instead a *response* to one of the clichéd attitudes of this audience.
That is, the poem pretends to be addressed to someone in the kind of
sixties popular audience delineated in "Annus Mirabilis."

"This Be the Verse" has as its base one of the complications of the
sexual revolution of the sixties, the widening division between genera-
tions. ("Annus Mirabilis" and "This Be the Verse" turn out to be the
same poem from two different perspectives. "Annus Mirabilis" sees the
generational shift of the sixties as something unique that the speaker
can never experience; "This Be the Verse" sees it as a part of a universal
pattern.) What is implied but not directly stated in the poem is an issue
addressed by numerous sociologists and cultural historians. The sixties
sexual revolt, as H. F. Mooney argues, was part of a much wider rejection
by the young of "the middle-class mores of their parents." In "The
Young Audience," a 1964 study of the British audience for popular
music, Stuart Hall and Paddy Whannel stress the generational divide:
"Parents are always one generation behind their children: today they
seem to be two generations behind." The attitudes of the young,
expressed for example in their dress, point "to real failures in the
relationships between children and parents, and the sense of being
misunderstood."[27]

The self-pitying, misunderstood quality of the young audience is

27. H. F. Mooney, "Popular Music since the 1920s: The Significance of Shifting
Taste," *American Quarterly*, XX (1968), 81; Stuart Hall and Paddy Whannel, "The Young
Audience," in *On Record: Rock, Pop, and the Written Word*, ed. Simon Frith and Andrew
Goodwin (New York, 1990), 28, 33.

conveyed as well in their music, examples of which Hall and Whannel supply. One of these, "Teenage Dream" sung by Terry Dene, states the attitude toward parents to which "This Be the Verse" responds:

> Mum says we're too young to love
> And Dad agrees it's so,
> But the joy and bliss I find in your kiss
> Is a thrill they'll never know.[28]

To this Larkin's poem replies, "They do fuck you up, your mum and dad, but not quite in the way that you think." It is first more a biological than a cultural phenomenon, as both the pun in the first line and the deepening coastal shelf of the last stanza suggest, and it is not a condition unique to sixties youth. The sudden shift in tone to "Man hands on misery to man. / It deepens like a coastal shelf" is a way of saying that traditional poetry (such as that of Housman, who seems to be speaking in these lines) has told us all we need to know about generation. Other readers have heard Hardy in the third stanza, although the identity of the poet is of no particular importance. What is significant is the effect of the momentary movement away from the tone of address to the popular audience, the nod to the "serious" audience that has become a kind of Larkin signature.

Once alerted by the juxtaposition of tones to the possibility of depth in the poem, this audience may recognize as well a level of ambiguity that sets it apart from the popular verse it pretends to be. "The poem teases us by not quite telling us how seriously to take it," Swarbrick writes. In an interview with John Haffenden Larkin agreed that it was funny, but added, "It's perfectly serious as well." And in defending himself against the suggestion that he had used the word *fuck* as a "shock tactic," he called Haffenden's attention to the ambiguity that gives the word (and the poem) its significance: " 'They fuck you up' is funny because it's ambiguous. Parents bring about your conception and also bugger you up once you are born." But it is not simply the opening phrase that is ambiguous. The irony of "This Be the Verse" as popular

---

28. Hall and Whannel, "Young Audience," 31.

poetry is that it furnishes an example of what Michael Riffaterre calls "the literary sign par excellence," the sign that marks the language of a text as literary discourse.[29]

In Riffaterre's distinction between a text's meaning and its significance, meaning is the contextual understanding demanded by grammatical considerations, a word's relation to other words, and significance is the product of a second and higher reading stage that separates the competent reader from the reader content with grammatical meaning, the reader of popular literature, for example. He uses the term *syllepsis* to characterize the trope that allows the second process—the move from contextual meaning to intertextual significance—to take place. The term refers to an expression understood at the same time as meaning and significance, and for this reason its presence points to the text's duality and marks it as "literary."[30]

"This Be the Verse" perfectly exemplifies Riffaterre's principle of literariness and at the same time mocks it. The duality of the text's message is evident from the first line to the last, but meaning and significance exist in such an odd relationship that it is difficult to know which is which. For example, the *literal* meaning of the expression in the first line ("They fuck you up") becomes the secondary or symbolic meaning because it is only in its idiomatic or slang meaning that the reader knows the expression and it is at a second reading stage that we recognize that the poem is asking us also to take the term *fuck* literally, thereby giving the cliché new life. And the same is true with the second line—"They may not mean to, but they do." Once we recognize the possibility of reading the first line in a way incompatible with our initial reading (so that it becomes something like "Your parents brought you into existence through the act of sexual intercourse"), we also recognize that the second may have a meaning incompatible with our first reading. Now rather than excusing the parents ("they don't necessarily mean to mess you up") the line suggests the possibility of blame of a different

29. Swarbrick, *Out of Reach,* 138; Haffenden, *Viewpoints,* 128–29; Riffaterre, "Syllepsis," 639.

30. Riffaterre, "Syllepsis," 637–38.

kind. The addressee's existence may be a matter of pure chance. He (and I determine the gender from line 11) may have been created not through the parents' intent but as a by-product of the pleasures of sexual intercourse.

This alternative reading for the first two lines introduces, in turn, a second incompatible reading for the last stanza. If the effect of generation is only increasing misery, each generation adding its own layer like a deepening coastal shelf, then the only resolution, the poem appears to say, is the Housman-like remedy of dying young and ending the process. In this reading "This Be the Verse" is an updated version of a Housman poem such as "To an Athlete Dying Young" or "If it chance your eye offend you." Its significance lies in the way its surface meaning—misunderstanding parents produce unhappiness—is undercut by its Housmanesque intertext—misery is simply the nature of existence; to be brought into existence is to be miserable, and the only way to escape it is to die early. But the poem introduces another possible reading in the last two lines incompatible with this reading. "Get out as early as you can, / And don't have any kids yourself" is not simply advice for departing this miserable world as soon as possible. It is also advice for indulging in worldly pleasure without "fucking someone up" by employing the birth-control technique of "pulling out early" (at least as early as you can, given the pleasure of the act itself) or *coitus interruptus*.

What makes "This Be the Verse" difficult to read according to Riffaterre's trope of syllepsis is that while it clearly can be understood in two different ways at once, as meaning and as significance, its two levels exist so close to each other and so close to the surface that the poem seems almost a parody of literariness and ambiguity, a parody of the poem with more than one level of meaning. But if this is the case, if it self-consciously works against the model of "serious" literary discourse, then that simply adds another level of significance that a "successful reading" must work through. My own reading, which may appear much too serious for such a lightweight poem, is intended to uncover the poem's complications, to indicate that although it has all the trappings of an appeal to a popular audience, it has been created to encourage and reward rereading. It *is*, as Larkin thought, a "serious" poem in more than one sense, and its significance, as he also saw, lies in its ambiguity, the duality of its performance.

The convention of the two audiences, the performance that is equally accessible as entertainment and as art, is best exemplified by Larkin's blues and jazz. Albert Murray, who has written extensively on the blurring of the line between folk art and fine art in the blues, finds it on the whole a healthy circumstance that jazz or blues should be written and performed at once for the two distinct audiences of the dance hall and the concert hall, and it is of course the existence of two different jazz audiences that forms the basis for Larkin's "Reasons for Attendance." Murray suggests also that "the phonograph record has served as the blues musician's equivalent for the concert hall almost from the outset." More than that, "it may have been precisely the phonograph record (along with the radio) that in effect required the more ambitious blues musicians to satisfy the concert-oriented listeners and Bacchanalian revelers at the very same time."[31] In "Writing Poems" Larkin associates his own composition with listening to records (*RW*, 84), and it seems natural to think of the jazz or blues recording as a part of the cultural matrix of "two-audience" poems like "Annus Mirabilis" and "This Be the Verse." (One could conceive of a study of the odd mixing of the phonographic, the photographic, and the pornographic in Larkin.)

It is surely significant that the greatest of the jazz musicians were also the perfect exemplars of the entertainer-artist model. In *All What Jazz* Larkin notes Louis Armstrong's "mixture of righteous jazz and vaudeville entertainment" (*AWJ*, 132), and Murray says of Armstrong: "On the one hand he was an irrepressible comedian or satirist; on the other he was the Prometheus of the blues idiom." The concert-hall crowd and civil rights leaders were scandalized, for example, when at the height of his fame as a great jazz artist Armstrong appeared in jungle costume and blackface as the King of the Zulus in the 1949 Mardi Gras parade, declaring that "being chosen for such a role was the fulfillment

---

31. Murray, *Stomping the Blues*, 183–84.

of a lifelong dream." (Ted Gioia argues that "Armstrong's reputation as an important jazz musician has been undeservedly tarnished by his considerable talents as an entertainer.")[32]

The "preeminent embodiment of the blues musician as artist was Duke Ellington," Murray writes. Ellington, "in the course of fulfilling the role of entertainer, not only came to address himself to the basic imperatives of music as fine art but also achieved the most comprehensive synthesis, extension, and refinement to date of all the elements of blues musicianship." Murray argues that Ellington "converted more of the actual texture and vitality of American life into first-rate universally appealing music than anybody else," and that he did so "in terms of such vernacular devices of blues musicianship as vamps, riffs, breaks, fills, call-and-response sequences, idiomatic syncopation, downhome folk timbres, drum-oriented horns, strings, and so on."[33]

"This Be the Verse" may be Larkin's most successful experiment in the artistic appropriation of vernacular devices or the poem that appears to make no distinction between entertainment and art. On the one hand, it has ransacked the cultural storehouse of commonplaces, clichés, and slang. On the other, it depends for its significance on incorporating the literary tradition of a line of poets that includes most prominently Hardy and Housman. In one of his most infamous early statements on the practice of poetry Larkin disavowed a belief in " 'tradition' or a common myth-kitty or casual allusions in poems to other poems or poets" (*RW*, 79). It would require an additional chapter to consider the Larkin poems that openly violate his statement, but, quite apart from that, it is odd that Larkin should have taken such a stance against an intertextual conception of literature given his knowledge of the intertextual nature of the popular art he holds up as a model against the excesses of modernism. More than once he ridiculed what he labeled the Ford T Model theory of literature, the view "that every poem must include all previous poems, in the same way that a Ford Zephyr has somewhere in it a Ford T Model."[34] Yet it is not inaccurate to say that every blues

32. Murray, *Stomping the Blues*, 191, 190; Gioia, *Imperfect Art*, 17.

33. Murray, *Stomping the Blues*, 214, 224.

34. Hamilton, "Four Conversations," 71.

song contains within itself earlier blues songs, or that almost all jazz is by definition intertextual, since jazz, at least Larkin's traditional jazz, may be defined as the variations or improvisations on the chord changes of an existing song, usually a blues or a standard.

Modern jazz presents us with an even more intriguing case of intertextuality, one perhaps closer to the literary model. In "The Silent Theme Tradition in Jazz," Frank Tirro points out that one practice of 1940s jazz, an "extension and variation of normal procedure" in traditional jazz, was to leave silent and hidden the "standard" on which the new piece was based. While the practice in traditional jazz is to play the melody in its entirety before beginning improvisations on it, in bop the preexistent melody may be present only through the harmonic pattern, so that Charlie Parker's "Scrapple from the Apple," for example, "contains" "Honeysuckle Rose" only in the sense that it is based on its chord progression. The new composition was renamed, and the musician never divulged the name of the original melody, "but every experienced bebop musician knew that *Groovin' High* was played to the chords of *Whispering,* that *Ornithology* was *How High the Moon,* and that *Anthropology* was an altered version of *I Got Rhythm.*"[35] Tirro is uninterested in the intertextual implications of this practice—the essay was published in 1967, and his interest is in the way the "Silent Theme" composition creates a music reserved for the elite—but the intertextuality of jazz is emphatic and instructive. Although variations on an unstated theme may be older than jazz, Tirro's bop examples constitute as clear an instance as one could find of new texts structured in response to (nearly) absent intertexts, one model for Larkin's response to jazz and blues.

In *All What Jazz,* Larkin cites Paul Oliver's characterization of the blues as a "music in which . . . 'a stockpile of traditional phrases' serves as 'an indispensable substitute for original thought' " (*AWJ,* 249). Oliver is discussing the intertextual character of the blues. After postulating a blues "stockpile" he cites a number of traditional phrases from it and concludes:

35. Frank Tirro, "The Silent Theme Tradition in Jazz," *Musical Quarterly,* LIII (1967), 314, 326–27. Tirro appends to his article a list of sixty-three "silent theme" compositions along with the standards on which they are based.

These words come from no special blues, but from a hundred, or a thousand. They are typical of the vast reservoir of blues resources and have been tapped by innumerable minor singers and major singers alike. . . . [T]he measure of their abilities is to be found in the ways in which old and familiar lines may be re-employed in their compositions to take on new meaning.[36]

Larkin's poems, the "entertainment" poems most of all, draw on a similar stockpile of phrases, commonplaces, and popular devices and techniques—his society's reservoir of idioms and clichés. His tradition and his myth-kitty are certainly not those of Eliot or Pound, but they are as crucial to the success of his poetry.

Larkin claimed that he objected to the concepts of the myth-kitty and poetic allusion because of their snobbish appeal. To incorporate myth and classical allusions "you have to be terribly educated, you have to have read everything to know these things, and secondly you've got somehow to work them in to show that you are working them in." Allusions to other poems or poets are "like the talk of literary under-strappers letting you see they know the right people" (RW, 79). The kitty from which Larkin's texts draw demonstrates, on the other hand, a kind of reverse snobbery, an extension of the complicated philistine manner Larkin and Amis first assumed at Oxford and never relinquished. In Amis's Lucky Jim the three most despicable characters are an organizer of chamber concerts, a would-be painter, and an amateur oboe player. The painter calls Jim Dixon, the character sometimes linked to Larkin, a "lousy little philistine,"[37] and in terms of the values the novel assumes the epithet is a badge of honor. The philistine pose of Larkin's poems and the love for jazz and other forms of popular music are clearly linked in ways difficult to unravel, but there is no question that jazz was for Larkin the epitome of an antielitist, unacademic art, the musical equivalent of a kind of poetry ("Annus Mirabilis" and "This Be the Verse" are examples) that would move twentieth-century verse away from The Waste Land and in the direction of Hardy and Housman, Ellington and Armstrong.

36. Oliver, *Aspects of the Blues Tradition,* 90–91.
37. Hamilton, "Four Conversations," 71–72; Amis, *Lucky Jim,* 188.

BIBLIOGRAPHY

Amis, Kingsley. "Farewell to a Friend." In *Philip Larkin: The Man and His Work*, edited by Dale Salwak. London, 1989.

———. *Lucky Jim*. London, 1965.

———. "Oxford and After." In *Larkin at Sixty*, edited by Anthony Thwaite. London, 1982.

Auden, W. H. *Collected Shorter Poems, 1927–1957*. London, 1966.

Auden, W. H., and Christopher Isherwood. *Plays and Other Dramatic Writings by W. H. Auden, 1928–1938*. Edited by Edward Mendelson. Princeton, 1988.

Baker, Houston A., Jr. *Blues, Ideology, and Afro-American Literature: A Vernacular Theory*. Chicago, 1984.

Bane, Michael. *White Boy Singin' the Blues*. New York, 1982.

Barlow, William. *"Looking Up at Down": The Emergence of Blues Culture*. Philadelphia, 1989.

Bayley, John. "Philip Larkin's Inner World." In *Philip Larkin: The Man and His Work*, edited by Dale Salwak. London, 1989.

———. "Too Good for This World." *Times Literary Supplement*, June 21, 1974, pp. 653–55.

Bechet, Sidney. *Treat It Gentle*. New York, 1960.

Beinhart, Larry. *American Hero*. New York, 1993.

Bennett, Alan. "Alas! Deceived." *London Review of Books*, March 25, 1993, pp. 3–9.

———. "Instead of a Present." In *Larkin at Sixty*, edited by Anthony Thwaite. London, 1982.

Berendt, Joachim. *The Jazz Book.* Translated by Dan Morgenstern and Helmut and Barbara Bredigkeit. New York, 1975.

Bergonzi, Bernard. *Reading the Thirties: Texts and Contexts.* London, 1978.

Berlin, Irving. *The Songs of Irving Berlin: Movie Songs.* Milwaukee, 1991.

Berry, Francis. *Poetry and the Physical Voice.* London, 1962.

Booth, James. *Philip Larkin: Writer.* New York, 1992.

Bristow, Joseph. "The Obscenity of Philip Larkin." *Critical Inquiry,* XXI (1994), 156–81.

Calinescu, Matei. *Rereading.* New Haven, 1993.

Carey, John. "Mail Chauvinism." *Sunday Times,* October 25, 1992, sec. 6, p. 5.

———. "Not a Hope in Hull." *Sunday Times,* April 4, 1993, sec. 7, p. 4.

Charters, Samuel B. *The Country Blues.* New York, 1975.

———. *The Poetry of the Blues.* New York, 1963.

Cobb, James C. *The Most Southern Place on Earth: The Mississippi Delta and the Roots of Regional Identity.* New York, 1992.

Cohn, Lawrence. *Nothing But the Blues.* New York, 1993.

Conquest, Robert. "A Proper Sport." In *Larkin at Sixty,* edited by Anthony Thwaite. London, 1982.

Coward, Noel. *Private Lives.* London, 1930.

Crow, Bill. *Jazz Anecdotes.* New York, 1990.

Culler, Jonathan. *The Pursuit of Signs: Semiotics, Literature, Deconstruction.* Ithaca, N.Y., 1981.

Davie, Donald. "Letters from Hull." *PN Review,* XIX (1993), 4–5.

———. *Thomas Hardy and British Poetry.* London, 1973.

Day, Roger. *Larkin.* Philadelphia, 1987.

Day Lewis, C. *Poems of C. Day Lewis, 1925–1972.* Chosen and with an introduction by Ian Parsons. London, 1977.

Dylan, Bob. *Bob Dylan Song Book.* New York, 1970.

———. *The Songs of Bob Dylan.* New York, 1980.

Eagleton, Terry. *Criticism and Ideology.* London, 1976.

Eliot, T. S. "Hamlet." In *Selected Prose of T. S. Eliot,* edited by Frank Kermode. New York, 1975.

Ellison, Mary. *Extensions of the Blues.* New York, 1989.

Esman, Aaron H. "Jazz—A Study in Cultural Conflict." *American Imago,* VIII (1951), 219–26.

Evans, David. *Big Road Blues: Tradition and Creativity in the Folk Blues.* New York, 1987.

Everett, Barbara. "Art and Larkin." In *Philip Larkin: The Man and His Work,* edited by Dale Salwak. London, 1989.

———. "Larkin's Edens." In *Poets in Their Time: Essays on English Poetry from Donne to Larkin.* London, 1986.

———. "Philip Larkin: After Symbolism." In *Poets in Their Time: Essays on English Poetry from Donne to Larkin.* London, 1986.

Ferris, William R. *Blues from the Delta.* Garden City, N.Y., 1978.

Frith, Simon. "Playing with Real Feeling—Jazz and Suburbia." In *Music for Pleasure: Essays in the Sociology of Pop.* New York, 1988.

———. "The Real Thing—Bruce Springsteen." In *Music for Pleasure: Essays in the Sociology of Pop.* New York, 1988.

———. *The Sociology of Rock.* London, 1978.

———. "Why Do Songs Have Words?" In *Music for Pleasure: Essays in the Sociology of Pop.* New York, 1988.

Fuller, Roy. "Fascinating Rhythm." In *Professors and Gods: Last Oxford Lectures on Poetry.* New York, 1973.

Furia, Philip. *The Poets of Tin Pan Alley: A History of America's Great Lyricists.* New York, 1990.

Garber, Frederick. "Fabulating Jazz." In *Representing Jazz,* edited by Krin Gabbard. Durham, N.C., 1995.

Garon, Paul. *Blues and the Poetic Spirit.* New York, 1978.

Gearin-Tosh, Michael. "Deprivation and Love in Larkin's Poetry." In *Critical Essays on Philip Larkin: The Poems,* edited by Linda Cookson and Bryan Loughrey. London, 1989.

Gershwin, George, and Ira Gershwin. *The George and Ira Gershwin Song Book.* New York, 1960.

Gioia, Ted. *The Imperfect Art: Reflections on Jazz and Modern Culture.* New York, 1988.

Gold, Robert S. *Jazz Talk.* New York, 1975.

Goodby, John. "'The Importance of Being Elsewhere,' or 'No Man Is an Ireland': Self, Selves, and Social Consensus in the Poetry of Philip Larkin." *Critical Survey,* I (1989), 113–21.

Grossman, Stefan, Stephen Calt, and Hal Grossman. *Country Blues Songbook.* New York, 1973.

Guillory, John. *Cultural Capital: The Problem of Literary Canon Formation.* Chicago, 1993.

Gushee, Larry. "King Oliver's Creole Jazz Band." In *The Art of Jazz: Essays on the Nature and Development of Jazz,* edited by Martin T. Williams. New York, 1959.

Haffenden, John. "Philip Larkin." In *Viewpoints: Poets in Conversation with John Haffenden.* London, 1981.

Hall, Stuart, and Paddy Whannel. "The Young Audience." In *On Record: Rock, Pop, and the Written Word,* edited by Simon Frith and Andrew Goodwin. New York, 1990.

Hamilton, Ian. "Bugger Me Blue." *London Review of Books,* October 22, 1992, pp. 3–4.

————. "Four Conversations." *The London Magazine,* IV (1964), 64–85.

————. "Self's the Man." *Times Literary Supplement,* April 2, 1993, pp. 3–4.

Harmon, William. "Larkin's Memory." *Sewanee Review,* XCVIII (1990), 206–21.

Hartley, George. "Nothing to Be Said." In *Larkin at Sixty,* edited by Anthony Thwaite. London, 1982.

Hartley, Jean. *Philip Larkin, the Marvell Press, and Me.* Manchester, 1989.

Hassan, Salem K. *Philip Larkin and His Contemporaries; An Air of Authenticity.* Foreword by Philip Hobsbaum. London, 1988.

Hesse, Hermann. *Steppenwolf.* Translated by Basil Creighton. New York, 1961.

Hobsbawm, Eric. *The Jazz Scene.* New York, 1993.

Hoggart, Richard. *The Uses of Literacy.* London, 1957.

Holderness, Graham. "Philip Larkin: The Limits of Experience." In *Critical Essays on Philip Larkin: The Poems,* edited by Linda Cookson and Bryan Loughrey. London, 1989.

Housman, A. E. "The Name and Nature of Poetry." In *A. E. Housman: Selected Prose,* edited by John Carter. Cambridge, U.K., 1961.

Jacobs, Eric. *Kingsley Amis: A Biography.* London, 1995.

Jakobson, Roman. "On Realism in Art." In *Readings in Russian Poetics: Formalist and Structuralist Views,* edited by Ladislav Matejka and Krystyna Pomorska. Ann Arbor, 1978.

James, Clive. "On His Wit." In *Larkin at Sixty,* edited by Anthony Thwaite. London, 1982.

Jardine, Lisa. "Saxon Violence." *Guardian,* December 8, 1992, sec. 2, p. 4.

Keil, Charles. *Urban Blues.* Chicago, 1966.

Kernfeld, Barry, ed. *The New Grove Dictionary of Jazz.* London, 1988.

Kimball, Robert, ed. *Cole.* Introduction by Brendan Gill. New York, 1971.

Knight, Arthur. "*Jammin' the Blues,* or the Sight of Jazz, 1944." In *Representing Jazz,* edited by Krin Gabbard. Durham, N.C., 1995.

Kuby, Lolette. *An Uncommon Poet for the Common Man: A Study of Philip Larkin's Poetry.* The Hague, 1974.

Laing, Dave. *The Sound of Our Time.* Chicago, 1970.

Lane, Anthony. "Writing Wrongs." *New Yorker,* March 10, 1997, pp. 86–92.

Larkin, Philip. *All What Jazz: A Record Diary, 1961–1971.* New York, 1985.

———. *Collected Poems.* Edited by Anthony Thwaite. New York, 1989.

———. *Jill: A Novel.* Woodstock, N.Y., 1976.

———. *Required Writing: Miscellaneous Pieces, 1955–1982.* New York, 1984.

———. *Selected Letters of Philip Larkin, 1940–1985.* Edited by Anthony Thwaite. New York, 1993.

———. "The True Voice of Feeling: An Auto Interview." In *Philip Larkin, 1922–1985: A Tribute,* edited by George Hartley. London, 1988.

Leavis, Q. D. *Fiction and the Reading Public.* London, 1939.

Leggett, B. J. *Early Stevens: The Nietzschean Intertext.* Durham, N.C., 1992.

Lerner, Laurence. "Larkin's Strategies." *Critical Survey,* I (1989): 113–21.

Levine, Lawrence. *Black Culture and Black Consciousness: Afro-American Folk Thought from Slavery to Freedom.* New York, 1977.

Lindrop, Grevel. "Being Different from Yourself: Philip Larkin in the 1970s." In *British Poetry since 1970: A Critical Survey,* edited by Peter Jones and Michael Schmidt. New York, 1980.

Lodge, David. "Philip Larkin: The Metonymic Muse." In *Philip Larkin: The Man and His Work,* edited by Dale Salwak. London, 1989.

———. "Where It's At: California Language." In *The State of the Language,* edited by Leonard Michaels and Christopher Ricks. Berkeley, 1980.

Lomax, Alan. *Mister Jelly Roll: The Fortunes of Jelly Roll Morton, New Orleans Creole and "Inventor of Jazz."* 2nd ed. Berkeley, 1973.

Longley, Edna. "'Any-angled Light': Philip Larkin and Edward Thomas." In *Poetry in the Wars.* Newcastle upon Tyne, 1986.

Macherey, Pierre. *A Theory of Literary Production.* Translated by Geoffrey Wall. London, 1978.

Marcus, Greil. *Dead Elvis: A Chronicle of a Cultural Obsession.* New York, 1991.

———. "Introduction." In *Stranded: Rock and Roll for a Desert Island,* edited by Greil Marcus. New York, 1979.

———. *Mystery Train: Images of America in Rock 'n' Roll Music.* Revised ed. New York, 1982.

———. "When You Walk in the Room." In *The Dustbin of History.* Cambridge, Mass., 1995.

———. "Who Put the Bomp in the Bomp De-Bomp De-Bomp?" In *Rock and Roll Will Stand,* edited by Greil Marcus. Boston, 1969.

Martin, Bruce K. *Philip Larkin.* Boston, 1978.

Middleton, Richard. *Pop Music and the Blues: A Study of the Relationship and its Significance.* London, 1972.

———. *Studying Popular Music.* Philadelphia, 1990.

Mooney, H. F. "Popular Music since the 1920s: The Significance of Shifting Taste." *American Quarterly,* XX (1968), 67–85.

Morrison, Blake. *The Movement: English Poetry and Fiction of the 1950s.* London, 1986.

Motion, Andrew. *Philip Larkin.* London, 1982.

———. *Philip Larkin: A Writer's Life.* New York, 1993.

Murray, Albert. *Stomping the Blues.* New York, 1976.

Newton, Francis. *The Jazz Scene.* New York, 1960.

Nietzsche, Friedrich. *The Dawn of Day.* Translated by J. M. Kennedy. Vol. IX of *The Complete Works of Friedrich Nietzsche,* edited by Oscar Levy. New York, 1964.

———. *The Joyful Wisdom.* Translated by Thomas Common. Vol. X of *The Complete Works of Friedrich Nietzsche,* edited by Oscar Levy. New York, 1964.

Oakley, Giles. *The Devil's Music: A History of the Blues.* New York, 1977.

Oliver, Paul. *Aspects of the Blues Tradition.* New York, 1968.

———. "Blues and the Binary Principle." In *Popular Music Perspectives,* edited by David Horn and Philip Tagg. Exeter, U.K., 1982.

———. *Blues Fell This Morning: Meaning in the Blues.* 2nd ed., foreword by Richard Wright. Cambridge, U.K., 1990.

The Oxford Book of Twentieth-Century English Verse. Chosen by Philip Larkin. London, 1973.

Panassié, Hugues. *The Real Jazz.* Revised ed. New York, 1960.

Partridge, Eric. *A Dictionary of Clichés.* London, 1978.

Paulin, Tom. Letter to the Editor. *Times Literary Supplement,* November 6, 1992, p. 15.

Powell, Neil. *Carpenters of Light: Some Contemporary English Poets.* Manchester, 1979.

Pritchard, William H. "Larkin's Presence." In *Philip Larkin: The Man and His Work,* edited by Dale Salwak. London, 1989.

Raban, Jonathan. *The Society of the Poem.* London, 1971.

Regan, Stephen. *Philip Larkin.* London, 1992.

Ricks, Christopher. "Can This Really Be the End?" In *Conclusions on the Wall: New Essays on Bob Dylan*, edited by Elizabeth Thomson. Manchester, 1980.

———. "Clichés." In *The State of the Language*, edited by Leonard Michaels and Christopher Ricks. Berkeley, 1980.

———. "Like Something Almost Being Said." In *Larkin at Sixty*, edited by Anthony Thwaite. London, 1982.

Riesman, David. "Listening to Popular Music." *American Quarterly*, II (1950), 359–71.

Riffaterre, Michael. *Fictional Truth*. Baltimore, 1990.

———. "Intertextual Representation: On Mimesis as Interpretive Discourse." *Critical Inquiry*, XI (1984), 141–62.

———. "The Intertextual Unconscious." *Critical Inquiry*, XIII (1987), 371–85.

———. "Interview." *Diacritics*, XI (1981), 12–16.

———. *Semiotics of Poetry*. Bloomington, 1978.

———. "Syllepsis." *Critical Inquiry*, VI (1980), 625–38.

———. *Text Production*. Translated by Terese Lyons. New York, 1983.

Rogers, James. *The Dictionary of Clichés*. New York, 1985.

Rossen, Janice. *Philip Larkin: His Life's Work*. New York, 1989.

Russel, Nick. "Larkin' About at St John's." In *Philip Larkin, 1922–1985: A Tribute*, edited by George Hartley. London, 1988.

Sackheim, Eric. *The Blues Line: A Collection of Blues Lyrics*. New York, 1969.

Sadie, Stanley, ed. *The New Grove Dictionary of Music and Musicians*. Vol. XVIII. London, 1980.

Schiff, Stephen. "The Poet of Embarrassment." *New Yorker*, September 6, 1993, pp. 92–101.

Sinfield, Alan. *Literature, Politics, and Culture in Postwar Britain*. Oxford, 1989.

Smith, Barbara Herrnstein. *Poetic Closure: A Study of How Poems End*. Chicago, 1968.

Swarbrick, Andrew. *Out of Reach: The Poetry of Philip Larkin*. New York, 1995.

Thwaite, Anthony. "Introduction." In *Larkin at Sixty*, edited by Anthony Thwaite. London, 1982.

Tilton, Jeff Todd. *Downhome Blues Lyrics*. 2nd ed. Urbana, 1990.

Timms, David. *Philip Larkin*. New York, 1973.

Tirro, Frank. "The Silent Theme Tradition in Jazz." *Musical Quarterly*, LIII (1967), 313–34.

Tolley, A. T. *My Proper Ground: A Study of the Work of Philip Larkin and Its Development*. Ottawa, Ontario, 1991.

Underhill, Hugh. "Poetry of Departures: Larkin and the Power of Choosing." *Critical Survey,* I (1989), 183–93.

Van Der Merwe, Peter. *Origins of the Popular Style: The Antecedents of Twentieth-Century Popular Music.* Oxford, 1989.

Vulliamy, Graham. *Jazz and Blues.* London, 1982.

Watson, J. R. "Clichés and Common Speech in Philip Larkin's Poetry." *Critical Survey,* I (1989), 149–56.

Watts, Cedric. "Larkin and Jazz." In *Critical Essays on Philip Larkin: The Poems,* edited by Linda Cookson and Bryan Loughrey. London, 1989.

Whalen, Terry. *Philip Larkin and English Poetry.* London, 1986.

Wilder, Alec. *American Popular Song.* Edited and with an introduction by James T. Maher. New York, 1972.

Yeats, William Butler. *Autobiographies.* London, 1956.

———. *The Collected Works of W. B. Yeats.* Vol. I: *The Poems.* Edited by Richard J. Finneran. New York, 1989.

INDEX

Yeats, W. B.: biographical attacks on, 6; audience for, 17; and discussions of jazz at Oxford, 26; on poem as piece of luck, 29; as influence on Larkin, 45, 117, 118, 120–21, 134, 138; compared with Larkin, 155;

—works: "When You Are Old," 77–78; "The Wild Swans at Coole," 82, 83–84; "The Fisherman," 134; "What Then?" 160–61